Righting a Wrong

Japanese Americans and
the Passage of the
Civil Liberties Act of 1988

ASIAN AMERICA

A series edited by Gordon H. Chang

The increasing size and diversity of the Asian American population, its growing significance in American society and culture, and the expanded appreciation, both popular and scholarly, of the importance of Asian Americans in the country's present and past—all these developments have converged to stimulate wide interest in scholarly work on topics related to the Asian American experience. The general recognition of the pivotal role that race and ethnicity have played in American life, and in relations between the United States and other countries, has also fostered this heightened attention.

Although Asian Americans were a subject of serious inquiry in the late nineteenth and early twentieth centuries, they were subsequently ignored by the mainstream scholarly community for several decades. In recent years, however, this neglect has ended, with an increasing number of writers examining a good many aspects of Asian American life and culture. Moreover, many students of American society are recognizing that the study of issues related to Asian America speak to, and may be essential for, many current discussions on the part of the informed public and various scholarly communities.

The Stanford series on Asian America seeks to address these interests. The series will include work from the humanities and social sciences, including history, anthropology, political science, American studies, law, literary criticism, sociology, and interdisciplinary and policy studies.

Righting a Wrong

*Japanese Americans and
the Passage of the
Civil Liberties Act of 1988*

Leslie T. Hatamiya

STANFORD UNIVERSITY PRESS
STANFORD, CALIFORNIA

Published with the assistance of a
special grant from the Stanford
University Faculty Publication Fund
to help support nonfaculty work
originating at Stanford.

Stanford University Press
Stanford, California

©1993 by the Board of Trustees
of the Leland Stanford Junior University

Printed in the United States of America

CIP data are at the end of the book

Original printing 1993
Last figure below indicates year of this printing:
03 02 01 00 99 98 97 96 95 94

Stanford University Press publications are distributed exclu-
sively by Stanford University Press within the United States,
Canada, and Mexico; they are distributed exclusively by
Cambridge University Press throughout the rest of the world.

For my parents,
Roy and Momoko Miriam Hatamiya

Preface

As a third-generation Japanese American and the daughter and grand-daughter of former internees, I have been directly affected by the U.S. internment of Japanese Americans during World War II and the subsequent quest for redress. On a personal level, the development of this book has been a search to figure out who I am, what my roots are, and where I am going. Although I have been aware of the evacuation and internment all my life, my research has helped me truly understand the ordeal that my parents and grandparents lived through, the injustice of it all, and my own good fortune.

Since World War II, the internment has been a focal point for the Japanese American community. It distinguishes Japanese Americans from all other Asian American groups. Although non-Asians often lump all Asian Americans into one catch-all group and although all Asian groups have faced some form of discrimination in this country, no other group—not even Chinese Americans, many of whom began immigrating to America before the vast majority of Japanese Americans, nor more recent immigrants from Korea and refugees from Southeast Asia—has experienced wholesale evacuation and internment. The internment experience has had a bonding effect on the Japanese American community; when one Japanese American meets another for the first time, inevitably the question of the camps comes up. The Nisei (second-generation Japanese Americans) and the few surviving Issei (first-generation immigrants) ask one another, "What camp were you in?" and then comment on whom they knew in the camps named. For the Sansei and Yonsei (third- and fourth-generation Japanese Americans), the question is, "Where were your parents or grand-parents sent?" Pre-war, post-war, redress—these are all reference points in Japanese American history, and they define many parts of the experience of the people of Japanese descent in this country. The terms "internment," "evacuation," and "Executive Order 9066" need no explanation in discussions between Japanese Americans.

The importance of both the internment and the subsequent quest for redress in Japanese American history was evident throughout the research and writing of this book. The emotions I encountered were strong, and I soon realized that the fight for redress has powerfully affected every person whose life it has touched. It was moving to listen to former internees, members of Congress, and their aides recount stories of internment and of events in the redress bill's long path to the White House; to learn about the bottled-up emotion released at the commission hearings on redress and about the Nisei World War II veteran who changed an influential congressman's mind about the bill; to hear Congressman Norman Mineta tell his story of boarding the train to a camp as a ten-year-old Cub Scout; and to read graphic descriptions of the awful conditions in which many internees lived. I saw the tears well up in the eyes of Carol Stroebel, Mineta's chief legislative aide, as she spoke about former internees telling her story after story of their internment experiences. I watched Mineta fall into a trance of emotional memories as I asked him to recount the congressional history of redress. I felt the tension in the voice of Grant Ujifusa of the Japanese American Citizens League as he explained how those incarcerated during the war were denied the opportunity to go to college and get jobs of their choice. These experiences not only gave me a personal connection to the bill, but also helped me to better understand my family and, ultimately, myself.

Although most Sansei and Yonsei understand the importance of what our parents and grandparents endured before, during, and after the war, I think too few of us give much thought to it or to the impact it has had on our lives. Having come of age after the civil rights struggles of the 1960s, many of us take the freedoms and opportunities we enjoy for granted and do not fully understand the historical context of the obstacles still before us. It is difficult to comprehend the reality of the camps and to conceive of living behind barbed wire for no reason other than hair color or eye shape. It seems unreal. Yet it happened—to my parents, as well as to 120,000 other Japanese Americans. My parents, grandparents, aunts, and uncles—

my family suffered such an atrocity. My family was herded into concentration camps. At the age of seven, my mother lived in a horse stall that only a
few weeks earlier had housed animals. My father and his young teenage
friends waved good-bye to other Japanese American families aboard trains
headed for the camps, knowing that in a few weeks or days they, too,
would be evacuated. Both my parents' families left established farming
businesses behind, and though both were able to rebuild their livelihoods
after the war, at the time they had no idea what the future held in store.

The legacy inherited by younger generations of Japanese Americans is
the responsibility to ensure that our parents' and grandparents' story is
never forgotten and that what they experienced will never again happen to
any group in the future of this nation. Although blatant racial discrimination is rarely openly condoned today, it is not unthinkable that other
minority groups could experience injustices similar to those suffered by
Japanese Americans during World War II. During the Iran hostage crisis of
the 1970s, there was talk of incarcerating all people of Iranian descent living in the United States. Some have suggested quarantining all people
infected by HIV, the virus that causes AIDS. And during the recent economic downturn, scapegoating of and attacks on the Japanese, all "for-
eigners," African Americans, and other minority groups have unnervingly
paralleled the anti-Japanese rhetoric of the 1940s. Justice for Japanese
Americans prevailed in the fight for redress, but, as the 1992 riots in Los
Angeles clearly showed, differences between various groups of Americans
continue to divide the nation. As the United States becomes increasingly
diverse—in the 1990 census, nearly 30 percent of the U.S. population identified itself as nonwhite or Latino, and the Asian American population
alone doubled in the 1980s—the nation's success in meeting the needs of
its citizens as well as providing leadership in the world depends on its ability to reconcile its racial divisions and to broaden the definition of "Americans" to include people of all races, ethnicities, religions, genders, and
lifestyles. If we fail, we will sacrifice our future and our children's.

Although there is widespread agreement on the significance of both
the internment and redress in American history, it has been both an academic and a personal challenge to balance differing viewpoints on the passage of the redress law. Discussions about redress can be contentious and
political, especially within the Asian American community. Politically progressive members of the community have attributed the legislation's success primarily to grass-roots efforts; more conservative members have
tended to give overwhelming credit to inside-the-Beltway maneuverings;

and others have taken stances somewhere in between. I do not believe that either side can accurately or completely tell the story; the legislation's success involved a combination of both grass-roots and inside-the-Beltway forces. By depicting the passage of the bill in this way, I have sought to give a more comprehensive and balanced view. I have disagreed with family members who place great emphasis on the grass-roots letter-writing campaign, and now, as a Senate staffer myself, I have seen firsthand the limited impact that constituent pressure sometimes has on the policy-making process. I write this book as a member of a group, but I do not speak for the group. Thus, I must cope with perceptions that I am betraying my heritage by downplaying the effectiveness of grass-roots movements and highlighting the white-male-dominated power structure in Washington, D.C. Critiques of this work from both within and outside the Asian American community are inevitable and healthy.

The history of the passage of the Civil Liberties Act of 1988 is an integral part of my past, present, and future, as well as my country's. The internment serves as a reminder of the fallibility of government, and the bill's passage renewed my faith in the American political system. Although the Asian American community has gone on to address new challenges— hate crimes directed at Asians, Japan-bashing, and a resurgence in nativist fears, to name a few—the struggle for redress remains a landmark event in American history. The lessons it has taught us—the danger of wartime hysteria and failed political leadership, the power of a small but sedulous minority group to effect change in this country, the politics required to secure passage of a piece of legislation, and the will of the American people to right a historical wrong—are so valuable for all of us, not just Japanese Americans, as we continue the quest for a more just and equitable America.

Many people made this book possible and deserve my deepest appreciation. I am indebted to the many individuals I interviewed for their time, knowledge, and insights. In particular, I want to thank Grayce Uyehara, Grant Ujifusa, Carole Hayashino, John Tateishi, and Carol Stroebel for their openness and generous assistance. I thank my friends for keeping me sane as I worked on this project and for putting up with my many late nights and weekends spent in the library and in front of the computer.

The efforts of a few people throughout the development of this book were indispensable, especially those of Laura Selznick of the Undergraduate Research Opportunities program at Stanford University, who helped me get my research off the ground, and Muriel Bell, my editor, who assisted me in developing an undergraduate paper into the work before you. Very special thanks go to David Brady of Stanford's Political Science Department for his unending faith in me and his commitment to this project. Only with his support was I able to make this book a reality.

Finally, I must thank my family for encouraging me throughout all stages of the project and for giving me the motivation and reason to research and write this book. It was my parents' active participation in the redress movement that sparked my interest in the legislation and gave me the idea to begin this project, and their continuous support saw me through to its completion. This book is a testament to the example of hard work and commitment that they set for me and my two brothers to follow.

And to all the former internees, I salute you. Your strength, resilience, and sense of justice during the war and throughout the fight for redress were inspirational.

L. H.

Contents

Chronology of Events   *xvii*

Introduction   *1*

1   The Wartime Experience   *6*

2   How Congress Works   *27*

3   Chances for Success   *38*

4   Electoral Interest Analysis of the Roll-Call Votes   *57*

5   The Commission on Wartime Relocation   *81*

6   The Institutional Setting in the 100th Congress   *99*

7   The Nikkei Members of Congress   *110*

8   Strange Bedfellows: Redress for Aleutian Islanders   *120*

9   A Community Comes to Terms with Its Past   *129*

10   Strategy for Victory   *146*

11   The Impact of Other Redress Efforts   *165*

12   The Battle for Appropriations   *181*

Conclusion   *191*

APPENDIX A: Organizational Endorsements of Redress   *199*

APPENDIX B: Executive Order 9066   *204*

APPENDIX C: Public Law 100-383 [H.R. 442]   *206*

Notes   *225*

References   *241*

Index   *247*

Chronology of Events

Dec. 7, 1941   Japan's military forces bomb the U.S. naval base at Pearl Harbor, precipitating the United States's entrance into World War II the next day.

Feb. 19, 1942   President Franklin Delano Roosevelt issues Executive Order 9066, permitting the exclusion of Japanese American residents from the West Coast.

Mar. 2, 1942   Lieutenant General John L. DeWitt, military commander of the Western Defense Command, issues Public Proclamation no. 1, announcing that the western halves of California, Oregon, and Washington, and the southern portion of Arizona, are military areas from which certain classes of people may be excluded.

Mar. 18, 1942   President Roosevelt signs Executive Order 9102, which establishes the War Relocation Authority to help those evacuated under Executive Order 9066.

Mar. 21, 1942   Congress passes Public Law 77-503, making anyone convicted of violating a military order subject to civil penalties, including imprisonment.

Mar. 24, 1942   A curfew is established requiring all Japanese Americans to be in their homes between 8 P.M. and 6 A.M.

Mar. 24–   All persons of Japanese ancestry are evacuated from Cali-
Nov. 3, 1942   fornia and parts of Arizona, Washington, and Oregon and moved to temporary detention centers throughout

	the four states and then to ten permanent internment camps in the deserts and swamplands of California, Arizona, Arkansas, Idaho, Wyoming, Colorado, and Utah. Approximately 120,000 Japanese Americans are evacuated and interned.
Mar. 28, 1942	Minoru Yasui is arrested for violating curfew in Portland, Oregon.
May 16, 1942	Gordon Hirabayashi turns himself in to the FBI in Seattle for failing to register for evacuation.
May 30, 1942	On a San Leandro, California, street corner, Fred Korematsu is picked up by the police for failing to report to the Tanforan assembly center with his family.
June 1942	Japan invades the Aleutian Islands off Alaska. American military officials order the immediate evacuation of all Aleuts, who are shipped to primitive camps until the United States regains control of the islands and allows them to return to their homes in 1944 and 1945.
Jan. 28, 1943	The U.S. War Department creates a segregated, all-Japanese American unit of the U.S. Army, the 442d Regimental Combat Team. Combined with the 100th Battalion, which began as an all-Nikkei unit of the Hawaii National Guard in 1942, the 442d becomes the most decorated American unit of its size in World War II.
June 21, 1943	In *Hirabayashi v. United States* and its companion case, *Yasui v. United States*, the U.S. Supreme Court unanimously upholds the constitutionality of the curfew restrictions as a military necessity.
Dec. 17, 1944	The War Department rescinds the exclusion and detention orders.
Dec. 18, 1944	The U.S. Supreme Court, in its 6–3 decision in *Korematsu v. United States*, holds the exclusion of a single racial group to be within the war powers of Congress and of the president.
Dec. 18, 1944	The U.S. Supreme Court announces its decision in *Ex Parte Endo*, ruling that the War Relocation Authority cannot detain loyal citizens in the camps nor bar them from the West Coast.
Mar. 20, 1946	The last of the concentration camps are officially closed.
July 2, 1948	Congress passes the Japanese American Evacuation

	Claims Act, which allows Japanese Americans to file claims against the government for losses of property that followed from the wartime evacuation and internment.
July 1970	The Japanese American Citizens League (JACL) National Convention passes its first resolution accepting redress as an issue of concern for the organization.
July 1974	The JACL National Convention creates the National Redress Committee.
Feb. 19, 1976	President Gerald Ford formally rescinds Executive Order 9066.
July 1978	The JACL National Convention accepts proposed guidelines for its National Redress Committee to follow; they include working toward securing redress for former internees in the form of individual payments of $25,000 and the creation of a trust fund to benefit Japanese Americans.
Nov. 25, 1978	The first "Day of Remembrance" program is held at Camp Harmony, the former Puyallup, Washington, assembly center.
Late Jan., 1979	The JACL National Committee for Redress meets with Senators Daniel Inouye and Spark Matsunaga and Congressmen Norman Mineta and Robert Matsui to discuss strategies for obtaining redress. A study commission is proposed.
Aug. 2, 1979	A bipartisan group of senators, led by Senators Inouye and Matsunaga, introduces S. 1647, the Commission on Wartime Relocation and Internment of Civilians (CWRIC) Act.
Sept. 28, 1979	Nine Democrats introduce H.R. 5499, the House companion bill to S. 1647, with over 110 cosponsors.
Nov. 28, 1979	Congressman Mike Lowry introduces H.R. 5977, the Japanese American Human Rights Violation Redress Act, calling for compensation of $15,000 for each internee plus $15 for each day in camp.
May 22, 1980	The Senate overwhelmingly passes S. 1647, which has been amended in committee to include the wartime experience of Aleutian Islanders in the commission's study.
July 21, 1980	The House passes H.R. 5499 by a vote of 297–109.
July 31, 1980	President Jimmy Carter signs the CWRIC Act into law.

July 14–
Dec. 9, 1981

The CWRIC holds twenty days of hearings in nine cities, at which over 750 witnesses testify.

Dec. 1982

The CWRIC releases its 467-page report, *Personal Justice Denied*. The report concludes that Executive Order 9066 was "not justified by military necessity" and was the result of "race prejudice, war hysteria, and a failure of political leadership."

Jan. 1983

Fred Korematsu, Minoru Yasui, and Gordon Hirabayashi each file a petition for writ of error *coram nobis* to reopen their wartime cases.

Mar. 16, 1983

The chair of the National Council for Japanese American Redress (NCJAR), William Hohri, files a class-action lawsuit against the U.S. government on behalf of 25 named Japanese American plaintiffs and all former evacuated and interned Japanese Americans in general, stating 22 causes of action, including 15 violations of constitutional rights, and suing for $27 billion.

June 1983

The CWRIC issues recommendations for remedies for the wartime violation of constitutional rights. Among its recommendations are that Congress and the president offer a national apology to the interned Japanese Americans and that Congress make compensation payments of $20,000 to each surviving evacuee and internee. The commission also recommends that restitution be paid to the surviving evacuated Aleuts.

Oct. 6, 1983

Congressman Jim Wright introduces H.R. 4110, which calls for acceptance and implementation of the CWRIC's findings and recommendations.

Nov. 10, 1983

U.S. District Court Judge Marilyn Patel grants Korematsu's petition for a writ of error *coram nobis*, vacating his 40-year-old convictions.

Nov. 16, 1983

Senator Spark Matsunaga introduces S. 2116, the companion bill to H.R. 4110.

Jan. 16, 1984

U.S. District Court Judge Robert C. Belloni grants a motion by the government to vacate Min Yasui's conviction but dismisses his petition for a writ of error *coram nobis*. Yasui appeals the dismissal of his petition to the Ninth Circuit Court of Appeals, but in Nov. 1986, before the court rules on his appeal, Yasui dies. Yasui's family asks

	the Supreme Court to review his case, but in 1987 the Court refuses to grant certiorari.
May 17, 1984	U.S. District Court Judge Louis F. Oberdorfer dismisses the entire Hohri class-action suit on the grounds of sovereign immunity and the statute of limitations.
Jan. 3, 1985	Majority Leader Jim Wright introduces H.R. 442, which is nearly identical to H.R. 4110 but renamed in honor of the 442d Regimental Combat Team, with 99 cosponsors.
May 2, 1985	Senator Matsunaga introduces S. 1053, the companion bill to H.R. 442, with 25 cosponsors.
June 17, 1985	Gordon Hirabayashi's *coram nobis* case goes to a full evidentiary hearing in Seattle.
Jan. 21, 1986	On appeal of Judge Oberdorfer's dismissal of the Hohri class-action suit, the U.S. Court of Appeals for the District of Columbia rules in favor of the NCJAR plaintiffs on the statute of limitations and reverses Oberdorfer's decision.
Feb. 10, 1986	In the Hirabayashi *coram nobis* case, U.S. District Court Judge Donald Voorhees rules that the suppression of evidence by the War Department was a fundamental error and vacates Hirabayashi's exclusion order conviction. He also rules that Hirabayashi's curfew conviction was not affected by the government's misconduct. On appeal, the Ninth Circuit Court of Appeals reverses Judge Voorhees on the curfew conviction and remands the case to him with orders to vacate both convictions.
Aug. 26, 1986	NCJAR appeals Judge Oberdorfer's sovereign immunity ruling in its class-action suit, filing a writ of certiorari to the Supreme Court.
Jan. 1987	New leadership emerges in the House of Representatives, as Jim Wright becomes Speaker, Tom Foley Majority Leader, and Tony Coelho Majority Whip. Congressman Barney Frank becomes chair of the Subcommittee on Administrative Law and Governmental Relations of the Judiciary Committee.
Jan. 6, 1987	Majority Leader Foley introduces H.R. 442, with 124 cosponsors.
Apr. 10, 1987	Senator Matsunaga introduces S. 1009, H.R. 442's companion bill, with 71 cosponsors.

May 13, 1987   The House Judiciary Subcommittee on Administrative Law and Governmental Relations approves H.R. 442 by voice vote.

June 1, 1987   In a unanimous decision, the Supreme Court vacates the D.C. Court of Appeals' decision in the Hohri suit and remands the district court appeal to be reheard by the U.S. Court of Appeals for the Federal Circuit. The federal circuit court subsequently rules in favor of the government.

Aug. 4, 1987   The Senate Committee on Governmental Affairs passes S. 1009 by unanimous voice vote.

Sept. 17, 1987   The House passes H.R. 442, without any major amendments, by a vote of 243–141 on the bicentennial of the U.S. Constitution.

Jan. 12, 1988   U.S. District Court Judge Voorhees sets aside Gordon Hirabayashi's curfew conviction. The government declines to ask for a review of this order.

Apr. 20, 1988   The Senate passes S. 1009 by a 69–27 margin.

July 26, 1988   The conference committee assigned to reconcile H.R. 442 and S. 1009 files its report. The Senate's provision for redress for evacuated Aleutian Islanders is included in the final bill and the time limit for the government to make all payments to internees is set at ten years.

July 27, 1988   The Senate accepts the conference report on H.R. 442 unanimously by voice vote.

Aug. 4, 1988   The House votes 257–156 to accept the conference report on H.R. 442.

Aug. 10, 1988   President Ronald Reagan signs H.R. 442, the Civil Liberties Act of 1988, into law.

Sept. 27, 1989   By a vote of 74–22, the Senate approves a $17.3 billion appropriations package for the Commerce, Justice, and State Departments that includes redress as an entitlement program to be paid out during fiscal years 1991, 1992, and 1993.

Oct. 19, 1989   House and Senate negotiators settle on the Senate's entitlement program for redress in conference committee.

Nov. 21, 1989   President George Bush signs H.R. 2991, establishing redress as an entitlement program.

Oct. 9, 1990   The first nine redress payment checks are distributed to a cross-section of the oldest living former internees.

Mar. 24, 1992   Majority Leader Richard Gephardt introduces H.R. 4551, the Civil Liberties Act Amendments of 1992, which would appropriate additional funds to be used for redress payments, because original estimates of the number of eligible recipients were too low.

Mar. 31, 1992   Senator Inouye introduces S. 2553, the companion bill to H.R. 4551.

Aug. 5, 1992   The Senate Governmental Affairs Committee approves S. 2553 by voice vote.

Aug. 11, 1992   The House Judiciary Committee approves H.R. 4551 by voice vote.

Sept. 14, 1992   The House unanimously passes H.R. 4551 by voice vote.

Sept. 15, 1992   The Senate unanimously passes H.R. 4551 by voice vote.

Sept. 27, 1992   President Bush signs H.R. 4551 into law, ensuring that all eligible Japanese American recipients will receive their redress money. In addition, a new group of eligible recipients—non-Japanese American spouses or parents who were interned—is created.

Righting a Wrong

*Japanese Americans and
the Passage of the
Civil Liberties Act of 1988*

Introduction

In December 1982, the Commission on Wartime Relocation and Internment of Civilians (CWRIC), a congressionally created body, concluded that the evacuation and incarceration of 120,000 Americans of Japanese ancestry during World War II were the result of racism, war hysteria, and a failure of the nation's leadership. Six months later, the commission recommended that the U.S. government offer a national apology and payments of $20,000 to the surviving internees as a form of redress. On August 10, 1988, those recommendations became law when President Ronald Reagan signed the Civil Liberties Act of 1988.

Although numerous bills are passed by Congress and signed by the president each session, the passage and signing of the Civil Liberties Act, with a price tag of $1.25 billion, were historic on three different levels. On its most basic level, the act's importance lay in its direct effect on the lives of the former internees and their families. For the approximately 80,000 surviving Japanese Americans whose rights were violated,[1] it signified the culmination of a 40-year struggle for an apology and monetary restitution from the United States government for the unjust evacuation and internment that they suffered during the war. On a more universal level, the bill's passage reconfirmed all citizens' constitutional civil rights and civil liberties. For this reason, passage was more than just a victory for Japanese Americans: it was a victory for all Americans. It was a promise by the U.S. government that it would never again incarcerate a group of its own citizens en masse, without due process of law, solely on the basis of ethnicity.

But the historical significance of the Civil Liberties Act of 1988 encompasses more than its content and symbolism. On an intellectual level, the case of redress is important in that contemporary political theories of how Congress operates and how legislation is passed have difficulty explaining the bill's passage. Before August 1988, few students of the U.S. Congress would have predicted that the redress movement would win the support of both houses. When redress was first introduced as congressional legislation in the late 1970s and early 1980s, many factors seemed to portend political disaster for the bill. Japanese Americans were a small fraction of the American population—approximately three-tenths of one percent—and were concentrated in a few West Coast states. Since Japanese Americans on the whole had not been very active politically, they had little influence over most of the reelection-minded members of Congress. Even more important, the Japanese Americans who were determined to fight for redress could not agree on the route the movement should take; cleavages within the Japanese American community further weakened the movement. Additionally, the federal deficit was at an all-time high, and with Gramm-Rudman-Hollings spending restrictions coming into play in 1985, it seemed highly unlikely that a bill authorizing over $1.25 billion in monetary compensation to a relatively prosperous minority group would be passed. Considering these factors against a backdrop of representatives' and senators' fixation with reelection, it seems a miracle, if political theorists are to be believed, that the Civil Liberties Act of 1988 was ready for the president's signature on August 10.

This study is not meant to be an all-inclusive history of the Japanese American redress movement, nor a sociological or psychological study of former internees and key players in the redress campaign. Nor is it the primary goal of this book to be a study of mass movements and the dynamics of ethnic communities. The entire redress movement encompassed a wide range of activities, including a class-action suit, a reopening of wartime court cases, community gatherings, and exhibitions—in addition to a legislative campaign—and, admittedly, this book does not begin to cover them all. Many other authors have attempted to record such accounts, and here I only include various events in the redress movement and highlight the activities of various community groups as they *directly relate* to the passage of H.R. 442. Moreover, I do not mean here to pass moral judgment on the individuals or organizations involved; there are no "good guys" or "bad guys." Nor is this book's focus on the legislative campaign meant in any way to belittle the other efforts or to downplay their significance to the Japanese American community as a whole.

This book is first and foremost about political reality and the policy-making process on Capitol Hill. Its purpose is to assess the importance and effectiveness of factors affecting the redress legislation throughout the policy-making process—from introducing the bill in Congress to obtaining cosponsors, to maneuvering through committees, to voting on the bill on the floor and signing it into law—*in terms of a successful legislative outcome.*

Moreover, this book places the legislative campaign for redress in the broader theoretical context of how Congress and the policy-making process work. The crucial question is how a small and politically incohesive minority group was able, at a time of massive federal budget deficits, to secure passage of a potentially controversial bill, authorizing $1.25 billion in redress payments, by members of Congress who would gain no electoral advantage by supporting that bill. Political-interest pressures could not have been the sole factors determining how representatives and senators voted on the legislation. Other institutional and external factors, such as the composition and leadership of both houses of Congress, the organization and lobbying power of opposition groups, the prevailing economic and social environment, and the nature of the legislation itself, must have contributed to the legislation's passage. This book thus seeks to explain why standard conceptions of the legislative process proved to be irrelevant and how various institutional and external factors developed and interacted to account for the passage of the Civil Liberties Act.

To address these questions, this study begins by setting forth the essential historical and theoretical background. Chapter One presents a brief overview of events leading up to the evacuation and incarceration of West Coast Japanese Americans during World War II, the government's rationale for its actions, the conditions in the camps, and the U.S. Supreme Court cases that challenged the constitutionality of the evacuation and detention orders. Chapter Two deals with the dominant political-science explanations of how Congress operates and the factors that typically affect the policy-making process.

Subsequent chapters examine how and why redress passed—the crucial factors involved and the arguments made for and against the bill—despite its potential for failure. Chapter Three analyzes the factors that were possible predictors of the redress legislation's chances for success, given the economic, social, and political situation in the United States at the time. Keeping in mind the historical background outlined in Chapter One, I draw on the political theory presented in Chapter Two to predict the most likely outcomes for the redress legislation in Congress. I also assess the state of certain institutional and external factors that could have affected the bill's fate. To a limited extent, the electoral interest theory discussed in Chapter Two can be used systematically to explain how particular representatives and senators voted on the Civil Liberties Act of 1988. I do this in Chapter Four, where I analyze the three House and four Senate roll-call votes in the 100th Congress that dealt with the redress legislation with respect to different variables that often influence congressional voting behavior—percentage of Asian American constituents, party affiliation, geographic region, and political ideology.

Chapter Five begins to shed light on the particulars of how the bill was passed. As a result of the bill's special nature, timing was crucial, and the 100th Congress provided an auspicious setting for H.R. 442, both institutionally and externally. This chapter analyzes the role of the CWRIC as the catalyst for support for the bill both in Congress and in the Japanese American community at large.

The next three chapters highlight the institutional factors that contributed to the act's passage. In Chapter Six, I examine the fortuitous lineup of House and Senate leaders that developed in the 100th Congress. Despite this advantageous lineup, it is unlikely that the bill would have passed and been funded had it not been for four Japanese American members of Congress, who used their influence and traded favors to persuade their colleagues to support the legislation; thus, in Chapter Seven, I highlight these four men, Senators Daniel Inouye and Spark Matsunaga and Congressmen Norman Mineta and Robert Matsui. In Chapter Eight, I discuss the portion of the Civil Liberties Act of 1988 that deals with redress for the Aleutian Island inhabitants evacuated during the war. The Aleuts' situation during the war was quite different from that of the Japanese American internees, but combining the two causes, a "political marriage of convenience," proved beneficial to both.

In Chapters Nine, Ten, and Eleven, the spotlight shifts to the other principal actor: the Japanese American community. Chapter Nine examines the evolution of key components of the grass-roots lobbying organization and its contribution to the bill's success. Chapter Ten describes how, by coordinating its grass-roots efforts with the lobbying of specific members, the Japanese American Citizens League's Legislative Education Committee (JACL-LEC) became an effective lobbying machine. Chapter Eleven examines the effects of other redress efforts led by the Japanese American community: the three *coram nobis* cases, the Hohri class-action lawsuit, and the role of sympathetic media. Although the passage of the Civil Liberties Act is by far the most significant accomplishment of the redress movement, Congress hardly discussed and passed H.R. 442 in a political and social vacuum; just as external forces might have given members reason to oppose the legislation, these other factors had a positive impact on the bill.

The first eleven chapters thus deal directly with the surprising combination of institutional and external factors that led to the passage of H.R. 442. Although an explanation of the bill's passage is the point of this study, its passage did not mark the end of the struggle for surviving internees. Chapter Twelve deals with the appropriations battle that ensued after H.R. 442 was enacted into law; that battle included another round of legislative maneuvers and politicking and resulted in the establishment of an entitlement program that began payments in fiscal year 1991. New legislation in 1992 authorized additional government funds to ensure that all eligible recipients would receive their compensation.

It need hardly be said that the Civil Liberties Act of 1988 was significant for the surviving Japanese American internees and their families, or indeed for all Americans, whose constitutional protections the act strengthened. But even in a theoretical and academic context, the passage of the act is important; it sheds new light on how policy is made in the U.S. Congress. Electoral interest pressure is not always the greatest determinant of congressional behavior, but rather, as this study shows, only one factor among many. In the case of the 1988 Civil Liberties Act, skillful leadership, the lack of coherent opposition, and a moral appeal to "right a wrong" made a crucial difference in ensuring passage of this landmark legislation.

CHAPTER ONE

The Wartime Experience

The Civil Liberties Act of 1988 was just one of many bills passed by the 100th Congress, yet its significance is hardly refutable, and the story behind it draws from an important but sometimes forgotten event in American history. It is the story of a small but sedulous minority group that has faced generations of personal and legal discrimination as well as economic and social success in the United States. The story involves one of the most extraordinary blows to constitutional rights in the history of this nation, when from 1942 to 1946, approximately 120,000 persons of Japanese ancestry, of whom 77,000 were American citizens, were denied their rights to life, liberty, and property without criminal charges or a trial of any kind. The entire West Coast Japanese American population was forced from its homes and communities and confined in ten internment camps in the nation's deserts and swamplands. With only a few days' or hours' notice, Japanese Americans—men, women, and children, the elderly and the disabled—had to sell or abandon their possessions and leave friends behind for an uncertain future behind barbed wire. The basis for the federal government's policy was the presumption that this group of people, solely because of their ancestry, had to be inherently disloyal to the United States. The story of the Civil Liberties Act does not begin with President Franklin D. Roosevelt's 1942 order authorizing the evacuation and internment, however. Rather, the story reflects a long-standing history of anti-Asian sentiment in this country and the struggle by one minority group, unjustly treated, to restore faith in this nation's system of government.

Although a few Japanese arrived in North America in the 1860s, Japanese immigrants first came to America in significant numbers in the 1880s, principally as contract farm laborers on the sugar plantations of Hawaii.[1] From 1884, when Japan agreed to permit workers to emigrate, to the mid-1890s, some 30,000 Japanese immigrated to Hawaii.[2] Significant immigration to the mainland United States began in the 1890s, with the migration of over 22,000 Japanese, mostly to California, from 1890 to 1900.[3]

Anti-Asian Sentiments on the West Coast

Prejudice against persons of Asian ancestry has an extensive record in American history. The early Japanese in America faced many of the same challenges—and prejudices—as their Chinese predecessors, who first made their way to Hawaii and the mainland in the 1850s. Although about 50,000 Chinese came to Hawaii as contract plantation laborers in the second half of the nineteenth century, many more flooded to the West Coast as a result of the California Gold Rush.[4] In 1848, white immigrants from the eastern United States had wrested control of California from Mexico as a result of the Mexican-American War; shortly thereafter, gold was discovered in the Sierra Nevada mountain range. As people from across the United States and around the world went in search of the golden nuggets, a fierce fight for control of the much-sought-after gold mines ensued between aspiring miners. During the Gold Rush, approximately one-fourth of the miners were Chinese. The dominant white immigrants did not like this new foreign competition and soon resorted to acts of terrorism to scare the Chinese from the mining areas.[5] Moreover, Chinese miners were the target of a Foreign Miners' Tax enacted in the 1850s, which was racially neutral on its face but was hardly enforced against other nationalities.[6]

The Chinese also faced legal discrimination when California gained statehood in 1850. Article XIX of the California State Constitution made it legal for cities to expel Chinese or restrict them to segregated areas and prohibited public organizations or companies from employing Chinese workers. Despite this sanctioned discrimination, the Chinese population in California increased. In the late 1860s, Chinese labor was irreplaceable in the construction of the first transcontinental railroad. At its peak, over 10,000 Chinese worked on the railroad, providing the manual labor needed to clear and grade the way through the snow and rough terrain of the Sierra Nevadas. Once the railroad was completed, these laborers were left unemployed, competing for jobs with the white population as a cheap labor source.[7] White labor unions pushed for the removal of all Chinese from the state. As "The Chinese must go!" became their rallying cry, California officials supporting the white laborers lobbied for federal restrictions on Chinese immigration and American citizenship proceedings. Congress responded by passing the Chinese Exclusion Act of 1882. The purpose of the act was to strip the Chinese of all legal rights and to prevent a permanent Chinese population from forming in the United States. The act gave Chinese people the status of "aliens ineligible for citizenship," prohibited nearly all immigration of Chinese to America, and barred Chinese men from bringing their wives to the United States.[8]

The Issei and the Nisei

The majority of the first Issei, or first-generation Japanese in America, found work in the California farming industry. Although they began as farm laborers, the industrious Japanese had expectations of moving up the social and economic ladder. As Japanese farmers saved enough money to buy or lease their own farmland, they became an integral part of the California agricultural industry. In California, where they made up only about 2 percent of the population, they produced up to 90 percent of some crops, while controlling 450,000 acres of the state's fertile farming land.[9] With the skills and knowledge they brought from Japan, "Issei farmers more often opened up new lands with their labor-intensive, high-yield style of agriculture, as opposed to the resource-intensive agriculture characteristic of American farming."[10] Thus, Japanese American farmers helped revolutionize American farming, contributing to California's ascension as an agricultural mecca.

Nevertheless, the white community viewed Japanese success in agriculture as fierce competition, and the anti-Asian sentiments that terrorized Chinese immigrants now focused on the Japanese. First manifested as verbal abuse and violence, the prejudices against them became institutionalized in law by local, state, and federal governments. In 1913, the California State Legislature passed the Alien Land Law, which prohibited aliens from buying land or leasing it for more than three years. Although it did not specifically name people of Japanese descent, the bill was designed to keep the Japanese out of the landowning class, declaring unlawful ownership of "real property" by "aliens ineligible for citizenship."[11] Other laws were passed that denied the Japanese citizenship, barred them from certain jobs, and kept them from marrying Caucasians.

As in the earlier Chinese exclusion movement, California officials lobbied the federal government to end the immigration from Japan. As a result, the United States and Japan concluded the "Gentleman's Agreement" of 1908, in which both nations agreed to decrease Japanese immigration to the United States.[12] The Asian Exclusion Act of 1924 barred all Japanese immigration for permanent residence. Even with the Exclusion Act, the Japanese population in the United States increased from 111,010 in 1920 to 126,947 in 1940. The immigrant community had a growing number of citizen offspring, who by 1940 made up 62.7 percent of the Japanese American population.[13]

By the time war broke out in 1941, the Japanese American community had undergone a major transformation from a predominantly Japanese-speaking immigrant group to an established ethnic community consisting primarily of English-speaking, American-born, American-educated citizens. While the Issei still identified with Japan to a certain extent, many of the Nisei, or second-generation native-born citizens, were almost entirely America-oriented. Except for the kibei, who were born in the United States but sent to Japan for schooling, Japan was a far-off nation for the Nisei, as foreign as Africa or Europe—the land of their ancestors, but little more. As early as 1920, the Nisei began to form their own organizations, such as the Japanese American Young Republicans and Young Democrats, and the Japanese American Citizens League (JACL).[14] Although other community groups, like the Japanese Association, had already been established, they were geared to the needs of the Issei in dealing with a new country.

JACL was founded in 1929 as a "civic and patriotic group concerned with the well-being and political and economic progress of American citizens of Japanese ancestry."[15] Originally a West Coast organization made up of local chapters, its purpose was to help the American-born Nisei deal with the economic, social, and political discrimination they faced. Although only a small number of Japanese Americans have been active members of JACL throughout its existence, before World War II it was the key organization of Japanese Americans[16] and has been since its inception the community's only national organization.

"Yellow Peril"

As the Japanese Americans organized in the 1930s, anti-Japanese activists intensified their efforts to exclude Japanese from the West Coast. They were aided by a new weapon—the media. "Yellow peril" hysteria in the coastal states was spread by all means of mass communication. As Japan rose as a military power, the media portrayed Japanese Americans as spies for Japan. The Hearst and McClatchy newspapers inflamed the "yellow peril" myths,[17] and motion pictures depicted Japanese people as sinister villains.[18] With no access to the media, Japanese Americans had no means of countering the false accusations and stereotypes. Although many of the Issei had lived in the United States for up to four decades and now considered it, not Japan, their home, racially biased laws denied them the right to become naturalized citizens. Even the Nisei, who as loyal American citizens knew no country other than the United States and spoke English as their native tongue, could not escape prejudice and discrimination in employment, housing, public facilities, and education.

Prejudice against Japanese Americans rose to an even greater height once World War II began. After Japan invaded China in 1937 and Germany invaded Poland in 1939, the United States was driven closer to entering the war. In conjunction with Britain and the Dutch East Indies, the United States placed a total embargo on exports to Japan in July 1941, cutting off Japan's oil supply. With relations between Tokyo and Washington quickly deteriorating, war with Japan seemed imminent. U.S. military intelligence had broken Japan's top secret military codes, and a September 24, 1941, message signaled that Pearl Harbor, Hawaii, was a possible target for Japanese attack. President Roosevelt immediately granted special investigative powers to Curtis B. Munson as special representative of the State Department. Munson had the top-secret task of obtaining "as precise a picture as possible of the degree of loyalty to be found among residents of Japanese descent, both on the West Coast of the United States and in Hawaii."[19] In November 1941, Munson submitted a 25-page report of "uncommon significance,"[20] which certified that Japanese Americans possessed an exceptional degree of loyalty to the United States and that they were no threat to America's security. Munson's conclusions were corroborated by over a decade of surveillance by both domestic and military U.S. intelligence services, including secret Federal Bureau of Investigation (FBI) and Naval Intelligence investigations. Reports by both the FBI and Naval Intelligence confirmed that almost 100 percent of the Japanese Americans were trustworthy. Yet, for reasons still uncertain, the extraordinary results of these investigations were not revealed to the public until the Pearl Harbor hearings of 1946, after the war had ended, and after 120,000 persons of Japanese descent had been rounded up and incarcerated in American concentration camps.[21]

War Breaks Out

On December 7, 1941, Japan's military forces dropped a series of bombs on the U.S. naval base at Pearl Harbor, and the next day the United States declared war on Japan. Japanese Americans' worst fears were soon realized: they were caught in the middle of a war between two unrelenting powers. Although nearly all were Americans at heart, they looked like the enemy. Though the Nisei were American citizens by birth, the Issei suddenly became enemy aliens, denied the right to become American citizens, but no longer true Japanese nationals either. Knowing that a Japanese attack could occur at any moment, the FBI was prepared for the war. Within hours of the bombing, it had arrested 1,291 alien Japanese American community leaders; by February 16, 1942, that number had increased to 2,192.[22] Japanese newspaper editors and publishers, Buddhist and Christian ministers, Shinto priests, community leaders, businessmen, and Japanese language schoolteachers were arrested and sent to detention centers because the FBI considered them suspicious persons.[23] None of the arrestees was ever charged with espionage, sabotage, or any other crime. Some arrestees were released within a few weeks; many others were secretly sent to one of 26 isolation camps throughout sixteen states and the territories of Hawaii and Alaska.[24]

The weeks immediately following the attack on Pearl Harbor were difficult for Japanese Americans. Their actions were severely restricted; their futures were uncertain. Since many adult men had been taken away, Nisei teenagers faced the responsibility of caring for their families. Pressure for harsher measures against the alien and citizen Japanese Americans mounted. Lieutenant General John L. DeWitt, at the time commander of the Fourth Army on the West Coast, was "convinced that the military security required [more assertive] measures."[25] As a result, by the end of December 1941, all enemy aliens in California, Oregon, Washington, Montana, Idaho, Utah, and Nevada were ordered to surrender all "contraband," including shortwave radios, binoculars, cameras, and some weapons.[26] At the discretion of the Justice and War Departments, enemy aliens were excluded from zones surrounding vital installations. In addition, by February 1942, a curfew between 9 P.M. and 6 A.M. and a five-mile travel limit were placed on alien Japanese Americans on the West Coast.[27]

In actuality, the first month of the war was relatively calm; few cases of public panic or hysteria occurred, and Japanese Americans were hardly treated differently than they had been before the war began. Some news-papers were even sympathetic to their predicament of looking like the enemy but being loyal Americans, and some government officials advised the public not to blame the Japanese in America for the war.

But the sympathy was not pervasive, nor did it last for long. The exclusionists who for so long had fought for the ouster of all Japanese Americans were not satisfied with the arrests of a few hundred prominent men; they wanted the entire Japanese American population removed from the West Coast. These anti-Japanese advocates, with feelings of anger and resentment that had been building for a decade, plunged into an all-out hate campaign. The Hearst papers vigorously attacked Japanese Americans. Henry McLemore, a syndicated Hearst columnist, wrote on January 29, 1942: "I am for the immediate removal of every Japanese on the West Coast to a point deep in the interior . . . let 'em be pinched, hurt, hungry. Personally, I hate the Japanese. And that goes for all of them."[28] Other articles with similar messages or fabricated stories of racial violence flooded the nation's newspapers daily. False stories of spies and Japanese activists were published. Actually, throughout the course of the entire war, not one episode of espionage or sabotage is known to have been committed by a Japanese American, citizen or alien.[29] On the other hand, a number of people who were not of Japanese ancestry—many of whom were Germans or of German descent—were charged and convicted of espionage or sabotage for Japan.[30]

Because of the extensive history of prejudice against Japanese Americans, it was all too easy for the general public to believe the fabricated stories of Japanese spies and secret agents. Racist attitudes toward Japanese Americans quickly spread up and down the coast, and groups such as the American Legion, the Native Sons of the Golden West, and the California State Grange vocally expressed their desire for the evacuation and incarceration of all Japanese Americans. To make matters even more dire for Japanese Americans, the liberal groups that were usually committed to civil rights and civil liberties did not defend them. Only some Quaker groups openly supported them.[31] Meanwhile, the California congressional delegation advised President Roosevelt to remove the entire West Coast Japanese population. They were joined by General DeWitt and California Attorney General Earl Warren. In a February 14, 1942, memorandum to Secretary of War Henry L. Stimson, DeWitt submitted a proposal for expanding the exclusion areas and for including all Japanese Americans in the program. Warren, who was later to become governor of California and chief justice of the U.S. Supreme Court when it outlawed racial segregation in the nation's schools, supported DeWitt's plan, expressing some of the most irrational justifications for the evacuation. DeWitt stated that "the very fact that no sabotage has taken place to date is a disturbing and confirming indication that such action will be taken."[32] Warren agreed with DeWitt in contending that American citizens of Japanese ancestry were even more of a threat to the United States than Japanese nationals.[33] These arguments stating that the very loyalty of Japanese Americans to the United States was reason to believe that they would soon be disloyal became a justification for the mass incarceration of Japanese Americans.[34]

In some areas, a few cases of violence against Japanese Americans, including shootings and killings, occurred. Local police and sheriff departments did not come to the defense of Japanese Americans who were abused and terrorized. These attacks on Japanese Americans were even used as a justification for confining and relocating them: it was for their own good, to protect them against racist violence. This argument, however, was the same as saying, "Put all citizens into detention centers so that they will be safe from the criminals outside"—the exact opposite of the fundamental philosophy of the American criminal justice system, that of punishing the criminal, not the victim.

As the exclusion movement began to gain momentum, Congressman John H. Tolan (D–Calif.) from Oakland called for the creation of the Select Committee Investigating National Defense Migration of the House of Representatives, 77th Congress, Second Session—commonly known as the Tolan Committee—in early February 1942. The declared purpose of the committee was to make a concerted effort to determine the facts and the arguments for and against the proposed exclusion. In the end, however, it served merely "to provide a platform for those advocating the removal of Japanese Americans from the West Coast."[35] Although the committee held hearings on the West Coast in February and March, President Roosevelt had given Secretary of War Stimson his approval to start formulating plans for a mass evacuation of all persons of Japanese ancestry from the West Coast on February 11—ten days before the Tolan Committee held its first hearing.[36]

Executive Order 9066

While Oregon and Washington supported California's lobbying, the rest of the country paid little or no attention to the Japanese Americans' situation; many other pressing war problems held their attention. As a result, there was little lobbying against evacuating West Coast Japanese Americans and incarcerating them in inland concentration camps, and President Roosevelt finally gave in to pressure from the West Coast states and dropped his own sort of "bomb" on America. On February 19, 1942, he signed Executive Order 9066, setting the stage for the evacuation of 120,000 aliens and citizens from California, Oregon, Arizona, and Washington. Executive Order 9066 specifically gave Secretary of War Stimson the authority to designate "military areas" from which "any and all persons may be excluded."[37] The order declared that "the successful prosecution of the war requires every possible protection against espionage and against sabotage to national-defense material, national-defense premises and national-defense utilities."[38] Although the order did not specifically name one group or allow for detention, high government and military officials understood that its purpose was to authorize the evacuation and internment of Japanese Americans only—even though less than 4 percent of the 1,100,000 nationals of enemy nations living in the United States in 1942 were Japanese nationals.[39] Although the United States was at war with both Italy and Germany, Executive Order 9066 did not affect persons of Italian or German ancestry, alien or citizen—even though people of Italian and German birth made up the two largest foreign-born ethnic populations in the United States.[40] President Roosevelt signed Executive Order 9066 despite strong opposition from U.S. Attorney General Francis Biddle, who declared the order unconstitutional,[41] and from FBI Director J. Edgar Hoover. Hoover went on record stating that the demand for the removal of all Japanese Americans on the West Coast was not justified on national security grounds; he said the plan was not based on factual evidence, but on public and political pressure.[42]

The issuance of Executive Order 9066 set off a rapid series of executive, military, and congressional events with critical implications for Japanese Americans on the West Coast. On February 20, 1942, Secretary of War Stimson named Lieutenant General DeWitt as the military commander of the Western Defense Command, in charge of executing Executive Order 9066.[43] On March 2, DeWitt issued Public Proclamation no. 1, announcing that the western halves of California, Oregon, and Washington, and the southern portion of Arizona, were military areas, and that certain persons or classes of persons might be excluded from those areas should the situation make it necessary.[44] Sixteen days later, on March 18, President Roosevelt signed Executive Order 9102, which established the War Relocation Authority (WRA) to help those people evacuated under Executive Order 9066.[45] Milton S. Eisenhower was named the WRA's first director, charged with the responsibility of seeing that an orderly evacuation of designated persons from the restricted military areas took place.[46] Although the order did not explicitly call for relocation camps, the newly created WRA was given wide discretion in deciding the fate of the Japanese Americans who were forced to leave their homes. On March 21, Congress backed the evacuation measures by passing Public Law 77-503. The law made anyone convicted of violating a military order subject to a civil penalty of a $5,000 fine, up to one year of imprisonment, or both.[47] During this time, although the West Coast was declared a theater of war, martial law was never declared and habeas corpus was not suspended. The civil court system was in full operation throughout the war, and anyone charged with espionage or sabotage could have been properly tried. Yet the federal government proceeded with its plans for a mass evacuation and incarceration of American citizens and resident aliens, based solely on race, without any individual review.

JACL Urges Compliance

Meanwhile, although in terms of membership JACL represented only a small portion of the Japanese American community, it took a leading role in reacting to the government's orders. As the president and the War Department made their wartime decisions involving West Coast Japanese Americans, the government notified and consulted with JACL, as a national Japanese American organization. JACL leaders testified at the Tolan Committee hearings and met with War Department officials to discuss evacuation plans.

JACL's most significant move during this time—one for which it has been both praised and severely criticized—was its decision to cooperate with the WRA's orders. Army officials had told JACL leaders Saburo Kido and Mike Masaoka about the evacuation decision before it was publicly announced, and after brief but excruciating deliberation, the two concluded that "there was no choice but to cooperate."[48] Although the first impulse was to refuse, Masaoka stated the reasons for cooperating:

> First of all was the matter of loyalty. In a time of great national crisis the government, rightly or wrongly, fairly or unfairly, had demanded a sacrifice. Could we as loyal citizens refuse to respond? The answer was obvious.

We had to reason that to defy our government's orders was to confirm its doubts about our loyalty.

There was another important consideration. We had been led to believe that if we cooperated with the Army in the projected mass movement, the government would make every effort to be as helpful and as humane as possible. Cooperation as an indisputable demonstration of loyalty might help to speed our return to our homes. Moreover, we feared the consequences if Japanese Americans resisted evacuation orders and the Army moved in with bayonets to eject the people forcibly. JACL could not be party to any decision that might lead to violence and bloodshed. . . . As the involuntary trustees of the destiny of Japanese Americans, Kido and I agreed that we could do no less than whatever was necessary to protect that future. I was determined that JACL must not give a doubting nation further cause to confuse the identity of Americans of Japanese origin with the Japanese enemy.[49]

Although for the most part Japanese Americans followed JACL's lead and complied with the WRA's orders, divisions within the community existed. Some individuals condemned JACL as selling out the community, and these conflicts sometimes resulted in violence. JACL, however, reacted strongly to such challenges and attempted to suppress and obstruct any opposition to the government's orders. The organization also refused to support individuals who challenged the constitutionality of the evacuation through the court system and, later, those who resisted the draft.[50]

Evacuation and Incarceration Begin

With the backing of Congress and the president, DeWitt proceeded with his plan to rid the West Coast of all persons of Japanese ancestry. Beginning on March 23, 1942, DeWitt issued a series of civilian exclusion orders and public proclamations that extended travel restrictions, curfew, and contraband regulations to all Japanese Americans, regardless of citizenship, and eventually called for all persons of Japanese ancestry in California and parts of Arizona, Washington, and Oregon to turn themselves in at temporary detention centers near their homes. The evacuation took a total of eight months, from March 24 to November 3.[51] Fifteen temporary detention centers were set up throughout the three coastal states and Arizona. They were mainly converted fairgrounds, race tracks, and livestock exhibition halls. In some cases, horse stalls, which had housed animals only weeks before, were used as living quarters for the evacuated Japanese Americans. The evacuees typically received notice of the evacuation only a few days prior to the required departure date and were allowed to take only those belongings that they could carry with them. Property and other possessions had to be hurriedly sold, often for much less than their value, abandoned, or given away, and many people left behind family pictures and other belongings with personal and sentimental value, not knowing if they would still be there when they returned—if they were ever to return. For many Japanese Americans, it was the destruction of a dream—the American dream—as they lost what they had worked so hard for years to gain.

The official government explanation for the evacuation from the West Coast was "military necessity": Japanese Americans were a threat to national security because their loyalty to the United States could not be proved.[52] It should be noted, however, that those persons considered "suspicious" by the FBI—mainly community and religious leaders—had been rounded up and detained immediately after the attack on Pearl Harbor. In the Supreme Court cases that challenged the constitutionality of the evacuation orders, DeWitt's evidence of Japanese American espionage and sabotage was questionable at best; much of it was "essentially sociological in nature and based on questionable authority"[53]—not the type of factual evidence on which major military decisions are supposedly based. Also, if the purpose of the evacuation orders was to protect the West Coast against espionage and sabotage, how can we account for the infants, elderly, and mentally and physically ill people who were included in the orders? Any person with any percentage of Japanese blood was interned. The only exceptions were imprisoned convicts, patients in asylums, and the few adults with $1/32$ or less Japanese ancestry who were able to prove that they had no contact with the Japanese American community.[54]

If military necessity had been the real issue, then both people of German and Italian descent and Japanese Americans in Hawaii should have been evacuated and interned as well. Yet only Japanese Americans on the West Coast endured across-the-board evacuation and internment under the military orders. People of German and Italian descent on the mainland as well as Japanese Americans in Hawaii were primarily arrested and detained only on an individual basis, if the government felt it had reason to be suspicious of them. By February 16, 1942, the Justice Department had rounded up 1,393 German and Italian nationals, who received loyalty hearings. In the spring of 1942, the War Department seriously considered applying Executive Order 9066 to German and Italian resident aliens. The mass evacuation and incarceration of these groups faced loud opposition, however. Although President Roosevelt approved a plan by Secretary of

War Stimson that allowed military commanders to exclude individuals—not whole classes of Germans and Italians—from militarily sensitive areas, only a few people endured individual exclusion.[55]

In addition, less than 2,000 of the 160,000 persons of Japanese ancestry in Hawaii during the war were imprisoned by the government. By December 10, 1941, 449 Japanese, German, and Italian nationals and 43 American citizens in Hawaii were interned.[56] Martial law was declared in Hawaii on the day Japan bombed Pearl Harbor, December 7, 1941.[57] Under martial law, a number of regulations, such as the imposition of a curfew and the censorship of mail, were imposed upon all people living in Hawaii, although a few were specifically directed at enemy aliens. For example, no Japanese alien could travel by air or change residence or occupation. On December 8, 1941, aliens were required to turn in their firearms, cameras, explosives, shortwave receivers, and other items; two months later these restrictions were extended to American citizens of Japanese, German, and Italian ancestry. In July 1942, President Roosevelt authorized resettlement on the mainland of up to 15,000 people from Hawaii who were considered potential threats to national security.[58] By the end of the war, a total of 1,875 Hawaiian residents of Japanese ancestry had been removed to the mainland: 1,118 to WRA camps and 757 to Justice Department camps. A small number "voluntarily" evacuated to the mainland. Nearly 1,500 Japanese were held in Hawaii's detention camps, created under Hawaii's declaration of martial law and run by the army.[59]

Why did the Japanese Americans on the West Coast face different treatment than these groups? First, as a practical matter it would have been logistically impossible to evacuate and intern all 690,000 Italians and 314,000 Germans living in the United States[60] and all 160,000 Japanese Americans in Hawaii.[61] Moreover, the removal of these populations had economic and political implications. Because Japanese made up 35 percent of Hawaii's total population, evacuating all of them would have crippled the islands' economy. Racial tensions also were muted to nonexistent in Hawaii, which was more ethnically mixed and more racially tolerant than the mainland. Although some anti-Japanese sentiment existed there, it was hardly as prevalent or as well organized as the half-century-old anti-Japanese antagonism on the West Coast. Both Italians and Germans were well integrated into mainstream American society and had achieved political as well as economic clout in many parts of the nation. Italians were more or less dismissed as a security threat. Although a stereotype of an unassimilable, Hun-like German was prevalent, anti-German sentiments never accumulated the organized and strong support of powerful interest groups, as the anti-Japanese movement did. Thus, political opportunism rather than military necessity dictated who was and who was not interned.

Finally, on June 2, 1942, DeWitt declared all parts of the West Coast to be exclusion areas, and no person of Japanese ancestry on the West Coast was free any longer. But on this day, another significant event occurred. At the Battle of Midway in the Pacific theater, the Japanese naval fleet was ruined. Japan was no longer a threat to the West Coast, or even to Hawaii. U.S. government and military leaders were aware that the danger of a Japanese invasion was effectively ended, but they continued their plans to build permanent relocation camps in the interior deserts and swamplands of the mainland United States. If "military necessity" was the real reason for the incarceration, the exclusion policy should have been terminated after the American victory at Midway, since no threat of invasion existed any longer.[62]

Despite the great cost and the wartime shortage of many materials, the government completed the construction of ten permanent concentration camps in the nation's wastelands: Manzanar and Tule Lake in California, Poston and Gila River in Arizona, Rohwer and Jerome in Arkansas, Minidoka in Idaho, Heart Mountain in Wyoming, Topaz in Utah, and Granada (Amache) in Colorado. Most of the Japanese Americans were moved from the temporary centers to the permanent camps hundreds of miles away. Each of the ten permanent camps held between 8,000 and 16,000 evacuees,[63] and a total of approximately 120,000 were ultimately detained.[64]

Life Inside the Camps

Enclosed by high barbed-wire fences, the inland camps were located in desolate areas, miles from the nearest town. Guard towers were placed at strategic locations, with armed soldiers keeping watch at all times. Living quarters were cramped; privacy was scarce. Assigned to specific barrack and block numbers, large families were squeezed into tiny, unpartitioned rooms, the biggest being 20 by 24 feet. Since the rooms had no running water or plumbing, internees were forced to use common latrine, shower, and laundry facilities. Meals were served in large dining halls, and makeshift schools that lacked enough qualified teachers, textbooks, and supplies were created.

As parents lost control of their children and families rarely ate together, internees watched in frustration as the family unit—one of the most important forces of traditional Japanese culture—crumbled.

The internees attempted to make life in the camps bearable by obtaining scrap materials to make furniture and room partitions. Some started small gardens; others used surplus materials to build schools and recreation rooms. The internees ran their own camp farms and produced much of the camps' food. Most of the adults worked as carpenters, teachers, custodians, dishwashers, and gardeners in the camp hospitals, schools, mess halls, and lavatories, even though many had the qualifications to be businessmen, secretaries, farmers, and engineers. The top salary paid was about $19 a month, while the majority of the workers made between $12 and $16 a month.[65]

While Japanese Americans were detained in the camps, Congress proposed and seriously considered blatantly racist legislation. One bill proposed to divest all American-born Japanese Americans of their citizenship and send them to Japan at the war's end. Others proposed that Japanese Americans be used as objects of retaliation for the mistreatment of American prisoners of war in Japan. One representative even suggested a mandatory sterilization program. Fortunately for Japanese Americans, none of these proposals was passed.[66]

After being imprisoned for almost one year, the internees were subjected to another indignity when the WRA distributed a leave clearance form to all internees 17 years of age or older. Questions 27 and 28 of the form, which in reality was a loyalty questionnaire, caused paranoia and created a serious dilemma for internees. Question 27 asked internees if they would serve in the U.S. armed forces whenever necessary, while question 28 asked whether they would "swear unqualified allegiance to the United States of America and faithfully defend the United States from any or all attack by foreign or domestic forces, and forswear any form of allegiance or obedience to the Japanese emperor, or any other foreign government, power or organization."[67] While the first question was straightforward, the second caused much confusion and outrage among Japanese Americans. For the Nisei, a "yes" answer was inapplicable, since they were born in America and had never had any ties with the Japanese government; how, then, could they forswear a previous allegiance to Japan that they had never had? But to answer "no" would mean that they were disloyal to the United States. For the Issei, the question was just as complicated. A "yes" answer would leave them stateless, since they would be renouncing their Japanese citizenship but still could not apply for American citizenship. On the other hand, a "no" answer would portray them as loyal Japanese nationals—spies or agents for the Japanese government. Clearly, both the Issei and the Nisei were in no-win situations.[68] Although most internees, both citizens and aliens, felt they had no other option than to answer "yes" to both questions, a small but significant number were angered by the "trap" set by the government and answered "no" to both; hence their label, "no-no boys." Many of those who answered "no" to both questions were sent to the Tule Lake camp, chosen as the segregation center for those the government considered disloyal, with the intent of sending them to Japan.

Over 6,000 people also petitioned for renunciation of their American citizenship as a way of demonstrating their opposition to the government's actions. The Justice Department approved nearly 5,600 of the applications. As the end of the war drew closer, however, many of these people asked to withdraw their petitions, and after the war, American Civil Liberties Union lawyer Wayne Collins took up their case. To fight their deportation to Japan, he filed suits on behalf of over 4,000 renunciants, arguing that they had acted under duress and coercion. After a series of court proceedings that lasted until 1950, the District Court declared that coercion had to be shown in each individual case. Collins filed over 10,000 affidavits on behalf of the renunciants; the last case was finally processed in 1968.[69]

In addition, by the end of 1945, over 16 percent of the internees had applied for repatriation or expatriation. This demonstration of protest and disillusionment gained momentum as the war progressed, as the 2,255 applications filed by the end of 1942 increased to over 20,000 requests three years later. Few of the applicants actually moved to Japan; once the exclusion order was lifted, many were free to resettle in the United States.[70]

Japanese Americans in the Armed Forces

Although the majority of the West Coast Japanese American population was interned in the camps, a small minority served in the U.S. armed forces. In 1941, when the United States entered the war, about 5,000 Japanese Americans were in the service, but once the nation went to war against Japan, most Japanese American servicemen were rendered Class 4-C by the Selective Service System: enemy aliens ineligible for service. After JACL protests, they were later reclassified as "not acceptable to the armed services because of nationality or ancestry."[71] Two groups were exempt: the

Military Intelligence Service Language School (MISLS), and the 100th Infantry Battalion, which began as an all-Nisei unit of the Hawaii National Guard in 1942.[72]

Since its 1942 convention in Salt Lake City, JACL had made the issue of letting the Nisei fight in combat a top priority; without a military record to prove their loyalty, they argued, the Japanese American community and JACL would not be able to obtain their postwar goals of equality and justice.[73] After negotiations among Colonel William Scobey, Assistant Secretary of War John J. McCloy, and JACL leaders, on January 28, 1943, the U.S. War Department announced its decision to let Japanese Americans volunteer to fight in Europe. President Roosevelt, the same man who had issued Executive Order 9066 less than a year before, blandly declared:

> The proposal of the War Department to organize a combat team consisting of the loyal American citizens of Japanese ancestry has my full approval. . . . This is a natural and logical step toward the reinstitution of Selective Service procedures which were temporarily disrupted by the evacuation from the West Coast.
>
> No loyal citizen of the United States should be denied the democratic right to exercise the responsibilities of citizenship, regardless of his ancestry. The principle on which this country was founded and by which it has always been governed is that Americanism is a matter of the mind and heart; Americanism is not, and never was, a matter of race or ancestry.[74]

At the beginning of 1944, military service for young Japanese American males was no longer voluntary, when the Selective Service reinstituted the draft. This action was met with considerable opposition from certain sections of the Japanese American community. An organized draft resistance formed, most strongly at Heart Mountain, where it was led by the Fair Play Committee.[75]

Forty-five hundred men from Hawaii and the mainland voluntarily joined forces to form a segregated unit, which, combined with the 100th Battalion, was called the 442d Regimental Combat Team. In seven major campaigns, over 18,000 men served with the 442d, which had a 300 percent casualty rate, including 600 men killed. The unit's major campaigns included capturing the French town of Bruyères, after three days of gruesome fighting, and rescuing the "Lost Battalion," a Texas battalion trapped in the Vosges Mountains of France, in its bloodiest assignment. The 442d eventually became the most decorated American unit of its size in World War II. The unit received seven Presidential Distinguished Unit Citations and earned 18,143 individual decorations, including one Congressional

Medal of Honor, 47 Distinguished Service Crosses, 350 Silver Stars, 810 Bronze Stars, and more than 3,600 Purple Hearts.[76] Forty years later, two decorated members of the 442d would spearhead the fight for redress in the Senate. For their fellow senators, the distinguished combat records of Daniel K. Inouye and Spark Matsunaga made a powerful case for passage of the redress legislation.

Although the 442d is the best-known Japanese American contribution to the war, altogether over 33,000 Nisei served in the nation's military forces, as medics, mechanics, and clerks in the Quartermaster Corps, in the WACs, and with the Office of Strategic Services and the Office of War Information, as well as in the 100th, the 442d, and the MISLS, which has been credited with shortening the Pacific War by two years through its skillful translations of battle plans, defense maps, tactical orders, intercepted messages, and diaries.[77] Ironically, these people were fighting for the country that held their families and friends in concentration camps. To quote the report of the Commission on Wartime Relocation and Internment of Civilians, "The question of loyalty had been most powerfully answered by a battlefield record of courage and sacrifice."[78]

Constitutionality Challenged: The Court Cases

Whereas most of the Japanese Americans obeyed the military orders as a way of demonstrating their loyalty to the United States, there were some equally patriotic individuals who challenged the constitutionality of the evacuation and internment orders. While over 100 Japanese Americans deliberately violated at least one of the orders,[79] the government carefully picked three cases for prosecution. Fred Korematsu was charged with refusing evacuation, Minoru Yasui with violating curfew, and Gordon Hirabayashi with violating curfew and failing to report for detention. All three were convicted in the federal courts for disobeying military orders and appealed their cases to the U.S. Supreme Court. Because they entailed violations of law, the cases of Korematsu, Yasui, and Hirabayashi were criminal cases. Conversely, in the fourth case, Mitsuye Endo cooperated with the military orders and broke no laws; thus, her case against the government was a civil suit. She agreed to become a test case challenging the government's right to imprison an American citizen without charge or trial. She filed a habeas corpus petition in July 1942. A year later the decision denying her release was announced, and she also appealed to the Supreme Court.[80]

All four appellants claimed that the military orders were unconstitutional. Unfortunately, prejudice and war hysteria affected even the judgment of the Supreme Court justices, and the judicial branch failed to uphold the Constitution. In the cases of *Hirabayashi v. United States*,[81] *Yasui v. United States*,[82] and *Korematsu v. United States*,[83] the Supreme Court upheld Executive Order 9066 and the army's subsequent evacuation procedures under the guise of "military necessity." It ruled that a group defined entirely by ancestry could constitutionally be placed under curfew and expelled from their homes, because Congress had declared war and the military had decided that it was impossible to separate the loyal from the disloyal. Ignoring the constitutional rights to life, liberty, and property and to due process of law, the Court made what have been called its most ignoble decisions.[84]

In the case of *Ex Parte Endo*,[85] in late 1944 the Court unconditionally released Endo from detainment, ruling unanimously that the WRA could neither detain loyal citizens nor prevent them from going to the West Coast. But Endo lost the point of her suit. The Court ruled that her exclusion from the West Coast and detention for three years without charges had been constitutional, but that since Endo was a proven loyal citizen, she had to be given her freedom.[86] The result of this decision, issued on December 18, 1944, was that the WRA no longer had the legal authority to keep in custody any Japanese American who could not be proven disloyal to the United States.

Secretly notified of the Supreme Court's decision in the Endo case ten days before it was announced, the War Department rescinded the exclusion and detention orders on December 17—one day before the landmark opinion was handed down. On the day of the decision, the WRA, anticipating the ruling's broad implications, announced that all the concentration camps would be closed within a year and that the entire WRA program would be terminated by the beginning of July 1946. Effective January 2, 1945, all Japanese Americans were free to return to their homes on the West Coast.[87] On March 20, 1946, the last camp, Tule Lake in northeastern California, was closed. All the camps were officially and finally empty.[88]

After the War: Rebuilding Lives

The return to the West Coast was not easy for the former internees. They faced acts of violence and pressure groups that desperately wanted to keep them out of their towns and communities. Many restaurants, gas stations, grocery stores, and other businesses refused to serve Japanese Americans after the war. Not surprisingly, Japanese Americans found it difficult to rebuild their lives. Upon return to their "home" towns, many found the belongings that they had been forced to leave behind destroyed, vandalized, or missing. For the Issei, their entire lives' earnings, the fruits of decades of hard work, were lost, and it was too late for them to start rebuilding their fortunes. About 20 percent of the surviving Issei were still below the poverty level in 1970. Many of the Nisei could not complete their college educations because they had to work to support their families.

The losses sustained by Japanese Americans were great. According to a 1942 estimate by the Federal Reserve Bank of San Francisco, wartime property losses alone for Japanese Americans were by then in excess of $400 million.[89] In addition to the loss of material goods, established professional careers as well as those on the rise and college educations were disrupted, at incalculable cost. Besides financial losses, enormous psychological damage was wrought. As families fell apart, individuals lost their self-esteem and pride—two characteristics important in Japanese culture. But most significantly, Japanese Americans had suffered the indignity of being falsely imprisoned by their own government. They had been innocent victims in a racist episode that betrayed the very principles on which the United States was founded.

A New Time, the Same Pain

Five decades have passed since that fateful day when President Roosevelt signed Executive Order 9066. Throughout the years, the stereotypes and racial prejudices applied to Japanese Americans have faded or been transformed. Similarly, the United States's status as a world power has declined in relative terms from that of a victorious bastion of democracy to that of a declining economic power challenged by the country it defeated a half-century ago, Japan. While much has changed, the feelings of anger, pain, and betrayal and the memories of their wartime experience have not been wiped away for many Japanese Americans. Many were so emotionally and psychologically scarred by the internment that they could not talk about the experience until decades later. But once they were able to express their feelings, their resentment toward the government and their anger at the humiliation they experienced were as strong as they had been 40 years earlier. Memories of living in horse stalls, of having to leave behind their homes, friends, and possessions, and of facing a completely uncertain destiny do not fade easily.

It was these deep and intense feelings that set off the grass-roots movement for federal redress. No more would Japanese Americans passively accept the legitimacy of the government's wartime actions. They wanted their story told, to awaken the consciousness of all Americans; they wanted the entire nation to know what they had suffered during the war to ensure that such an injustice would never happen again. But feelings of outrage and betrayal do not easily translate into the successful passage of any congressional bill, much less a substantive piece of legislation like the Civil Liberties Act of 1988. The legislative process is complex and often difficult to fathom, with legislative outcomes the result of a mixture of institutional and external factors. Yet the Civil Liberties Act did somehow overcome all the obstacles before it to reach President Reagan's desk for signing on August 10, 1988. How did this happen? How did a bill first introduced in 1983 become law in 1988? These are the central questions this book will attempt to answer.

CHAPTER TWO

How Congress Works

Constitutionally established as the legislative branch of the federal government, the U.S. Congress is the body in which a substantial portion of public policy is originated, researched, and made into law. The legislative process by which policy is made defies simple definition; it consists of a complex intermingling of personal preferences, institutional structures, and external factors. According to contemporary political theory of how Congress operates,[1] these three elements are hardly neutral in terms of policy-making. Each has implications for how members of Congress behave, and taken together they ultimately determine legislative outcomes. Thus, for a comprehensive explanation of how legislation is passed, contemporary conceptions of the legislative process first emphasize the significance of the electoral institutions of Congress, especially the development of the personal vote, to representatives' and senators' motivations and goals. Once the members' personal goals are established, three other sets of critical variables—organized interest groups, the institutional structure of Congress, and external factors—come into play.

The Rise of the Personal Vote

An important phenomenon in congressional elections of the last four decades has been the rise of the personal vote. Until the 1950s, party affiliation was the dominant factor determining the candidates for whom voters cast their ballots. Since then, however, the tendency to vote along party lines has noticeably declined, with congressional candidates appealing to voters on the basis of their personalities and service to constituents rather than their party affiliations. Voters no longer tend to vote the straight party line. This change is primarily the net result of three developments: the rise in ticket-splitting at the turn of the century, the expansion of the federal bureaucracy in the 1930s and the postwar period, and the Eisenhower presidency, particularly Eisenhower's reelection in 1956.

The history of congressional elections reveals that the advent of the personal vote was a post–World War II phenomenon. In the nineteenth century, the voting mechanism explicitly prevented ticket-splitting, as voters could vote for only one party's candidates in all races. Starting in 1888, however, a reform movement to clean up the American political scene after the Civil War and the contested presidential election of 1876, which pitted Samuel J. Tilden against Rutherford B. Hayes, resulted in the adoption of the Australian ballot—on which one votes for an individual candidate in each race, rather than for one party's slate of candidates in all races—marking the beginning of ticket-splitting. By 1893 almost every state had adopted the Australian ballot. With ticket-splitting, voters could for the first time vote for a presidential candidate of one party and a senatorial or congressional candidate of another.

The personal vote was slow to develop, however, because until 1908, parties still held nearly absolute control over the congressional nominating process. In 1904 the Progressives advocated direct-mandated primaries, in which the general public votes for a party's nominee, and by 1914, 40 of 48 states had direct-mandated primaries. The personal vote still did not blossom until the 1950s, though, because an electorate of strong party identifiers continued to exist; as a result, candidates had no incentive to swing voters of other parties to vote for them.

Beginning in the 1950s, the growth in bureaucracy gave members of Congress a mechanism to appeal to voters of the opposite party. According to Morris Fiorina, an institutional change—the expansion of the bureaucracy—encouraged a behavioral change among members, which in turn led to a behavioral change among some voters.[2] With a more activist federal government, voters found themselves increasingly dealing with bureaucratic agencies, whether to locate a lost social security check or to receive a veterans' benefit. Possessing the unique power to expedite bureaucratic activity, representatives and senators gained many more opportunities, through casework and pork-barrel activities, to help meet their constituents' needs and to shine in their eyes.

At the same time the bureaucracy was expanding, members of Congress discovered ways to advertise these services through increased use of the franking privilege and the media. Most important, the newborn medium of television began to fill American living rooms in the 1950s. Thus, congressional candidates became visual media figures; the way they looked and spoke became as important as what they said about political issues. Not only could incumbents publicize their constituent services to a wide audience, but all candidates could use personality and style to their electoral advantage.

Finally, perhaps the single most significant factor in the rise in the personal vote was the election of 1956. In 1952 Dwight D. Eisenhower won the presidency and the Republican Party gained control of the House. In 1954 House Democrats regained a majority, and in accordance with the 1832–1946 "rule" that presidential election outcomes were predicted by which party controlled the House in the previous off-year election,[3] it appeared that a Democrat would win the presidency in 1956. Democratic incumbents in Congress, however, drawing on newly developed polling techniques that predicted Eisenhower's defeat of Democratic presidential candidate Adlai Stevenson, knew it would have been political suicide to campaign against such a popular American hero as Eisenhower. As a result, they developed strategies to distance themselves from their own presidential candidate to improve their chances for reelection. In the 1950s, then, congressional candidates had both the ability and the incentive to appeal to voters as individual personalities; thus began the use of the personal vote.

The rise in the personal vote means that reelection has become the primary concern of members of Congress. They are preoccupied with appealing to their constituencies because it is as individuals, not as members of one party or the other, that they win or lose elections. According to David Mayhew, even though members of Congress have other goals, such as making conscientious public policy and achieving prestige within their respective chambers, "the electoral goal has an attractive universality to it. It has to be the *proximate* goal of everyone, the goal that must be achieved over and over if other ends are to be entertained."[4] Because partisan ties are weak, members spend more time and energy catering to their constituents, regardless of party, through nonpartisan constituent services and pork-barreling. They serve individual voters, for example, by tracking down lost social security checks or by creating jobs at a new Air Force base in the district. To scare off potential competitors, they also build up huge caches of campaign funds, through contributions from individuals, businesses, political-action committees, and organized interest groups.[5]

The policy consequences of this "reelection mentality" are significant. The very idea that members of Congress predominantly focus on party-neutral, uncontroversial constituent-service activities works counter to the congressional role as the legislative, policy-making branch of the federal government. Mayhew's model of the "electoral connection"—that members of Congress engage in advertising, credit claiming, and position taking to enhance their chances for reelection—takes this problem to the extreme. Admittedly, Mayhew's model fails to account for public policy at all, but even in more nuanced models of congressional behavior, responsible public policy-making is still difficult to find. Members are captured by local single interests; they are concerned about luring a NASA contract to their district or keeping a nuclear waste site out. They are especially responsive to organized interest groups that can rally a large number of voters on election day and make major financial contributions to their campaigns—groups such as labor unions, industry associations, religious groups, and professional organizations. Although responsiveness and accountability to one's constituents may seem benign—in concept at the very root of representative democracy—devotion to organized local interests comes at the expense of responsible national policy. The phrase "more responsive, but less responsible" is a fitting description of Congress in this situation. On the whole, representatives and senators are less interested in what is good public policy for the entire nation, as on such issues as homelessness, AIDS, or public education, than they are in pleasing local interests.

The rise in personal voting and members' consequent preoccupation with their own reelection make getting bills passed by both houses of Congress difficult. A bill's chance of passage depends less on what a representative or senator thinks is just or in the national interest than on other variables. The legislative process varies greatly from one situation to another. It is possible, however, to outline the conditions that are most likely to ensure legislative success for any given bill.

The Power of Organized Interest Groups

The first important set of variables involves the organization and mobilization of interests concerned about a specific piece of legislation and the intensity of their lobbying efforts for or against it. Concerned about securing both votes and campaign funding, members of Congress are most responsive to the best-organized interest groups, those that can be the greatest help (or greatest threat) at election time. Although it may appear that countless organized interest groups are at work at all times—from the NAACP to the AFL-CIO to the American Association of Nurserymen—their ability to pressure members to pass or block legislation varies greatly from issue to issue, from group to group, and from situation to situation. In general, the power of a particular group depends on the preferences of its members, the intensity of those preferences, their incentive to take action, and their ability to do so.

What are the factors that affect a given interest group's likelihood of vigorously pressuring Congress to pass a bill that it favors? To put the situation in economic terms, on the demand side—that is, the demand for action to influence policy-making—one must examine the number of substitutes for the legislation that are acceptable to the group, the magnitude of the legislation's benefits as a whole, and the magnitude of per capita benefits. If an interest group has few or no acceptable alternatives to the proposed bill, it is more likely to work hard to pressure Congress to pass it, all other factors being equal, than if many substitutes are available. An interest group that would accrue a moderate to high level of benefits from the legislation is more likely to lobby Congress in an organized fashion than a group whose benefit would be small. Similarly, the larger the per capita benefit, the more likely members of the group are to take action.

On the supply side, the size of the group's membership, its costs of organizing, its coverage across the nation, and its resources are all important. It is debatable whether groups with large or small memberships will take the most vigorous action. The larger the membership, the larger the number of votes that can be dangled to pressure members of Congress. Long-established groups with large memberships may be more mobilized for action than newer and smaller groups. On the other hand, the larger the group, the more diverse its membership and the more difficulty it may have organizing around any one vote. For those reasons, at times smaller groups may more effectively mobilize themselves for action than their more cumbersome counterparts. Thus, organizational costs matter: the lower the organizational costs, the more time and energy a group can invest in lobbying for a bill.

More important than sheer size is a group's distribution of members across the country. The larger the geographic area over which the group is organized, the more representatives and senators the group can pressure and the greater its potential impact on legislation. For example, although the aircraft industry is important to the nation's military forces, the aircraft lobby is a less powerful interest group than a group like the Auto Dealers Association, since aircraft manufacturing plants are situated in only a few areas of the country, whereas car dealerships are located in virtually every town and city. Important, too, are a group's resources, notably money. An interest group with insufficient resources to pay for lobbying efforts and campaign contributions will have little impact on legislation regardless of its size.

Of course, not every one of these conditions must be met for an interest group to lobby Congress successfully, but the more of them that are present at one time, the higher the likelihood that the group will influence the legislative outcome. For the purpose of this study, the important point is that a piece of legislation would be most likely to pass when the benefits are concentrated in a large, organized group and the costs are dispersed among a wide number of unorganized interests. In this situation, the proponents of the bill would probably be organized and the opposing forces probably would not put forth much resistance.

How Institutional Features of Congress Affect Policy

The organization of interest groups is only one factor affecting the potential success of legislation. The second significant factor is the institutional structure of the policy-making process, specifically the committee system, the composition of the House and Senate, and the rules of each chamber. Institutional structures in Congress may prove to be the greatest obstacle to legislation; no matter how well organized an interest group for a particular cause may be, the chances of legislative success will be diminished if, for example, the chair of the relevant committee is a vehement opponent of the bill. The way in which the institution is structured—its rules, leadership, and composition—is hardly neutral; rather, it has a significant effect on all legislative outcomes.

The committee system is probably the most crucial institutional determinant of the fate of proposed legislation. The functional role that committees play in policy-making, the way committees are composed, and the differences among the various committees all have far-reaching policy implications. The functional importance of committees is obvious: committees are the institutional mechanisms that review, research, and mark up legislation for the chamber as a whole. A committee has three primary powers, known as ex ante, ex post, and gains in trade. The ex ante power, often referred to as monopoly and gatekeeping power, is the power to set the agenda for policy issues under the committee's jurisdiction. Once the president or a legislator proposes a piece of legislation, it is sent to the committee that has jurisdiction over it, where it is in turn assigned to the relevant subcommittee. At this point the subcommittee chair may decide to hold hearings on the bill, with presentations by witnesses for and against it, to educate members on the bill's substantive merits and possible pitfalls. At the conclusion of the hearings, the subcommittee "marks up" the bill, amending and rewriting it for presentation to the full chamber. Alternatively, the chair may decide against holding any hearings, in effect killing the bill before it has a chance to be considered by the body as a whole or even by the entire committee.[6] A committee's ex post power refers to its role after similar bills have passed in both houses. The chair selects the members who will sit on the conference committee charged with reconciling the two bills for final votes by both houses. In many cases the compromises reached in the conference committee determine whether or not the legislation will secure the votes needed in both chambers for final passage.[7] Finally, the concept of "gains in trade" means that if members let one committee use its ex ante and ex post powers to bolster the reelection chances of its members, they allow other committees to behave in similar fashion.

Although the functional powers of committees are obviously important, the effect of committee composition on policy-making is even more direct. According to the widely accepted "preference outlier" theory of the committee system, the members of a committee are usually representatives or senators with specific electoral interests in that committee's legislative realm. They also tend to be more favorably disposed toward government aid and intervention in that realm than the body as a whole. Thus, when the committee exercises its three powers (ex ante, ex post, and gains in trade), legislation emerging from the committee tends to be much closer to the preferences of the median member of the committee than to those of the median member on the floor. For example, the members of the House Committee on Agriculture tend to be from predominantly rural areas and are more likely to favor increased federal aid to farmers than the House overall. Because the committee sets the agenda, controls the conference committee, and benefits from gains in trade, the final legislative outcome is likely to be closer to the committee's pro-aid stance than to the stance of the House as a whole. Thus, the tendency of committees to be composed heavily of members who stand to benefit from its policy-making powers routinely results in the passage of preference-driven legislation.[8]

While this preference outlier theory is the prevailing general theory of how committees operate, the wide variation among committees also has critical consequences for policy-making. Richard Fenno explored this aspect of the committee system in depth in *Congressmen in Committees*. Assuming that congressional committees matter, Fenno argues that these committees differ, and that these differences greatly affect how a committee operates and what type of legislation emerges from it. Committees differ, according to Fenno, across five different variables: member goals, environmental constraints, strategic premises, decision-making processes, and decisions.[9] Members of Congress have three basic goals, Fenno contends: to ensure their own reelection, to gain influence within the parent chamber, and to make good public policy. The opportunities to achieve these goals vary widely from committee to committee. For example, members of the Interior committees often use their positions to help their constituents and thus increase their chances for reelection, whereas Education and Labor committee members often emphasize strong personal concerns for the content of public policy in the committees' areas of jurisdiction.[10] Committees also differ in the environmental constraints they experience. Other parties with interests in the committee's policy domain—whether they be congressional colleagues, members of the executive branch, members of clientele groups, or members of political parties—contribute to the environmental constraints on a given committee. For example, the policy coalitions of the Foreign Affairs committee are executive-led; House members have little direct interest in foreign affairs, whereas the president uses the committee to legitimate his foreign policy.[11] With their divergent goals and environmental constraints, committees also differ in their strategic premises, which are the decision rules that come into play as they try to meet the members' goals. As a result of the diversity in the first three variables, committees also differ in their decision-making processes, particularly in the levels of partisanship and specialization that come into play, and in the actual decisions that they make.

The implications of these three aspects of the committee system— committee powers, composition, and variation—are tremendous. First, the way in which a bill is written is crucial; members go to great lengths to draft a bill in such a way that it will be sent to a favorably disposed committee. Even more important, these institutional features give committee chairs and subcommittee chairs power to determine the fate of any given bill. Although committee chairs are in no way autocratic rulers over the business of their committees, they do control large committee staffs and play a strategic role in deciding which bills their committees will take up.

Chairs who oppose legislation proposed by the president may delay taking up the bill, water it down, or substitute their own legislation on the same subject. Both committee and subcommittee chairs may use committee hearings on a bill strategically, manipulating the timing and length of the hearings to favor the side they support.

The magnitude of power held by committee and subcommittee chairs varies from the House to the Senate, and from committee to committee. In the smaller and more collegial Senate, the majority of the review of and debate over legislation takes place at the committee, rather than subcommittee, level. Conversely, in the House, subcommittees play a large role in the legislative process. Thus, in the House, subcommittee chairs often have as much power as full committee chairs to manipulate the future of a given bill, whereas in the Senate, committee chairs are best able to exercise significant leverage in determining whether a piece of legislation makes it to the floor for consideration by the full chamber. Even within each house, there is variation in the power of committee and subcommittee chairs. As noted earlier, the goals of committee members vary, and as a result, committee and subcommittee chairs play different roles depending on the type of committee they oversee. For example, in the House, chairs of policy committees like Judiciary and Foreign Affairs are "policy combatants competing for committee endorsements of their own policy preferences rather than solitary leaders with the power simply to implement those preferences."[12] The chairs of constituency committees like Veterans' Affairs and Small Business, on the other hand, are encouraged to build "a committee consensus or a system of mutual noninterference, depending on the nature of the constituency interests served."[13] Despite the differences in power distribution, though, in both houses it is to the advantage of any legislation to be handled by a committee and subcommittee with chairs supporting it. It can hardly hurt a bill to have the relevant full committee or subcommittee chair using all possible powers to clear the way for a favorable legislative outcome.

Once a bill comes out of committee and arrives on the floor, two additional institutional features have significant policy consequences: the composition of the House and Senate and the rules governing each body. Because almost all members of the House represent much smaller geographic areas and much less diverse constituencies than members of the Senate, they are more closely tied than senators to specific local interests. House members' districts tend to be predominantly urban or predominantly rural, economically depressed or well-off, and racially or ethnically homogeneous. Senators, conversely, tend to represent constituencies that contain much more diverse elements. Most states have major metropolitan areas as well as small towns, economically prosperous as well as depressed regions, and predominantly white as well as predominantly nonwhite and racially mixed areas. Senators, then, have a broader base of electoral support than members of the House. As a result, senators are much freer than House members to vote for a bill they believe to be in the best interests of the nation as a whole, without worrying greatly about electoral backlash from one specific segment of their constituencies.

Moreover, the geographical distribution of organized interest groups across the nation is more crucial to getting a bill passed in the House than in the Senate. To cause senators to take notice of it, a clientele group need only be an organized and powerful force in *parts* of each state; but for it to influence each representative, it must be an organized electoral force in *most districts* of every state. Thus, a bill that is in the best interests of the nation as a whole but lacks strong organized backing throughout the nation is more likely to pass in the Senate than in the House.

The different formal rules of the House and Senate also help determine a bill's chances for success in each house. For example, in the Senate, when a bill is stalled in committee because of a hostile chair or some other constraint, a senator can attach the legislation as a "rider" to a bill on the floor, often on a completely different issue, that seems likely to pass, thereby bypassing the committee process completely. This is not possible in the House, which has a strict rule of germaneness.[14] Another important difference is that the Senate permits filibusters and the House does not. Senators can use the filibuster to prolong debate on a bill and thereby to stall the legislative machinery for an extended period of time.[15] A successful filibuster may permit two kinds of outcome in the Senate that cannot occur in the House. First, it may be able to pass a bill that would not have survived in the House because in the extra time provided by the filibuster, proponents gather additional support. A filibuster may also be used to block legislation by bringing almost all legislative activity in the Senate to a dead halt.

The Impact of External Factors

The final set of variables that influences a bill's chances of success consists of external factors that affect members' votes. These are forces that are outside the institutional structure of the policy-making process and beyond the control of concerned interest groups. These extrainstitutional factors are relatively nebulous and vary widely from situation to situation, ranging from the president's current popularity to international crises to natural disasters. These factors reflect, more or less, the current political, social, and economic conditions of the nation—and in some cases of the world—at the time the legislation is under consideration. Some such factors may be crucial to one bill, yet play no role whatsoever in the fate of another. However nebulous they may be in general theory, though, their impact on legislative outcomes can hardly be doubted.

The external factor most relevant to the Civil Liberties Act of 1988 was economics. The state of the national economy is extremely important when members of Congress consider bills that allocate large sums of government money, as in this case. When the federal deficit is alarmingly large, as it has been throughout the past decade, representatives and senators scrutinize monetary allocations much more severely than when the economy is thriving. Thus, even if members of Congress acknowledge the merits of a particular bill, they may still decline to vote for it if it entails large expenditures at a time of fiscal budgetary constraints. Clearly, such extrainstitutional factors have a significant impact on legislation even though they are beyond the control of both Congress and interest groups.

Representatives and senators can hardly be viewed solely as disinterested national legislators seeking to serve the best interests of the country as a whole. As reelection-minded public servants, they use the policy-making process, within the constraints of institutional structures and external forces, to appeal to their constituents and supporters. But what did this mean for the movement to redress the wartime experience of Japanese Americans on the West Coast? What were the chances of a bill designed to accept and implement the findings and recommendations of the Commission on Wartime Relocation and Internment of Civilians? These questions form the foundation for this study, and it is to them that I now turn.

CHAPTER THREE

Chances for Success

It is a rare accomplishment to have a bill passed by Congress and signed into law by the president. Even though thousands of bills are introduced in each Congress, only a small percentage emerge from committee, and even fewer secure passage on the floor. For example, of the 11,282 different bills and resolutions introduced in the House and Senate in the 100th Congress, only 761 were enacted into law. As we saw in the previous chapter, legislation succeeds only when favorable institutional and external factors converge. Often, the convergence of these factors is purely coincidental. The ideal circumstances for legislative success are specific to each bill, and for any one bill, the chance of having all, or even most, of the favorable factors in place is small. Such was the situation facing the original redress bills in the early 1980s.[1] The relevant institutional and external factors seemed to predict almost certain failure. It looked as if the bill would never get out of committee; passage by both houses of Congress seemed inconceivable. Demographically and organizationally, the Japanese American community did not appear to have the size, the resources, or the capacity for mobilization to launch an effective lobbying campaign in support of the bill, whereas opposition groups, including some veterans' and historical organizations, seemed to have the potential to block it. External factors ranging from the federal budget deficit to strained race relations seemed to presage failure.

Institutional Barriers to Redress

It took four years from the introduction of H.R. 4110 and S. 2116 before the two redress bills—by then renumbered H.R. 442 and S. 1006, respectively—made it out of committee. At the time of their introduction in the fall of 1983, both bills faced major institutional stumbling blocks. In the House of Representatives, the committee system provided the primary barrier, while in the Senate it was the distribution of power between the Democratic and Republican parties. Although redress had the support of Congressman Peter Rodino (D–N.J.), the chair of the House Judiciary Committee, the Subcommittee on Administrative Law and Governmental Relations and its chair in the 98th Congress, Texas Democrat Sam Hall, appeared to be insurmountable obstacles. Elected to represent the First Congressional District of Texas, a rural area in the northeastern corner of the state that most resembles the deep South, Hall hardly had the credentials of a staunch supporter of redress. With the most conservative record among Texas Democrats, Hall had a low Americans for Democratic Action (ADA) rating of 5 percent[2] and an American Civil Liberties Union (ACLU) rating of 8 percent in 1982,[3] while his American Conservative Union (ACU) rating tended to be one of the highest among Democrats.[4] Not surprisingly, the issue of redressing the loss of constitutional rights of Japanese Americans during World War II was not a priority for Hall. He held hearings on the legislation, but was not willing to bring it to the full Judiciary Committee. His opposition meant the bill would not go before the full House for final vote. Hence, it did not matter in this case what support could be expected in the chamber as a whole; death in committee would put an end to surviving internees' hopes of obtaining redress from Congress for their wartime losses. The bill could only make it out of committee if Hall were to change his position on the matter, or if a more sympathetic chair were to replace him. Neither seemed likely to happen, at least in the near future, given Hall's voting record on civil rights and his seniority on the committee.

In the Senate, the situation was slightly different, but equally problematic for the bill. At least in the House there existed the small chance that the bill could get out of committee. In the Democrat-dominated House, the bill would have then had some possibility of being passed. But in the upper house, S. 2116 faced a Republican majority. Thus, control of the relevant subcommittee and committee—the Federal Services, Post Office, and Civil Service subcommittee of the Governmental Affairs Committee—was in Republican hands. Although Ted Stevens of Alaska, an ardent supporter of the Senate bill, was chair of the relevant subcommittee, William V. Roth, the senior senator from Delaware, was chair of the Governmental Affairs Committee and a known opponent of redress. A relatively consistent conservative whose ADA ratings hovered around 20 percent and whose ACU ratings were in the 70s and 80s,[5] from a state with only a minuscule percentage of Asian Americans,[6] Roth had been reluctant even to assign the bill to the subcommittee. Even if it had managed to make it out of committee in 1983, the redress bill would have faced a Republican-dominated body created on the coattails of President Ronald Reagan, a right-wing conservative. In general, Republicans tend to be less sympathetic than Democrats to civil-rights and civil-liberties issues, so a vote on redress in the Senate would likely have had a negative outcome. All in all, therefore, in both the House and the Senate, institutional factors seemed stacked against the bill. The importance of these barriers cannot be overstated; the failure of the bill even to be reported out of committee made other potential factors, such as the organization of interest groups, essentially irrelevant. Securing the support of key powerholders in Congress, then, would be critical if redress were ever to have a chance to pass—or even to be debated by the full chambers.

The Japanese American Community

Even if the redress legislation overcame institutional obstacles and reached the floor of both House and Senate, at the time of the 98th Congress the Japanese American community was hardly in a position to be an effective lobbying force on Capitol Hill. As an organized interest group, the Japanese American population lacked many of the qualities outlined in Chapter Two that are most vital for successful lobbying: Japanese Americans made up a minute percentage of the American population, and that percentage was heavily concentrated in a few Pacific Rim states; Japanese Americans, on the whole, had not been active in national politics; in monetary terms, the benefit the bill promised to each interned Japanese American was small relative to the losses sustained during the war; and cleavages among various sectors of the community precluded a unified effort to support the bill. In short, it was unlikely that the Japanese American community would mount a successful lobbying campaign; the community appeared to have neither the will nor the resources to see redress through to the end.

As we saw in the last chapter, in assessing the potential effectiveness of an interest group as a congressional lobby, the first indicator is the group's size and distribution. According to 1980 census data, Japanese Americans comprised just 0.3 percent of the U.S. population;[7] in 1990, that percentage remained virtually unchanged.[8] All Asian Americans together made up only 1.5 percent of the U.S. population in 1980.[9] Although Asian Americans were the fastest-growing ethnic group in the 1980s, they had only grown to 2.9 percent of the U.S. population by 1990.[10] Furthermore, they are concentrated in a few Pacific states—California, Hawaii, Washington, and Oregon—and in a few metropolitan areas elsewhere, such as New York City and Chicago. In certain congressional districts, such as in Gardena, California, and Hawaii, the Japanese American population is clustered with enough density to form a potential voting bloc. With the exception of Hawaii, however, the population of which is about 62 percent Asian American,[11] Japanese Americans do not wield much political influence over their elected officials. Again excluding Hawaii, even within the states and areas where they are mainly concentrated, they still constitute a small fraction of the voting public, and their potential political power within individual districts is limited, because unlike other minority groups such as Latinos or African Americans, Asian Americans "do not live in geographically isolated enclaves, and when they do, they aren't big enough to make politics worth pursuing on an ethnic basis."[12] The evacuation and internment dispersed an already small population throughout the country. Prior to the war, Japanese Americans tended to live in enclaves, so-called Japantowns, predominantly around California's fertile agricultural areas. After the war, though some returned to the same areas, many others relocated. Some, fearful of the anti-Asian racism still prevalent on the West Coast, headed east and settled in such areas as New York City and Philadelphia. Even in the West they are dispersed enough to prevent strong communities from developing, and in most other parts of the country, the number of Japanese Americans is negligible.

Even in the areas where Japanese Americans make up a substantial percentage of a representative or senator's constituency, they often do not form a powerful voting bloc, partly because on the whole Japanese Americans have not been very active in national politics or predominantly committed to either party. Statistics on the level of Japanese American political contributions and on the percentage of Japanese Americans who vote in elections point to a politically apathetic population. Although Asian Americans on the whole have increasingly become large campaign contributors,

Japanese Americans tend to be among the least generous.[13] According to a survey conducted by the University of California, Irvine, and the California Institute of Technology, only 77 percent of California's Asian Americans who were eligible to vote were registered to do so, compared to 87 percent of whites and 88 percent of blacks; moreover, the survey revealed that among Asian Americans, Japanese Americans were particularly unlikely to register and vote.[14] With the exception of Hawaii—which, with a sizable Japanese American population, has seen Japanese Americans elected to such positions as U.S. senator, U.S. representative, and governor—few states have elected Japanese Americans to high office. California has elected two Japanese American representatives, Norman Mineta from the Thirteenth Congressional District centered in San Jose and Robert Matsui from the Third District in Sacramento, but both have predominantly non-Japanese and non-Asian American constituencies.[15] California elected S. I. Hayakawa for one term as U.S. senator in 1976, but as a Canadian by birth, Hayakawa had not lived through the Japanese American wartime experience and was never a supporter of redress.

On the state and local levels, some Asian Americans have made inroads into electoral politics. California's secretary of state, March Fong Eu, was elected in 1974 and remains in office today. In 1984, Chinese American physicist S. B. Woo successfully ran for lieutenant governor of Delaware, a state with a negligible Asian American population, but he lost to Republican incumbent William Roth in his 1988 bid for a U.S. Senate seat. In California, however, the state with the largest Asian American population other than Hawaii, the first Asian American to serve in the state legislature since Assemblyman Paul Bannai left in 1980, Republican Nao Takasugi, was not elected until 1992. Los Angeles City councilman Michael Woo and former Villa Park, California, mayor Carol Kawanami did run successfully for local office. Prior to their service in Congress, Bob Matsui was a Sacramento city councilman, and Norman Mineta served as mayor of San Jose. Within local communities, some Asian Americans have also been active participants in social protests and movements, such as in the organization of garment and restaurant workers and in the creation of advocacy groups. As a force in electoral politics on the federal level and in the power games of Capitol Hill, however, their impact has been limited.

The limited political activism, both within the Asian American community as a whole and specifically among Japanese Americans, can be explained by a number of primarily sociological factors. After the war, Japanese Americans had to focus on survival—finding homes for their

families, looking for new jobs, securing educations for their children—
essentially rebuilding their lives after the humiliation and economic and
social devastation of internment. The last thing on their minds was the
next congressional election. After all, Japanese Americans had good reason
to be leery of a government that for no reason other than their ancestry
had locked them and their families up in concentration camps for as
much as four years. The memories of such an experience do not fade
quickly; neither does the loss of trust in the government that put them
behind barbed wire. This focus on family security and apprehension
toward government might also explain why much of the political activism
that does exist within the Asian American community has involved setting
up social-service agencies, such as legal-aid organizations, health clinics,
and support for children and the elderly. Their civic involvement has been
predominantly community-oriented, rather than in mainstream American electoral politics.

One reason why the Asian American community in general has been
politically passive is that neither the Democrats nor the Republicans have
made special attempts to organize the community, as they have with
African Americans and, to a lesser extent, Latinos. Another probable cause
is that Asian Americans, like other minority groups, have viewed the
American political arena as off-limits and any attempts to break into the
white, upper-class establishment as futile. Confucian cultural values emphasize the professions, such as medicine and business, that promise to
bring both wealth and prestige to the family; after all, many Asian Americans immigrated to the United States in the hope of becoming prosperous and living a better life than was possible in their native country. Asian
culture disdains many qualities necessary for political success, such as
assertiveness and aggressiveness, emphasizing instead qualities such as
deference and obedience. As Judy Chu, an elected official of Monterey
Park, California, a predominantly Chinese American suburb of Los Angeles, said, "All the things that are required in Western politics go against
Asian culture."[16]

Most important, Asian Americans can hardly be characterized as a
cohesive, unified community. The divisions within it are numerous and
severe. Although they are often thought of as one monolithic group, Asian
Americans make up one of the most diverse minority groups in the United
States, with over 60 different ethnic groups, each with its own history,
language, and culture. They have their origins in more than two dozen
countries, including China, Japan, North Korea, South Korea, Hong Kong,

Taiwan, Vietnam, Thailand, Cambodia, Laos, Burma, Singapore, Indonesia, Pakistan, India, and the Philippines. Some segments of the population have been in the United States for many generations; others have arrived only recently. Though a large portion of this population is financially well-off, many are poor. In fact, some cleavages between Asian nationalities are deeper than those between Asian Americans and people of other races; for example, because of the Japanese occupation of Korea from 1910 to 1945, there is great antagonism between some Korean Americans and Japanese Americans. In a very basic sense, the term Asian American is a creation of non-Asian America, imposed on very diverse groups of people because of shared physical characteristics. The result is an extremely heterogeneous and often conflictual group that does not have a cohesive political agenda.

The second measure of an interest group's potential for effectively lobbying Congress is the number of alternatives that the group has to the proposed legislation. It is thought that the fewer the alternatives, the greater the incentive for an interest group to be unified and vocal in support of the legislation. In the case of obtaining redress for the government's wartime actions, many different opinions and options were espoused by various factions, creating deep cleavages within the Japanese American community. Concerning the legal route to take, there were three main views: (1) to take action through the legislative branch; (2) to fight for redress through the judicial branch; or (3) to do nothing. The fundamental differences among these possibilities and the variations in level of conviction that members of the community felt toward them meant that the redress legislation lacked the strong and consistent support needed from a majority of the Japanese American community to give the bill a chance of success.

Members of the Japanese American community who were actively involved with the redress issue generally favored the legislative route. It was felt that the legislative branch of the government was the proper place for passage of an apology to the interned Japanese Americans on behalf of the nation. It was the president's Executive Order 9066 that had authorized the evacuation and internment, and Congress's Public Law no. 503 that had established civil penalties for those violating the military orders. Thus, according to this line of thought, those branches of the government should be the ones to make restitution. Besides, it was only through passage of a federal law that the various recommendations of the Commission on Wartime Relocation and Internment of Civilians—a national apology, an education fund, and individual payments of monetary compensation—

could be mandated; no court decision could encompass all these provisions. These supporters saw the legislative route as the only realistic possibility; they felt that the expired statute of limitations on the internees' claims against the government created an insurmountable obstacle to judicial relief.

Although the legislative route had the widest support among Japanese American groups involved in the redress campaign, dissension surfaced when the Japanese American Citizens League decided that its first step into the congressional arena would not be to ask for outright redress in the form of a national apology and monetary compensation for those interned. JACL's strategy was first to seek the creation of a commission by Congress that would study the issue and make recommendations for redressing the situation. Once they had the credibility of a federal study's recommendations behind them, Japanese Americans could then approach Congress for the redress measures themselves. As John Tateishi, former chair of JACL's National Redress Committee, explained, when the committee decided to push for the commission, in his heart he wanted to go directly for redress: "If I thought it was possible, I'd go for it. But given the reality of Washington politics, I knew that we'd have to put our energies into getting the commission created first."[17] I will examine JACL's support for congressional creation of a study commission in more detail in Chapter Five.

One faction of the Japanese American community split off from the JACL view and opted to push for redress through the courts. Led by William Hohri of Chicago, the National Council for Japanese American Redress (NCJAR) was created in May 1979 in opposition to JACL's decision in the late 1970s to lobby for a study commission.[18] NCJAR members felt that a commission should only be a fallback if efforts to win full monetary compensation failed; any other approach would be a cop-out. Once JACL had successfully lobbied for the commission in 1979, NCJAR decided that the congressional route was a lost cause and that the best alternative was to go to the courts for redress.[19] Although legal analysis of the facts deemed the case a long shot, Hohri filed a class-action suit with 22 causes of action against the federal government on behalf of 25 Japanese American plaintiffs and NCJAR in March 1983. As I will outline in further detail in Chapter Eleven, the suit sought $10,000 per cause of action per individual, for a total of $27 billion.[20]

The final alternative was simply to do nothing. Although it might at first seem that people who were unjustly incarcerated by their own government would seek redress as a matter of course, at the beginning of the redress movement doing nothing was the most widespread preference among Japanese Americans. Some felt that any attempt to make up for what the government had done during the war would just trivialize their suffering. Many disliked the idea of putting a price tag on their constitutional and property losses; how could a mere $20,000 check from the government possibly compensate for the emotional and economic losses they had endured? One attitude was that asking for redress was improper, a disgrace. Such Japanese words as *gaman* (endurance), *haji* (shame), and *shiyo ga nai* (it can't be helped) reflected an attitude that the wartime events were unavoidable and that to ask the government for compensation now was audacious and deplorable. Others, believing that Japanese Americans would never be able to mount an effective redress campaign for all the various reasons outlined in this chapter, felt that any effort to gain redress would be futile and ultimately a waste of time, money, and energy, not to mention a great embarrassment for the community. Another group feared a racist backlash, fueled by recent U.S.-Japan trade tensions, reminiscent of the anti-Asian sentiments that had led to their internment. Finally, there were some Japanese Americans, even among former internees, who were essentially ambivalent about the whole idea; they just did not care, one way or the other, about obtaining redress.

Thus, the Japanese American community was hardly in agreement on the legal route to take. Moreover, even within the group supporting legislative action, factions formed. The issue was the method by which to mount a successful lobbying campaign. On one side was JACL, which opted for a strategy of low-key grass-roots letter-writing and phone-calling efforts, coordinated with personal lobbying of members of Congress both in their home districts and in Washington, D.C. JACL realized the value of coalition-building and used the network of contacts with other powerful organizations in Washington, such as the Leadership Conference on Civil Rights, that it had been developing throughout its 60 years in existence. Although JACL knew that an education campaign was a vital part of the redress movement, its strategy was not to focus on high media visibility as a way of influencing members of Congress, but to use personal contacts and Washington insiders to persuade representatives and senators to support the bill. On the other side was the National Coalition for Redress / Reparations (NCRR), which took a high-visibility grass-roots approach. Focusing on press releases and free media exposure, NCRR staged rallies and massive letter-writing campaigns with the philosophy that "when the bottom moves, everything moves on top."[21] Self-characterized as a coalition of progressive-minded grass-roots organizations that emerged from the 1960s, NCRR acted out of the belief that the mobilization of grass-roots support was the key to winning redress.[22] Although the approaches of JACL and NCRR were not necessarily in conflict, the relationship between the two groups was tense, with verbal backbiting from both sides. These differences prevented the formation of a unified Japanese American community, which led to many efforts being duplicated or uncoordinated. Had the community been united, it could have launched a much more efficient and cohesive campaign, enhancing the Japanese American population's chances of becoming a powerful force in Washington.

The incentives for Japanese Americans to take vigorous action in support of redress existed, but they were limited. Passage of the bill would secure a national apology by Congress, an education fund, presidential pardons for those convicted of breaking curfew on the basis of ethnicity, and individual cash payments of $20,000 for all internees. As a package, these measures appear to benefit the Japanese American population substantially, but on a per capita basis their value decreases, which in turn decreases the incentive for individuals to take action in support of redress. Twenty thousand dollars may seem like a substantial sum, but it is negligible when one considers the value of the constitutional rights the internees lost, not to mention the current value of lost wages, property, education, and belongings. In addition, the redress legislation proposed to pay only the actual victims of internment who were alive at the time of its enactment. This meant that only about 80,000 people, less than 15 percent of the Japanese American population, would reap direct benefits from the bill's passage. As noted earlier, the overwhelming majority of Hawaiian Japanese Americans, the only group large enough and concentrated enough to have significant influence over its elected officials, was not interned during the war and therefore had no direct stake in the redress bill. Moreover, in order to be heard as a powerful political voice on Capitol Hill, Japanese Americans would need the support of all Asian Americans. Japanese Americans by themselves are not viewed as a political entity in Washington, but rather as a subset of the Asian American voting bloc. But, as we have seen, Asian Americans are hardly a cohesive group, and the other Asian American groups, such as the Chinese Americans, Vietnamese Americans, and Korean Americans, none of whom had been interned and some of whom were hostile to Japanese Americans, had no direct personal stake in the redress issue.

The main incentive for Japanese Americans to lobby for redress was the symbolic, as opposed to the economic, value of the legislation. Although the payments to former internees may have been small, the emotional and psychological value of redress was overwhelming and meaningful to both individual internees and the Japanese American community collectively. It seemed unlikely, however, that this single incentive would overcome all the disincentives that existed for the organization of Japanese Americans.

The Opposition to Redress

While the Japanese American community was attempting to galvanize its forces, the opposition launched its attack on the redress movement. Two principal camps emerged in opposition to redress: (1) certain veterans' groups, and (2) a Southern-California–based organization called Americans for Historical Accuracy (AFHA).

At first glance, it would seem that veterans' groups would be the most vehement opponents of redress. The military, under the authority of General DeWitt, had originated and implemented the curfew, evacuation, and internment plans during the war. Passage of the bill would literally stamp in the history books that what the military did during the war to Japanese Americans was due to "race prejudice, war hysteria, and a failure of political leadership."[23] It was doubtful that veterans, proud of their record in combat, would take such criticism without protest. Moreover, it seemed logical that many of the men who had fought in World War II, as well as their families, would object to giving $1.25 billion to Japanese Americans who suffered a tremendous inconvenience but were still clothed, fed, and housed, while members of the U.S. armed forces placed their lives on the line in battle, many of them losing limbs, friends, or their own lives to Japanese opponents. A typical response might be: "Why should Japanese Americans get compensated for their losses? Many of us died in battle in defense of our country. In time of war everybody makes sacrifices and everybody suffers. We haven't been compensated for our sacrifices and suffering. Why should they be compensated for theirs?" Thus, veterans had some motivation to oppose the redress legislation. They also had the organizational structure to front a powerful opposition lobby. Veterans' groups such as the powerful American Legion and Veterans of Foreign Wars (VFW) have effectively lobbied Congress on numerous issues important to them. They have local chapters nationwide, as well as a mobilized national organization and the resources to launch an anti-redress campaign. There was one extremely important element, however, that tempered the veterans' groups' vocal opposition: the Nisei veterans of World War II, primarily members of the 442d Regimental Combat Team and the 100th Infantry Battalion and of the Military Intelligence Service. With these veterans in American Legion and VFW chapters across the country reminding other veterans of the 442d's stellar record and of the fact that they had fought for the country while their parents, brothers, and sisters were locked up in concentration camps, some of the opposition was defused. Although some individual VFW and American Legion chapters as well as groups like American Ex-Prisoners of War and American Defenders of Bataan and Corregidor, Inc., passed resolutions against redress,[24] veterans' groups overall did not organize an active campaign against redress.

Americans for Historical Accuracy (AFHA), a group led by Lillian Baker, however, appeared to be a determined force with which the groups supporting redress would have to reckon. Based in Gardena, California, AFHA characterized itself as a "Coalition Against the Falsification of U.S.A. History." AFHA publications include two books by Baker, *The Concentration Camp Conspiracy: A Second Pearl Harbor* and *Dishonoring America: The Collective Guilt of American Japanese.* AFHA maintained that the internment was hardly an unpleasant experience for Japanese Americans—the camps were a pleasant haven in a time of war. It was ludicrous, its supporters contended, for former internees to be asking for monetary compensation and a national apology when the government fed, clothed, and housed them while the rest of the nation was fighting a war. The internment had been necessary for national security reasons, and any attempt to apologize or make up for that legitimate act was ridiculous.[25] The group's stalwart leader, Lillian Baker, is a historian whose papers are in the archives of the Hoover Institution at Stanford University. Baker's husband was killed in the Pacific theater during World War II, and as a result, she is hostile toward nearly anyone or anything remotely Japanese.[26] Although Baker's group was relatively small, it had the motivation and some resources to put up a fight. While it was in no way as powerful as, say, the labor lobby or Jewish lobby, it seemed to provide a moderate-sized hurdle for redress supporters to overcome.

Even more important, pressure from constituencies, independent of pressure from opposition groups, was a potential obstruction to the redress legislation. A number of factors outside the institutional structure of

Congress and the organization of interest groups created conditions that could have made it electorally difficult for representatives and senators to justify a vote in favor of the bill or politically convenient for them to rationalize a nay vote. These external factors included the federal budget deficit, strained U.S.-Japan trade relations, the "model minority" myth, and the problem of setting precedent.

External Factors: Justifying a Vote Against Redress

The Federal Deficit

The first and probably most important external factor working against redress was the federal budget deficit. In the early years of the Reagan Administration, the United States witnessed a historic and unprecedented rise in the federal budget deficit, from $59.6 billion in 1980 to $195.4 billion in 1983, when the redress bills were first introduced.[27] The escalating deficits prompted passage of the Gramm-Rudman-Hollings restrictions, which put stringent caps on federal spending in a congressionally mandated effort to lower the deficit. Passed by Congress in December 1985, the Gramm-Rudman-Hollings bill, officially titled the Balanced Budget and Emergency Control Act of 1985, called for a balanced budget by fiscal year 1991, with intermediate targets that decreased continually from 1986 to 1990. Under the legislation, if the estimated deficit for an upcoming year were to exceed its target (with a $10 billion tolerance range), then an automatic sequestration process would be triggered and across-the-board reductions for each federal account would be made. The combination of massive budget deficits and Gramm-Rudman-Hollings restrictions would have made it difficult for reelection-minded representatives and senators to explain to their constituents why they had voted for a bill giving $1.25 billion to a small but relatively well-off group at a time when numerous other federal programs were facing substantial cutbacks. It was possible that voters across the country, many of whom knew little about the internment, would not view spending such a large amount of money as appropriate and responsible fiscal management.[28] Because Asian Americans, particularly Japanese Americans, made up a tiny electoral bloc in most congressional districts and states, voting for the redress bill would have earned most members of Congress little electoral support and might have invited a nasty backlash.

Related to this economic concern was the argument that the federal government, as well as some state and local governments, had already paid compensation to the former internees. In 1948, Congress passed the Japanese American Evacuation Claims Act, which allowed Japanese Americans to file claims against the government for the loss of property that occurred as "a reasonable and natural consequence of the evacuation or exclusion."[29] This law did not allow claims for lost income or physical hardship and mental suffering, only loss of physical property. Because proof of loss was required and few internees had managed to gather and pack detailed records in the rush before departing for camp, only 26,568 claims totaling $148 million were filed under the act, with the government distributing a total of $37 million. Although there exist no accurate estimates of the extent of property loss, it seems reasonable to conclude that $37 million could not have fairly compensated the internees' economic losses.[30] In addition, in 1972 Congress amended the Social Security Act to allow Japanese Americans to claim social security for time spent in detention.[31] Federal civil service retirement provisions were amended in 1978 to let Japanese Americans over age 18 have credit for civil service retirement for the time interned.[32] In four other instances, state or county employees received partial compensation as reparations.[33] The redress legislation did not attempt to duplicate the 1948 act or any other government effort to compensate for material losses. It was intended to make up for a loss of *constitutional rights*—not property. The claim that the government had already compensated the internees once was a compelling argument for reelection-minded members to use, however, especially in conjunction with the deficit argument.

Two camps seemed to emerge from the objection to redress on economic grounds. The first group comprised members of Congress who acknowledged the injustice of the wartime events and supported a national apology, but could not responsibly vote for monetary compensation, given the state of the budget. The second group consisted of representatives and senators who objected to the very idea of monetary compensation. The reasons for opposing monetary compensation were numerous. One was the "everyone suffers during a war" argument; some were opposed to the "general concept of paying reparations to one specific group affected in World War II, while a lot of others remain uncompensated."[34] Others, notably Congressman Dan Lungren (R–Calif.), the only member of the CWRIC to object to its recommendation of individual payments, were in favor of a national apology, but did not agree that "we must have monetary redress . . . as a disincentive for us to repeat these actions in the future."[35] It was not possible, the reasoning went, to right past injustices through individual cash payments; putting a price on the loss of constitutional rights only cheapens the real value of such rights. As Congressman Norm Shumway (R–Calif.) stated, "Let us not resolve this problem by just throwing money at our problems as a balm to our conscience."[36] Although some members might have held this view regardless of the state of the economy, the alarming rate of increase in the federal deficit may have given many others good reason to espouse this "money cannot correct past mistakes" argument.

U.S.-Japan Trade Relations

The second external factor that might have engendered opposition to the redress bill was the state of trade relations between the United States and Japan. Although the United States has been the economic frontrunner for the past half century, recently Japan has seriously challenged the United States, emerging from the ruins of war as the second-largest economy and the leading exporter in the world today. In recent years, Japan has had a tremendous trade imbalance with the United States (a $58.9 billion trade surplus in 1986),[37] much to the dismay of American business and labor. Many American companies have been driven out of business by Japanese competitors, and in certain industries, such as automobiles and consumer electronics, domestic companies have seen their market share rapidly decline. Much debate has focused on whether Japan's "unfair" and "protectionist" trade policies or a decline in U.S. productivity has been the primary cause of the trade imbalance. But regardless of where the blame lies and although the issue in this case is between the United States and a foreign nation, the result has been an extremely anti-Japanese atmosphere in certain parts of the country, such as Detroit, which has even led on occasion to anti-Asian violence. A well-publicized example is the murder of Vincent Chin, a young Chinese American man who was killed by two out-of-work auto workers who mistook Chin for Japanese. In such cases, because the trade imbalance with Japan hurt the domestic economy, causing inflation and unemployment, some people vented their anger on Americans of Japanese ancestry. As a result, even though their constituents' anger was based on ignorance, representatives and senators might have been reluctant to support redress for fear of an electoral backlash.

This discussion of U.S.-Japan trade tensions leads to a broader phenomenon—the accepted prevalence of Japan-bashing in the United States. Criticism and mockery of Japan have become an American pastime. As *Fortune* magazine reported, "Suddenly, the Japanese have become the people it is OK to hate."[38] This antagonism toward Japan is transposed to anything remotely Japanese, including legislation affecting Japanese Americans. The phenomenon is significant because it reveals an important source of much of the opposition to the redress legislation, namely, the failure to differentiate between Japanese Americans and Japanese citizens in Japan. This common misperception is the predicament of all Asian Americans and members of other identifiable ethnic groups—being ostracized to the status of "permanent foreigner." It is this line of thinking that led to the evacuation and internment—in 1943 General DeWitt proclaimed, "A Jap's a Jap. . . . You can't change him by giving him a piece of paper"[39]—and created a problem for the redress campaign. Although few would admit to being racist, many people—not necessarily members of Congress themselves, but more commonly their constituents—did not distinguish in their minds between the Japanese with whom the United States was at war in the 1940s and the Japanese Americans—either American-born or resident aliens unable by law to gain U.S. citizenship—who served in the U.S. armed forces or were sent to detention camps during the war. The primary problem here was ignorance; many people across the country, even on the West Coast, did not know the facts behind the internment or, still worse, were not even aware that it had happened. Few American history textbooks devote space to the internment; those that mention it at all typically give it only a few sentences or paragraphs. Thus, a lack of understanding and a failure to distinguish between Japanese Americans and Japanese nationals meant that any event that fostered a negative attitude toward Japan reflected negatively on the efforts of Japanese Americans to secure redress for what their own government, the government of the United States of America, had done to them 40 years earlier.

The "Model Minority" Myth

The third external factor that posed a problem for the redress campaign was similarly rooted in misconceptions about Asian Americans: the "model minority" myth. A popular conception of American society is that Americans of Asian descent do not suffer the social and economic inequities that plague other minority groups, like blacks and Hispanics, and that Japanese Americans in particular do well. To some extent, statistical evidence supports this vision: in the category of median family income, Japanese Americans rank not only above African Americans and Latinos but also above whites. In 1989, the median income of Asian American families was $35,900—3 percent higher than that of non-Hispanic white families. The median income for black families was $20,200, and for Hispanic families, $23,400. In addition, in 1989, 39 percent of all Asian Americans lived in households that had incomes above $50,000, compared to only 32 percent of non-Hispanic whites.[40] Moreover, when it comes to excellence in education, the common picture at universities across the country today is that Asian Americans are at the head of the class. According to a *Newsweek* article on Asian Americans and education, "Asian American students form the fastest-growing segment in American higher education, not just on the West and East coasts, but nationally—and more often than not at the best universities."[41] Because of their above-average enrollment at the nation's colleges, Asian American students do not qualify for affirmative action in college admissions or special financial-aid programs. Asian Americans, the line goes, may be low in numbers in the United States, but not in motivational drive or in academic and economic success.

Although this view is not meant to be derogatory—and in fact is often meant as a compliment—it is still a stereotype that does not accurately portray this segment of the population. It leaves out Asian Americans who are not enrolled at Stanford or Harvard and are not doing well economically. It masks the fact that the per capita income of Asian Americans is lower than that of non-Hispanic whites—in 1989 it was $14,000 for Asian Americans and $14,900 for whites—primarily because of the relatively large size of Asian families.[42] This stereotype also overlooks the upward trend of the poverty rate among Asian Americans. The poverty rate of Asian Americans increased during the 1980s, from 13 percent in 1979 to 17 percent in 1988 and 14 percent in 1989. This rate is nearly twice that of non-Hispanic whites (8 percent).[43] Moreover, in the case of Japanese Americans, this generalization was detrimental to the redress efforts. Avoiding the basic issue of constitutional rights, it became possible for members of Congress simply to say, "They don't need the money. Look at them today. They're doing much better financially than many people in my district." Although few representatives or senators were likely to base their votes on the redress legislation entirely on the "model minority" myth, its existence contributed, along with the other factors mentioned here, to a political climate in which members of Congress could easily justify a nay vote in the name of electoral responsibility.

The notion of political climate leads to another argument against redress: that it would provoke a "backlash" against Japanese Americans. The argument went as follows: in an environment of concern over the federal deficit, strained U.S.-Japan trade relations, and the prospering of a "model minority," the passage of a bill awarding $1.25 billion to 80,000 Japanese Americans would invite, or even encourage, anti–Japanese American sentiments. As Congressman Shumway contended:

> I believe that this bill may revive some of the bias that we saw during our World War II and the years shortly thereafter against good Japanese American citizens. . . . I think that we do not want to do anything to revive that bias. We now count Japanese Americans citizens as some of the most respectable, hard-working, loyal Americans that we have in our country. To separate them out this fashion, to make them the recipient of a stipend which is an effort to pay them for something I think could revive some bias and I think the bill is dangerous for that reason.[44]

In this view, the passage of any redress legislation would bring more problems than benefits for Japanese Americans. Thus, by expressing concern for the welfare of the very persons that redress aimed to benefit, proponents of this view created another argument for representatives and senators to use to justify opposing the legislation.

Setting Precedent

The final external factor adversely affecting the redress movement was the situation of other minority groups in the United States and the fear of setting a dangerous precedent for redressing wrongs done to those groups. African Americans suffered an egregious injustice when the shackles of slavery chained them to a second-class status; similarly, the U.S. government did Native Americans a wrong when it literally stole their land and forced them onto reservations. If Congress granted monetary payments to the Japanese Americans who suffered during World War II, then what was to stop it from doling out money to every minority group that justifiably complained of government wrongdoing? As Congressman Lungren put it, "Attempting to put a price tag on misbegotten policies of the past poses the spectacle of unwieldy precedent. The principles of equity involve more than the satisfaction of wrongs in this specific case. Rather, similar treatment for those with similar grievances is required. American Indians and blacks are but two examples of possible claims to recompense under such elevated principles of retroactive justice."[45]

Proponents of redress point out the differences in situation that reduce the credibility of this "precedent" argument. As John Tateishi, former chair of JACL's National Redress Committee, replied, although slavery was much worse than the Japanese Americans' situation, the slave trade was run as free enterprise, not under government sponsorship, even though it was sanctioned under the Constitution. For Native Americans, the issue was one of broken treaties between separate nations. Neither case involved an act of the U.S. government against its own citizens. The internment of Japanese Americans is the only case in the history of the United States in which the U.S. government took a group of citizens and imprisoned them en masse without just cause. Although this rebuttal has merit, the "precedent" argument seemed to appeal to some members of Congress, and it contributed to an already antiredress environment.

The Odds Against Redress

Overall, the political environment at the time the first redress bills were introduced in Congress predicted almost certain failure for the legislation. At best, it would face tremendous difficulty in getting passed. The most important variables regarding the passage of legislation, according to contemporary conceptions of how Congress operates, seemed to be overwhelmingly negative. At the very least, it seemed certain that the provisions for individual monetary recompense would have to be deleted to secure the votes needed for passage of the redress bill.

Despite these negative tendencies, the redress legislation did pass—with monetary payments intact—by an overwhelming majority in the Senate and by a comfortable margin in the House. What could explain this apparent deviation in congressional behavior? What changes in the bill's institutional and external environment enabled the victory to occur? What role did luck play? Is the Civil Liberties Act of 1988 a fluke or can it be explained rationally? The rest of this book will attempt to answer these questions by analyzing the bill's road to success.

CHAPTER FOUR

Electoral Interest Analysis of the Roll-Call Votes

Although the relevant subcommittees in both houses held hearings on the redress legislation in 1984, both bills died in committee in the 98th Congress, an unsurprising outcome given the odds the bills faced.[1] With the arrival of a new Congress in 1985, a second set of bills to implement the recommendations of the Commission on Wartime Relocation and Internment of Civilians was introduced in both the House and the Senate. On January 3, 1985, Majority Leader Jim Wright introduced H.R. 442, which was nearly identical to H.R. 4110 but was renamed in honor of the 442d Regimental Combat Team, with 99 cosponsors. Four months later, on May 2, Senator Spark Matsunaga introduced S. 1053 with 25 cosponsors. Though the House Judiciary subcommittee held hearings on H.R. 442 in the 99th Congress, the Senate Governmental Affairs subcommittee held no hearings at all on S. 1053; neither bill made it out of subcommittee. In the 100th Congress, the final redress bills were introduced—H.R. 442 by Majority Leader Tom Foley (D–Wash.) in the House on January 6, 1987, with 124 cosponsors, and S. 1009 by Senator Matsunaga in the Senate on April 10, with 71 cosponsors. After holding hearings, the House Judiciary Subcommittee on Administrative Law and Governmental Relations approved H.R. 442 by voice vote on May 13, 1987. The subcommittee made a few minor changes, including reducing the amount to be authorized from $1.5 billion to $1.25 billion—leaving the $20,000 individual payments intact but cutting the educational trust fund—and removing the portion of the bill dealing with the Aleutian Islanders. After hearings by the Subcommittee on Federal Services, Post Office, and Civil Service in August 1987, the Senate Governmental Affairs Committee passed S. 1009 by unanimous voice vote. In mark-up, an amendment was added to the bill stretching individual monetary payments over five years. By that time, 75 senators—three-fourths of the chamber—had committed support to the legislation as cosponsors.

Finally, on September 17, 1987, the House passed H.R. 442, without any major amendments, by a vote of 243–141, with provisions for a public apology from the U.S. government and payments of $20,000 to each surviving internee. On April 20, 1988, S. 1009 was passed by a 69–27 margin, which sent the two bills to conference committee for reconciliation. The conference committee filed its report on July 26, 1988. The key compromises reached in the conference committee were that the section of the Senate bill providing for compensation to Aleutian Islanders who had been removed from their homes during the war would be retained in the final bill, and that the time limit for the government to make all payments to internees would be ten years. The next day, July 27, the Senate passed the conference bill unanimously by voice vote. On August 4, the House voted 257–156 to accept the conference report, sending the legislation to President Reagan for his signature.

In the light of the odds outlined in the last chapter, the congressional history of the redress legislation is amazing, its victory a remarkable feat. When it started its journey through the policy-making process, even some leading supporters had their doubts about its potential for success. But in 1988, redress made legislative history as Congress condemned the government's wartime actions and authorized monetary payments to individuals mistreated by the U.S. government solely on the basis of ancestry, to compensate for their loss of constitutional rights. An analysis of the roll-call vote in both houses in relation to variables that typically influence congressional votes can shed light on the success of the bills up to a point. According to the electoral interest model outlined in Chapter Two, certain characteristics of members of Congress and of their electorates are likely to influence the way legislators vote on a particular issue. In the case of redress, six factors appeared to be most relevant: (1) the percentage of Asian Americans in a state or congressional district; (2) the region of the country from which the member of Congress came; (3) the party affiliation of the member; (4) the member's Americans for Democratic Action rating;[2]

(5) the member's American Conservative Union rating;[3] and (6) the member's American Civil Liberties Union rating.[4] The percentage of Asian Americans in each state or congressional district serves as the best measure of the constituency pressure on a senator or representative to vote for redress, according to typical electoral interest analysis; that is, those members with large concentrations of Asian Americans in their constituencies would be more likely to support redress than those with few Asian American constituents. The other variables could give additional insights on the legislation's passage.

Constituent percentage of Asian Americans is not the ideal measure of electoral interest; the percentage of Japanese Americans specifically would have been a truer indicator of constituent pressure because only Japanese Americans benefited directly from the legislation. I used Asian Americans, however, because the U.S. Bureau of the Census does not tabulate statistics giving the percentage of Japanese Americans in each district.[5] Moreover, because Japanese Americans were such a minute percentage of the constituency of most individual congressional districts, usually less than 1 percent, their percentages would not have shown much stratification between districts and the possible impact on representatives' voting behavior. Percentages for Asian American constituencies, although also small, range more broadly and thus can more clearly show whether or not constituent pressure played any role in how individual members of Congress voted on the redress legislation. In addition, I found it acceptable to use Asian American percentages because other Asian American community organizations, such as the Chinese American Citizens Alliance, joined the Japanese American community in support of the redress legislation. To varying degrees, many parts of the Asian American community became involved in the redress movement and contributed to the coalition of lobbying organizations that made success possible.

To see if a strong relationship existed between any of the six variables and the actions of members of the House and Senate, I compared each variable to the votes cast in both houses. The data analysis proved relatively inconclusive. For three variables, these simple correlations revealed little or no relationship between how a member voted—on any of the amendments or on the bills themselves—and the member's ADA, ACU, or ACLU rating. The other three variables, however—party, region, and district percentage of Asian Americans—have, to varying degrees, some explanatory power for votes of both the House and the Senate. To clarify the relation between the variables and the roll-call vote, I ran selected regressions, analyzing the fit and significance of each variable. I will next present the results of this analysis, ending with general conclusions about the explanatory power of electoral interest theory and other variables that affected voting on the redress legislation.

Analysis of the House Roll-Call Vote

The House had three critical votes: the vote on the Lungren Amendment to eliminate the monetary payments and the initial full chamber vote on H.R. 442, both in September 1987, and the final vote on the conference report nearly a year later. The three votes were closely related, and analyses of the three yield relatively similar results: each variable seems to have had a consistent impact on all three votes.

The Lungren Amendment

On September 17, 1992, the only amendment to H.R. 442 proposed on the House floor was defeated by a margin of 162–237. This sound rejection of a proposal to strike the monetary compensation provision from the bill is surprising, given that the most powerful and most frequently made argument against the legislation was the large amount of federal funds that would be required to compensate former internees. As predicted, the percentage of Asian Americans in a particular congressional district[6] had some impact on the outcome of the vote. The larger the percentage, the more likely representatives were to vote against the amendment, and the smaller the percentage, the more likely representatives were to vote for the amendment. As Table 1 shows, the percentage of House members voting against the amendment increased with the percentage of Asian Americans in their constituencies. This variable is not as powerful as it might seem, however. Although it had a noticeable effect on those representatives from districts that were at least 1 percent Asian American, it seemed to be less of a factor in districts that were less than 1 percent Asian American. In that population grouping, the difference between those members who voted in favor and those who voted against the amendment was less than 5 percent. Thus, House members with constituencies less than 1 percent Asian American were nearly as likely to oppose the amendment as to support it. This finding contradicts the predicted outcome that the potential disadvantages and lack of electoral benefits in voting for the unamended version of the bill would motivate representatives with small Asian American constituencies to support the amendment in order to deflect potential backlash

TABLE 1
Vote by Percentage of Asian Americans per District

	Asian Americans within a congressional district[a]				
Vote	0%	1%	2–5%	6–20%	Over 20%
Yes	95	51	18	1	0
	48.5%	32.5%	29.5%	5.3%	0%
No	86	97	43	15	2
	43.9%	61.7%	70.5%	78.9%	100%
Present	0	0	0	1	0
	0%	0%	0%	5.3%	0%
N.V.[b]	15	9	0	2	0
	7.7%	5.7%	0%	10.5%	0%

SOURCE: Author, based on *Congressional Record* and Barone and Ujifusa, *Almanac of American Politics 1990.*
NOTE: All yea or nay votes in all tables include the votes of all members present as well as all paired and announced votes.
[a]As a percentage of its total population.
[b]In all tables, N.V. means the number of members for whom no vote was recorded.

TABLE 2
Vote by Geographic Region

Vote	West	South	Rest of nation
Yes	13	77	75
	21.3%	54.6%	32.2%
No	44	52	147
	72.1%	36.9%	63.1%
Present	1	0	0
	1.6%	0%	0%
N.V.	3	12	11
	4.9%	8.5%	4.7%

SOURCE: Unless otherwise noted, all tables were prepared by the author with information from the *Congressional Record.*

TABLE 3
Vote by Party Affiliation

Vote	Dem.	Rep.
Yes	51	114
	19.7%	64.8%
No	187	56
	72.2%	31.8%
Present	1	0
	0.4%	0%
N.V.	20	6
	7.7%	3.4%

TABLE 4
Vote by Geographic Region and Party Affiliation

	West		South		Rest of nation	
Vote	Dem.	Rep.	Dem.	Rep.	Dem.	Rep.
Yes	0	13	39	38	12	63
	0%	54.2%	41.1%	82.6%	9.4%	59.4%
No	35	9	45	7	107	40
	94.6%	37.5%	47.4%	15.2%	84.3%	37.7%
Present	1	0	0	0	0	0
	2.7%	0%	0%	0%	0%	0%
N.V.	1	2	11	1	8	3
	2.7%	8.3%	11.6%	2.2%	6.3%	2.8%

over monetary payments to former internees. In districts with higher concentrations of Asian Americans, then, the percentage seems to have had an impact on members' voting behavior; in districts with virtually no Asian Americans, however, the measure does not serve as an adequate predictor of voting behavior.

Similarly, the region variable appears to explain the vote to a certain degree, but not completely. For the purposes of this analysis, the country is divided into three regions: the West, the South, and the rest of the nation. The West consists of California, Oregon, Washington, Alaska, and Hawaii, all states whose representatives had an electoral reason to support redress unamended: the Japanese American internees were principally relocated from the three Pacific coast states, Hawaii has a large Asian American (and specifically Japanese American) population, and the Aleutian Islanders included in the Senate and conference versions of the bill were Alaskans. The South consists of 15 deep South and border states that have few Asian Americans, and whose inhabitants and representatives are typically conservative and less inclined for various reasons to support redress. These states are Alabama, Arkansas, Florida, Georgia, Kentucky, Louisiana, Maryland, Mississippi, North Carolina, Oklahoma, South Carolina, Tennessee, Texas, Virginia, and West Virginia. The final region comprises the remaining 30 states, none of which provided its representatives with a compelling reason to support redress unreservedly. As expected, a large majority of the representatives from the West—72.1 percent[7]—voted against the Lungren Amendment (see Table 2). Outside the West and the South, there was also a tendency to vote against the amendment, though it was smaller, at 63.1 percent. In the South, the House vote was more evenly divided, with 54.6 percent supporting the amendment. Thus, there exists some relationship between region and vote on the Lungren Amendment, although it is most powerful for the West and weakest for the South.

Party affiliation seems to be a relatively accurate predictor of the vote on the Lungren Amendment (Table 3). Republicans in general had a much greater tendency to support the amendment than Democrats. The dichotomy appears to be relatively clear and well defined. A slightly different picture emerges, however, when party identification is analyzed by region (see Table 4). Outside the West and South, the ratio of Democrats against the amendment compared to Republicans for the amendment (84.3 percent to 59.4 percent) is not markedly different from the national ratio, but in the West and South, the results are interesting. In the West, even though Republicans still favored the amendment, both Democrats and Republicans were more likely to oppose the amendment than they were in the nation overall. In the five western states, almost 95 percent of Democrats voted against the amendment and none voted for it. Conversely, over 54 percent of western Republicans supported the amendment, whereas slightly less than 38 percent did not. Thus, for western representatives, region had a slight impact on voting behavior, although there was still a noticeable difference in the votes cast by the two parties. In the conservative South, Republicans, at over 82 percent, were much more likely to support than to oppose the amendment, as predicted. Among southern Democrats, however, the picture contrasts considerably with the expected outcome. Southern Democrats were nearly as likely to support the amendment as they were to oppose it, 41.1 percent to 47.4 percent, although typical electoral interest analysis would suggest that House members from the South, even Democrats, would have been more likely to side with Lungren and avoid as much political backlash as possible. In this region, therefore, party affiliation can predict the Republican votes in general, but it does little to explain why slightly more Democrats voted against the amendment than for it.

The Full House Vote on H.R. 442

On the same day the Lungren Amendment was rejected, the redress legislation was passed, unamended, on the floor of the House by a vote of 243–141, with 63 percent of those present in favor of it. As expected, representatives from districts with a substantial percentage of Asian American voters were much more inclined to vote for the legislation than those with fewer Asian Americans among their constituents (Table 5). For representatives from districts with an electorate less than 1 percent Asian American, however, it is much harder to explain the outcome. Over 45 percent of members from such districts voted for the bill, whereas 44.9 percent voted against it. It is easy to understand why those who opposed the legislation did so; with virtually no Asian American constituency pressure, the electoral benefits of voting for the legislation were close to nil, while the potential backlash was great. But electoral interest analysis hardly explains why just as many representatives in this category voted in favor of the legislation. Constituency pressure could not have been the sole factor influencing their decision to support the entire redress package; other factors must have been at work.

Region and party affiliation had predictable results: those representatives from the West, at 77.1 percent, were most likely, and southerners, at

TABLE 5
Vote by Percentage of Asian Americans per District

Vote	Asian Americans within a congressional district[a]				
	0%	1%	2–5%	6–20%	Over 20%
Yes	89	101	44	16	2
	45.4%	64.4%	72.1%	84.2%	100%
No	88	42	16	1	0
	44.9%	26.8%	26.2%	5.3%	0%
Present	0	0	0	1	0
	0%	0%	0%	5.3%	0%
N.V.	19	14	1	1	0
	9.7%	8.9%	1.6%	5.3%	0%

SOURCE: Author, based on *Congressional Record* and Barone and Ujifusa, *Almanac of American Politics 1990*.
[a]As a percentage of its total population.

TABLE 6
Vote by Geographic Region

Vote	West	South	Rest of nation
Yes	47	54	151
	77.1%	38.3%	64.8%
No	11	71	65
	18.0%	50.3%	27.9%
Present	1	0	0
	1.6%	0%	0%
N.V.	2	16	17
	3.3%	11.3%	7.3%

TABLE 7
Vote by Party Affiliation

Vote	Dem.	Rep.
Yes	187	65
	72.2%	36.9%
No	43	104
	16.6%	59.1%
Present	1	0
	0.4%	0%
N.V.	28	7
	10.8%	4.0%

TABLE 8
Vote by Geographic Region and Party Affiliation

Vote	West		South		Rest of nation	
	Dem.	Rep.	Dem.	Rep.	Dem.	Rep.
Yes	35	12	46	8	106	45
	94.6%	50%	48.4%	17.4%	83.5%	45.3%
No	0	11	34	37	9	56
	0%	45.8%	35.8%	80.4%	7.1%	52.9%
Present	1	0	0	0	0	0
	2.7%	0%	0%	0%	0%	0%
N.V.	1	1	15	1	12	5
	2.7%	4.2%	15.8%	2.2%	9.4%	4.7%

38.3 percent, were least likely, to vote for the legislation (see Table 6), and Democrats had a much greater tendency to support the legislation than their Republican counterparts (Table 7). Once one examines the roll-call vote by party and region (Table 8), however, this analysis has less power. In the West, as anticipated, Democrats voted for the bill at the rate of 94.6 percent, with none opposing it. Western Republicans also supported the legislation at an above-average rate for Republicans of 50 percent and opposed it at a below-average rate of 45.8 percent. In the South, the results were slightly more surprising. Over 80 percent of southern Republicans predictably opposed the legislation, but the picture for southern Democrats is more complex, with 48.4 percent voting yea, 35.8 percent nay. It seems unlikely that so many conservative southern Democrats would have voted for the bill simply on the basis of constituent pressures. For the rest of the nation, the data are equally surprising. Although there seemed to be no pressing electoral need to vote for the bill, over 83 percent of the Democrats did so, with only 7.1 percent opposing it. As expected, more Republicans voted against the legislation than for it, but at the small margin of 52.9 percent to 45.3 percent. Contemporary theories of congressional behavior can at least partially explain why the nonwestern and nonsouthern Democratic and Republican representatives who voted against the bill did so, but they cannot shed light on why the vast majority of Democrats and nearly half the Republicans voted for it. Factors other than constituent pressure must have existed.

The Final Vote on the Conference Report

On August 4, 1988, the House accepted the conference committee's report by a roll call vote of 257–156. The analysis of the vote according to district percentage of Asian Americans, party identification, region, and a combination of party and region was similar to that of the September 1987 vote on H.R. 442 (see Tables 9, 10, 11, 12). Members of the House from districts with high concentrations of Asian Americans were more likely to vote for the legislation; Democrats were much more likely to vote for the bill, whereas Republicans tended to vote against it. Westerners, especially western Democrats, were the most likely to support the legislation, and southerners were more likely to oppose it; representatives from other areas tended to vote for it. Again, typical electoral interest politics can explain why many westerners, particularly western Democrats, and members from districts outside the West with substantial Asian American populations supported the legislation, and why many southerners and those from

TABLE 9
Vote by Percentage of Asian Americans per District

Vote	Asian Americans within a congressional district[a]				
	0%	1%	2–5%	6–20%	Over 20%
Yes	81	110	47	18	2
	41.3%	70.1%	77.0%	94.7%	100%
No	100	42	12	1	0
	51.0%	26.7%	20.0%	5.3%	0%
N.V.	11	3	2	0	0
	5.6%	1.9%	3.3%	0%	0%
N.M.[b]	4	2	0	0	0
	2.0%	1.3%	0%	0%	0%

SOURCE: Author, based on *Congressional Record* and Barone and Ujifusa, *Almanac of American Politics 1990.*
[a]As a percentage of its total population.
[b]In Tables 9–12, N.M. means the number of districts that did not have a member of Congress at the time of the vote. This category consists of congressional seats that were vacant at the time of the August 4, 1988, vote or whose representative changed during the 100th Congress between the September 17, 1987, vote and the August 4, 1988, vote. Such seats include those of the Twenty-first District of Illinois (changed from Melvin Price to Jerry Costello), the Fourth District of Louisiana (changed from Buddy Roemer to Jim McCrery), the Fifth District of Virginia (changed from W. C. Daniel to Lewis Payne), the Third and Nineteenth Districts of New York, and the Second District of Tennessee, the last three of which were vacant for the 1988 vote.

TABLE 10
Vote by Geographic Region

Vote	West	South	Rest of nation
Yes	54	48	156
	88.5%	34.0%	66.9%
No	7	80	68
	11.5%	56.7%	29.2%
N.V.	0	10	6
	0%	7.1%	2.6%
N.M.	0	3	3
	0%	2.1%	1.3%

TABLE 11
Vote by Party Affiliation

Vote	Dem.	Rep.
Yes	187	71
	72.2%	40.3%
No	55	100
	21.2%	56.9%
N.V.	12	4
	4.6%	2.3%
N.M.	5	1
	1.9%	0.6%

TABLE 12
Vote by Geographic Region and Party Affiliation

Vote	West		South		Rest of nation	
	Dem.	Rep.	Dem.	Rep.	Dem.	Rep.
Yes	37	17	42	6	108	48
	100%	70.8%	44.2%	13.0%	85.1%	45.3%
No	0	7	43	37	12	56
	0%	29.2%	45.3%	80.5%	9.4%	52.8%
N.V.	0	0	8	2	4	2
	0%	0%	8.4%	4.3%	3.1%	1.9%
N.M.	0	0	2	1	3	0
	0%	0%	2.1%	2.2%	2.4%	0%

districts sparsely populated by Asian Americans voted against it. But, as before, it has difficulty in explaining why so many nonwestern representatives with few Asian American constituents were moved to vote in favor of H.R. 442. Given the disadvantages and the lack of potential rewards of voting for it, it seems that the shrewd political choice would have been to play it safe and vote nay.

Analysis of the Senate Roll-Call Vote

The Senate had four important votes regarding S. 1009, including three motions to kill vitiating amendments to the legislation and the final vote on the bill as a whole. Unlike the House, the Senate took a voice vote on the conference report; thus, no analysis of a roll-call vote is possible. In general, in all four votes, those senators whom electoral interest analysis would expect to vote in favor of the unamended legislation did so, but among those predicted to oppose the bill or favor amending it, there existed considerable deviation from the predictions. The results tended to be generally the same across all four votes and similar under analysis to the House votes.

The Motion to Kill the Hecht Amendment

Senator Chic Hecht (R–Nev.) proposed an amendment to S. 1009 that eliminated the authorization of appropriations for individual monetary payments to former internees. On a motion by Senator Ted Stevens (R–Alaska), the Senate voted 67–30 to table the amendment, in essence killing the proposal. The lopsided vote is surprising, especially since financial constraints seemed to be the most persuasive argument against the legislation and the most potent source of political backlash from constituents concerned about the large amount of federal funds to be authorized. Hecht's argument that the provision would set a dangerous precedent and be fiscally irresponsible at a time of federal budget deficits had little impact on his colleagues.

The percentage of Asian Americans in a state tended to affect the votes of its senators; the larger a state's Asian American population, the more likely the state's senators were to vote to table the amendment (see Table 13). Nearly 61 percent of the senators from the 24 states with populations less than 1 percent Asian American and 73.1 percent of those from states with populations from 1 to 5 percent Asian American voted for Stevens's motion; the two senators from Hawaii, the only state whose population is over 5 percent Asian American, both voted in the affirmative

TABLE 13

Senate Roll-Call Vote on the Motion to Table the Hecht Amendment, Apr. 20, 1988,
by Percentage of Asian Americans per State, Party Affiliation, and Geographic Region

Vote	Asian Americans within a state[a]			Party		Region		
	0%	1–5%	Over 5%	Dem.	Rep.	West	South	Rest of nation
Yes	28	38	2	46	22	10	16	42
	60.9%	73.1%	100%	85.2%	47.8%	100%	53.3%	70%
No	17	13	0	6	24	0	13	17
	37.0%	25.0%	0%	11.1%	52.2%	0%	43.3%	28.3%
N.V.	1	1	0	2	0	0	1	1
	2.2%	1.9%	0%	3.7%	0%	0%	3.3%	1.7%

SOURCES: Asian Americans, author, based on *Congressional Record* and Barone and Ujifusa, *Almanac of American Politics 1990*; party and region, author, based on *Congressional Record.*
[a]As a percentage of its total population.

TABLE 14

Senate Roll-Call Vote on the Motion to Table the Hecht Amendment, Apr. 20, 1988,
by Geographic Region and Party Affiliation

Vote	West		South		Rest of nation	
	Dem.	Rep.	Dem.	Rep.	Dem.	Rep.
Yes	4	6	15	1	27	15
	100%	100%	68.2%	12.5%	96.5%	46.9%
No	0	0	6	7	0	17
	0%	0%	27.3%	87.5%	0%	53.1%
N.V.	0	0	1	0	1	0
	0%	0%	4.5%	0%	3.6%	0%

as well. Although it was predictable that the Hawaiian senators would vote for the motion, it is somewhat surprising that nearly three-fourths of the senators from states with smaller Asian American populations would vote for the bill. Moreover, while it is easy to justify the decisions of the 37 percent of the senators from states with constituencies less than 1 percent Asian American who voted against the motion, it is more difficult to explain why nearly 61 percent of them voted for it.

Party affiliation and region had mixed results as predictors of Senate behavior (see Table 13). As expected, Democrats were much more likely to vote for the motion than Republicans. Over 85 percent of Democratic senators voted in favor of tabling the amendment, while only 11.1 percent voted against it. The Senate Republicans were more evenly divided, with 47.8 percent for the amendment and 52.2 percent against it. Thus, Democrats were extremely likely to vote for the motion, but it was almost as likely that a Republican would vote for the motion as against it. By region, we find that 100 percent of the western senators voted for the motion, as

electoral interest theory would predict. The results for the southern senators are surprising, however: although theoretically they would be more
inclined to vote against the motion, 53.3 percent of them voted for it,
whereas only 43.3 percent voted in opposition. As for senators from the
rest of the nation, an overwhelming 70 percent voted with Stevens and
only 28.3 percent against him. As with the House votes, electoral interest
theory fails to explain why nonwesterners in the Senate, especially those
from the South, voted as they did. Analysis of party and region together
gives a somewhat clearer picture (Table 14). In the West, party played no
role: all senators voted for the motion. In the South, party had a
significant impact, as 68.2 percent of Democrats voted for the motion to
table and 87.5 percent of Republicans voted against it. For the rest of the
country, party played a moderate role. For Democrats, a yea vote was
almost automatic: 96.5 percent voted for the motion. For Republicans,
party was less of a predicting factor, with 46.9 percent voting in favor of
the motion and 53.1 percent against it. Thus, the impact of a senator's
party identification seemed to vary by region. Neither party nor region by
itself was a controlling factor; in the South party was important, in the
West it had no impact, and in the rest of the country it played some role.
Electoral interest theory consequently has only limited power to explain
the vote's outcome; other factors must have been involved.

The Motion to Kill the First Helms Amendment

Senator Jesse Helms (R–N.C.) proposed to amend S. 1009 so that no
funds would be appropriated in any year in which there was a federal budget deficit, citing fiscal responsibility and his opposition to imposing a
$1.25 billion burden on Americans who had nothing to do with the war-
time decisions. Senator Matsunaga made a motion to table the amendment, with which the Senate agreed by a vote of 61–35. As with the Hecht
Amendment, the Helms proposal seemed likely to appeal to senators worried by constituent concerns about the budget deficit, so it was surprising
that the Senate overwhelmingly defeated it. The results of analysis of the
roll-call vote were nearly the same as those of the previous amendment
(see Table 15). As the percentage of Asian Americans in a state increased,
so did the percentage of senators voting for the motion to table. Although
these results follow the predicted pattern, more senators voted for the
motion than against it in every category. Democrats were more likely to
vote for the motion: 77.8 percent of them supported it, whereas over half
(56.5 percent) of the Republicans sided with Helms. By region, the western

TABLE 15

Senate Roll-Call Vote on the Motion to Table the First Helms Amendment, Apr. 20, 1988, by Percentage of Asian Americans per State, Party Affiliation, and Geographic Region

Vote	Asian Americans within a state[a]			Party		Region		
	0%	1–5%	Over 5%	Dem.	Rep.	West	South	Rest of nation
Yes	25	34	2	42	19	10	13	38
	54.3%	65.4%	100%	77.8%	41.3%	100%	43.3%	63.3%
No	20	15	0	9	26	0	15	20
	43.5%	28.8%	0%	16.7%	56.5%	0%	50.0%	33.3%
N.V.	1	3	0	3	1	0	2	2
	2.2%	5.8%	0%	5.6%	2.2%	0%	6.7%	3.3%

SOURCES: Asian Americans, author, based on *Congressional Record* and Barone and Ujifusa, *Almanac of American Politics 1990*; party and region, author, based on *Congressional Record*.
[a]As a percentage of its total population.

TABLE 16

Senate Roll-Call Vote on the Motion to Table the First Helms Amendment, Apr. 20, 1988, by Geographic Region and Party Affiliation

Vote	West		South		Rest of nation	
	Dem.	Rep.	Dem.	Rep.	Dem.	Rep.
Yes	4	6	12	1	26	12
	100%	100%	54.5%	12.5%	92.2%	37.5%
No	0	0	9	6	0	20
	0%	0%	40.9%	75.0%	0%	62.5%
N.V.	0	0	1	1	2	0
	0%	0%	4.5%	12.5%	7.1%	0%

senators again voted unanimously to kill the amendment, and nonwestern, nonsouthern senators favored the motion by 63.3 percent to 33.3 percent. In the South, however, senators tended to vote against the motion to table, with 43.3 percent voting for it, 50 percent against. Unlike the vote on the Hecht Amendment, this ratio accords to a certain extent with electoral interest theory, which predicts that southerners would vote against the motion. But even in this case, the support for the Helms Amendment is weaker than one would expect. Looking at the impact of party identification by region, the results are also very similar to those for the Hecht Amendment (Table 16). In the West, party affiliation had no influence, with all six Republicans and all four Democrats voting for the motion. In the South, party had a great impact, with three-fourths of the Republicans opposing the motion and nearly 55 percent of Democrats supporting it. The only difference appears in the remaining states, in which party played a role for both the Republicans and the Democrats. Whereas the margin between Republicans voting for and against the motion was small in the previous vote, it was much more clear-cut this time, with 37.5 percent voting in favor and 62.5 percent voting against it. For the Democrats, again every senator present voted for the motion; the only difference is that this time two senators did not vote. Therefore, again, both party affiliation and region played only a small role in explaining the outcome of the vote.

The Motion to Table the Second Helms Amendment

The ever-resourceful Senator Helms suggested a second amendment to S. 1009 that would withhold monetary payments to individual internees until the Japanese government compensated the families of U.S. citizens killed in the December 7, 1941, bombing of Pearl Harbor. Senator Stevens quickly made a motion to table the amendment, which was resoundingly accepted by a vote of 91–4.[8] The illogic of Helms's proposition was such that this vote hardly requires examination. In defense of the amendment, Helms argued that the proposed change emphasized "the horror, the terror, the grave apprehension that motivated the then president of the United States operating on intelligence information provided to him,"[9] and that it prevented the bill from making a mockery of the nation's budget priorities. The assumption of the amendment was that the interned Japanese Americans had "something to do with the bombing of Pearl Harbor,"[10] and it failed to distinguish between law-abiding Americans of Japanese ancestry and the armed forces of Japan. Even senators who opposed the monetary compensation included in S. 1009 would not buy Helms's reasoning.

Senate Floor Vote on the Redress Bill

On April 20, 1988, the final vote to accept and implement the findings of the CWRIC, including the provisions for a national apology and individual payments of $20,000 to former internees, marked the passage of the Senate version of H.R. 442, which the House had already passed. The three variables of state percentage of Asian Americans, party affiliation, and region of the country all help illuminate why the bill was passed, but none is fully conclusive (see Table 17). As expected, the higher the percentage of Asian Americans in the state from which a senator hailed, the more likely the senator was to vote for redress. As with the other votes, electoral interest analysis can reasonably justify the nay votes of senators from states where Asian Americans are virtually absent, but is less effective in explaining why the vast majority of them voted for the bill.

In the Senate, unlike the House, neither political party membership nor region had much impact on the vote. As predicted, more Democrats

TABLE 17

Senate Roll-Call Vote on H.R. 442, Substituted with the Text of S. 1009, Apr. 20, 1988,
by Percentage of Asian Americans per State, Party Affiliation, and Geographic Region

Vote	Asian Americans within a state[a]			Party		Region		
	0%	1–5%	Over 5%	Dem.	Rep.	West	South	Rest of nation
Yes	29	39	2	45	25	10	16	44
	63.0%	75%	100%	83.3%	54.3%	100%	53.3%	73.3%
No	17	10	0	7	20	0	13	14
	37.0%	19.2%	0%	13.0%	43.5%	0%	43.3%	23.3%
N.V.	0	3	0	2	1	0	1	2
	0%	5.8%	0%	3.7%	2.2%	0%	3.3%	3.3%

SOURCES: Asian Americans, author, based on *Congressional Record* and Barone and Ujifusa, *Almanac of American Politics 1990*; party and region, author, based on *Congressional Record*.
[a]As a percentage of its total population.

TABLE 18

Senate Roll-Call Vote on H.R. 442, Substituted with the Text of S. 1009, Apr. 20, 1988,
by Geographic Region and Party Affiliation

Vote	West		South		Rest of nation	
	Dem.	Rep.	Dem.	Rep.	Dem.	Rep.
Yes	4	6	15	1	26	18
	100%	100%	68.1%	12.5%	92.9%	56.3%
No	0	0	7	6	0	14
	0%	0%	31.8%	75.0%	0%	43.8%
N.V.	0	0	0	1	2	0
	0%	0%	0%	12.5%	7.1%	0%

supported than opposed the bill, 83.3 percent to 13.0 percent, and Democrats were more likely to vote for the legislation than Republicans. Republicans still had a greater tendency to vote for the legislation than against it, however, indicating that party affiliation was not a critical factor in this case. Moreover, region has little explanatory power, since in all three regions senators were more likely to vote in favor of H.R. 442 than against it. The variable had the greatest impact in the West, where every senator voted yea. In the other two regions, political theory can only partially explain the 13 votes from the South and the 14 votes from the rest of the nation that opposed the legislation; it cannot fully explain why 53.3 percent of the southern senators and 73.3 percent of the others voted in the affirmative. When we examine the voting data by both region and party, the variables still have relatively weak explanatory power (Table 18). For western senators, party made no difference, as all ten voted for the bill. In the South, party identification did play a role; three-fourths of the southern Republicans voted in opposition to the final bill, whereas over 68 percent of southern Democrats supported it. In the rest of the country, party seemed to be important for Democrats, with all of those present voting for the legislation. Party made less of a difference among Republicans, as only slightly more voted yea (56.3 percent) than nay (43.8 percent).

Party affiliation, therefore, had a smaller impact on voting behavior in the four Senate votes than in the House votes, and all three variables had as little explanatory power in the Senate as in the lower chamber, or even less. This finding is not surprising, since senators tend to be less influenced by constituent pressures than members of the House because their constituencies tend to be more diverse and they face reelection less frequently. Also, Senate Democrats seem to be more uniformly liberal; although there does exist some variation between Ted Kennedy on the left and Bennett Johnston on the right, the range is much wider among Democrats in the House. Furthermore, the smaller Senate is much more tight-knit and collegial than the much larger House; as a result, favor-trading among members tends to be more common and to have more influence on votes in the Senate than in the House. Therefore, electoral interest politics, at least in this case, is even less able to explain the Senate vote than the House vote.

Conclusions

Overall, from the data on the three House votes and the four Senate votes, it appears that the passage of the Civil Liberties Act of 1988 is consonant with typical conceptions of electoral interest pressure. In each case, the percentage of representatives and senators voting for the bill (or voting against the hostile amendments) increased along with the percentage of Asian Americans in their constituencies; this result follows the thesis that reelection-minded members of the House and Senate react to pressure from their constituents and, accordingly, that the larger the percentage of Asian Americans in their electorates, the more likely they were to support the unamended redress legislation. Similarly, the percentage of representatives and senators voting against the redress legislation in its original form decreased as the percentage of Asian Americans in their electorates increased.

It would be unwise, however, to conclude that electoral interest analysis can explain redress's unlikely passage on the basis of these data regarding the percentage of Asian Americans in each constituency. The results of this analysis must be qualified. First, as I stated earlier, the percentage of Asian Americans is not a wholly satisfactory or useful measure in the case of this specific bill. The 1980 census classification of "Asian American," from which all the data in this study come, includes, among others, people of Chinese, Filipino, Asian Indian, Korean, Vietnamese, and Hawaiian descent. Although Japanese Americans were the only ones to benefit directly from the legislation, they made up just 19 percent of Asian Americans. Thus, the only people with a direct, personal reason to pressure their elected representatives to vote for the legislation made up only one-fifth of the already small percentage of the overall population (not quite 2 percent in 1980) of Americans of Asian descent. Moreover, Japanese Americans tend to be concentrated in a few places—in California, Oregon, Washington, and Hawaii—and are virtually nonexistent in others. Thus, even if a particular congressional district in the South, such as the Fourth District of Georgia, had a population at least 1 percent Asian American, it is not necessarily the case that one-fifth of that 1 percent was Japanese American; on the contrary, it is possible, even likely, that the district had a considerably smaller percentage of Japanese Americans. Therefore, the all-inclusive Asian American category does not fully fit the electoral interest model; as a variable, it has limited power, and any conclusions drawn from it must be qualified.

In addition, Asian Americans tend to vote in smaller percentages than the population as a whole. Although estimates vary, the percentage of qualified Asian Americans who are registered and vote is considerably smaller than that of whites, blacks, and Hispanics,[11] and one study of California voting patterns indicated that of all Asian Americans, those of Japanese descent are particularly unlikely to register and to vote.[12] As a result, using the 1980 U.S. census data—that is, the entire Asian American population—as a measure of Asian American electoral power slightly skews the analysis, since it overstates the size of the Asian American electorate. Thus, the percentage of Asian Americans in each state and congressional district is not a wholly accurate measure of the potential voting influence of Asian Americans on their congressional representatives.

Moreover, although it appears that as the percentage of Asian Americans in a congressional district or state increases, so does the chance that the representative or senator voted for redress, it is important to look closely at the actual data. On the House side, the categories are (1) less than 1 percent Asian American, (2) 1 percent, (3) 2 to 5 percent, (4) 6 to 20 percent, and (5) more than 20 percent; the percentages of congressional districts in each category are 45 percent, 36 percent, 14 percent, 4 percent, and 0.5 percent. Thus, nearly half the representatives fall into the "less-than-1-percent" range, yet it is that category which electoral interest analysis has the most difficulty explaining. Only the two Hawaiian districts have Asian American constituencies of more than 20 percent, and only nineteen districts, predominantly on the West Coast, fall into the 6 to 20 percent range; it is these districts in which Asian Americans make up a large enough portion of the population to have a noticeable effect on congressional voting behavior. Of the 435 congressional districts, 196 have populations less than 1 percent Asian American, 157 have populations that are 1 percent Asian American, and 61 have populations that are 2 to 5 percent Asian American. These groupings do not show a large stratification; 80 percent of all representatives come from districts with populations no more than 1 percent Asian American. But 1 percent, or even 2 to 5 percent, is not a highly significant portion of the population. Even if a representative has a constituency that is 1 percent Asian American, it is unlikely that the member is considerably more inclined to vote for the legislation than a colleague from a district less than 1 percent Asian American, simply on the basis of constituent pressure. Moreover, these small percentages are even less meaningful once we recall that 1 percent Asian American may translate into 0.2 percent Japanese American, a number so small that it has no value as a measure of constituent pressure on a particular member. The percentage is even smaller when it is considered that a relatively high percentage of Asian Americans are not registered voters. In the Senate, the measure is even less meaningful, since only one state—Hawaii at 60 percent—has a population that is more than 5 percent Asian American; the remaining 49 states are almost evenly divided between those with populations less than 1 percent Asian American (23) and those with populations 1 to 5 percent Asian American (26).

As a result, in most states and congressional districts, redress was a "throwaway" vote; the members' constituencies included neither a noticeable Japanese American (or Asian American) community nor a vocal and organized opposition. Consequently, the member was free to vote either for or against the legislation without fear of constituent backlash. For example, Jim Kolbe, a Republican representing the Fifth Congressional District of Arizona, received virtually no constituent mail supporting or opposing the bill. Since no vocal force within his constituency seemed to care—either in support or in opposition—electoral interest factors hardly played a role in determining how he cast his vote.[13] Precisely because redress was a free vote for many representatives and senators, factors other than constituency pressure are critical in explaining the passage of H.R.

442. As a throwaway vote, redress allowed inside lobbying and the trading of favors between representatives and between senators to influence the votes of particular members, as later chapters will show. For example, a senator for whom H.R. 442 was a throwaway vote might vote for the legislation to repay a favor owed to one of the bill's main supporters. Moreover, the throwaway nature of the vote allowed representatives and senators to vote their consciences, to let their own ideological and personal beliefs, rather than their constituents' needs and wants, dictate their voting decisions.

The results of multiple regression analysis corroborate the conclusion that the percentage of Asian American constituents has little explanatory power (see Table 19). Since the data for the three House votes are similar, we need to examine only the most important vote. Analysis of the September 17, 1987, roll-call vote on H.R. 442, when the chamber initially passed the legislation, suggests that the percentage of Asian Americans in a district is not a very powerful variable. The t-statistic is 2.59, showing that the data are significant, but barely. Although the estimated coefficient, or B, is positive (0.08)—and therefore its direction indicates that the expected relationship exists—the relationship is extremely slight. With a standard error of 0.03, the regression is unstable, but because of the estimated coefficient, the instability matters little. Most importantly, the fit of the data is extremely low; R-squared is only 0.015. For the Senate, the results are similar. For the final roll-call vote, by which the legislation was passed, the estimated coefficient is 0.028—again, in the correct direction, but barely—with a standard error of 0.027, signifying instability. With a t-statistic of 1.05, the data are not significant, and with an R-squared of 0.011, the fit is low. The regression results for the other two Senate votes on the redress legislation are comparable.

Next, we turn to two standard indicators of voting behavior: party and ideology (see Table 20). In the September 17, 1987, House roll-call vote on final passage of H.R. 442, the estimated coefficient is 1.51, with a standard error of 0.27. The significance is much greater than in the previous analysis, with a t-statistic of 5.63. Also, the fit is somewhat better—R-squared is 0.068—although still low. In the Senate, analysis of the roll-call vote on the redress bill reveals an estimated coefficient of 1.52 and a standard error equal to 0.43. With a t-statistic of 3.56, the data are significant, and the R-squared is 0.11.

The regression implies that the party to which representatives or senators belong played a larger role than the percentage of Asian Americans in

TABLE 19

Regression of Roll-Call Votes (H.R. 442) on Percentage of Asian Americans per District

Independent variable	House, Sept. 17, 1987[a]			Senate, Apr. 20, 1988[b]		
	B	Standard error	t-statistic	B	Standard error	t-statistic
Intercept	3.47	0.14	24.41[d]	2.383	0.231	10.33[d]
Asian Americans[c]	0.08	0.03	2.59[d]	0.028	0.027	1.05

[a] R-squared = 0.015. For Tables 19–21, roll-call votes are coded so as to indicate a positive slope if the hypothesis is confirmed.

[b] R-squared = 0.011.

[c] As a percentage of district population.

[d] Significant at the .05 level.

TABLE 20

Regression of Roll-Call Votes (H.R. 442) on Party Affiliation

Independent variable	House, Sept. 17, 1987[a]			Senate, Apr. 20, 1988[b]		
	B	Standard error	t-statistic	B	Standard error	t-statistic
Intercept	1.23	0.40	3.09[c]	3.15	0.31	10.04[c]
Party	1.51	0.27	5.63[c]	1.52	0.43	3.56[c]

[a] R-squared = 0.068.

[b] R-squared = 0.11.

[c] Significant at the .05 level.

their constituencies in determining their votes on the redress legislation. Yet according to electoral interest analysis, constituency makeup should have had a much larger impact than party affiliation, since redress is not intrinsically a partisan issue. Democrats would have been more likely to support redress than Republicans because they are typically more liberal on civil rights and minority issues. Democrats, however, ranging from the very liberal to the ultraconservative, did not have any more specific reason to support the legislation than Republicans did. For the vast majority of all members of both houses, the political rewards to be won from supporting redress were few compared to the potential backlash of voting for such a costly bill with so many compelling arguments in opposition. Moreover, although both the Democratic and Republican parties included an endorsement of redress in their 1984 platforms, redress was neither controversial nor important for either party. In contrast to the situation with the Democratic Party and blacks, Asian Americans were not a critical support group for either national political party. They did not constitute a solid voting bloc for the Democratic Party; in fact, many Asian Americans have tended to be conservative and vote Republican, although not as a mobilized group of voters.

What multiple regression analysis of the roll-call votes in both the House and the Senate seems to demonstrate is that ideology had as much to do with the passage of the Civil Liberties Act of 1988 as electoral pressure or party—much more than one would at first expect. Although the surface evaluation of the three ideological variables—the ADA, ACLU, and ACU ratings—showed no comprehensive relationship between the vote a representative or senator cast on the legislation and the member's ideological leaning, ordinary least-squares estimation shows to some extent the opposite. In both House and Senate votes, the ideological-rating variables have a much greater fit than Asian American district percentages or party affiliation, and their significance is considerably greater as well. Since the results for regressions on ADA, ACLU, and ACU ratings are relatively similar, we need not examine all three; for the purposes of this analysis, the results of the regression on ADA ratings in both House and Senate should be adequate (see Table 21.) In relation to the September 17, 1987, House vote on H.R. 442, the estimated coefficient for ADA ratings as the independent variable is 0.04, indicating a slight relationship, with a standard error of 0.003. Its t-statistic of 12.03 is much greater than those of party and district percentage of Asian Americans (see Tables 19 and 20). Moreover, its fit is also much greater, with an R-squared equal to 0.25, compared to 0.068 and 0.015 for the other two variables, respectively.

The regression on ADA ratings for the Senate vote on H.R. 442 in April 1988 reveals similar results. The estimated coefficient, B, is 0.03, and its standard error is 0.006. With a t-statistic of 5.68, the variable is more significant than Asian American constituency (1.05) and party (3.56); although the differences between the numbers are smaller than those for the House vote, they are still important because they similarly imply that ideology played a larger role than party identification or electoral pressure. Also, the R-squared for the regression on ADA ratings is 0.25, which is twice the fit for party affiliation and 20 times the fit for percentages of Asian Americans. Although ideology at first glance seemed to have little explanatory power in this case, in fact it goes further than party or even electoral interest pressure as a variable for explaining the passage of H.R. 442.

TABLE 21

Regression of Roll-Call Votes (H.R. 442) on ADA Ratings

Independent variable	House, Sept. 17, 1987[a]			Senate, Apr. 20, 1988[b]		
	B	Standard error	t-statistic	B	Standard error	t-statistic
Intercept	5.40	0.207	26.11[c]	3.88	0.335	11.55[c]
ADA rating	0.04	0.003	12.03[c]	0.03	0.006	5.68[c]

[a] R-squared = 0.25.
[b] R-squared = 0.25.
[c] Significant at the .05 level.

Although none of the regressions indicated a strong relationship between the different variables and members' votes, the data do imply that the conclusion earlier in this chapter that the size of the Asian American population in congressional members' constituencies affected the roll-call vote outcomes, as the straight percentages in Tables 1, 5, 9, 13, 15, and 17 show, is in fact misleading. It would be overstating the case to conclude that electoral interest pressure played absolutely no role in the final vote on the legislation, but it is also incorrect to contend that it explains very much. As we saw in Chapter Two, electoral interest typically only plays a role in influencing congressional voting behavior when the constituency involved has a direct interest in the issue, is vocal about it, and has substantial power to affect electoral outcomes, through the ability either to mobilize massive numbers of votes or to influence large campaign contributions. Grass-roots support tends to have the greatest impact when the issue is very specific and when constituents pressure their senators or representatives with a specific message.

One recent example in which electoral pressure made a significant difference is the issue of the Social Security "notch," a complicated issue that has been debated in Congress since the 1970s. In 1972, Congress changed the Social Security benefit formula so that retirement benefits were adjusted each year to compensate for the rising cost of living. The new formula was flawed, however, in effect compensating retirees twice for cost of living increases and possibly leading the Social Security program to bankruptcy. In 1977, Congress passed amendments designed to correct 1972's flawed formula in order to preserve the solvency of the program. To prevent those already on fixed incomes from having to endure an abrupt reduction in their benefits, these amendments did not alter their benefit rates; as a result, retirees born before 1917 continue to receive double cost-of-living increases. The 1977 law contained transition provisions for the new formula, making the adjustment easier for those nearing retirement age. Therefore, while individuals born during the "notch" years (1917–21) do not receive the double increase that older retirees may be getting, they receive a higher rate of benefits than retirees born after 1921. Since the 1977 changes, legislation has been introduced to deal with the notch. The current proposal before Congress, the Social Security Notch Adjustment Act, would not eliminate the notch. The legislation would extend the flawed 1972 formula to people born between 1917 and 1926, thereby creating a new notch for those born after 1926. Only by fully repealing the 1977 amendments could the notch be totally eliminated. This change would cost $860 billion over ten years, however, threatening the solvency of the entire Social Security system. Although many representatives and senators understand the complexity of the issue and disagree with "correcting" the notch, constituent pressure—through lobbying and massive amounts of mail to congressional offices—has led almost half of the senators and over 250 representatives to cosponsor the notch legislation. Their decisions were not based so much on their belief that the legislation is fair and the right thing to do, but rather on the influence of a large, powerful electorate that (1) votes, (2) contributes to campaigns, and (3) is mobilized by an effective lobby headed by the National Committee to Preserve Social Security and Medicare.

Japanese American redress and the notch legislation, however, are very different issues. When we compare the electoral and economic clout of all retired people with that of the Japanese American community, we see that constituent pressure played a significantly smaller role in the case of the redress legislation. As we saw in the last chapter, Japanese Americans—or the broader group of Asian Americans—did not make up a model organized interest group. Their numbers were too small and concentrated in only a few areas of the country; historically, they had had limited political activity on the national level; the benefits of the bill were small relative to the losses incurred during the war; and the community was divided on the issue. As a result, unlike the situation with the notch legislation (where the effect of targeted pressure by a powerful constituency is obvious), mass pressure cannot satisfactorily explain the passage of the legislation. Redress supporters might have served as a noisy irritant in a small number of specific congressional districts, but not overwhelmingly across the country.

Redress, simply put, is not a typical electoral interest story. Even ideology, although it has more explanatory power than both a constituency's percentage of Asian Americans and the representative's party affiliation, does not satisfactorily explain the roll-call votes. Rather, other factors, both institutional and external, necessarily played pivotal roles in assuring passage of the legislation. It is to those factors that we now turn.

CHAPTER FIVE

The Commission on Wartime Relocation

H.R. 442 differed significantly from most issues that come before the U.S. Congress; it was not of the sort that representatives and senators vote on daily, like resolutions establishing National Ballroom Dancing Week or bills calling for three new dam sites in Mississippi. Although such measures have direct implications for the members of Congress whose constituents they benefit, they are neither grave nor momentous matters. And even though such measures as tax reform and overhauling the federal budget do have momentous consequences for the nation as a whole, for the most part even they lack the emotional nature of the redress issue. The issue at stake was not one of dollars and cents, nor even of loyalty to foreign allies. Rather, it was a matter of constitutional rights and justice, of setting the historical, political, and moral record straight. It was not only about vindicating a small minority group, but about clearing the conscience of the nation.

Although at first glance the redress issue appeared to affect only the surviving 60,000 former internees and their families, it was not special-interest legislation, like a pork-barreling measure or even an affirmative-action measure, and its impact was more far-reaching. The issue was "all-American," touching the fundamental pillars of the U.S. Constitution, notably the Fifth Amendment guarantee of due process. Since the purpose of the monetary compensation and apology that the legislation sought was solely to redress the loss of constitutional rights, not to compensate for any personal property losses, groups other than Japanese Americans had a stake in the bill's passage. The redress bill was not a simple case of organized interest-group pressure or Mayhew's "electoral connection." The desire to make sound and just public policy, not the desire to be reelected, was the dominant factor in the decision to vote for redress.

For many Americans, however, the redress legislation was not a clear-cut answer to a complicated issue. The proposition of redressing the injustices suffered by one or two groups of people during a war of World War II's magnitude evoked a wide range of emotions. Few people could argue that Japanese Americans had not suffered during the war. But most Americans alive then had felt the effects of war firsthand, often through their own service or the service of a family member in the armed forces, and any reminders of the war brought back memories of their own pain and grief. Compensating Japanese Americans for their wartime loss of rights did not necessarily seem fair or right, since so many other people had suffered as well. A national apology might have been acceptable, but many people were unsure whether monetary compensation was the proper way to redress the loss of constitutional rights. Moreover, many people felt uncomfortable with the commission's strong indictment of popular American leaders. It was easy to look back at the events of World War II 40 years later and decide that the evacuation and internment were wrong, but was it reasonable to castigate government officials during the war, who did not have benefit of hindsight, for racism and failed political leadership? For many people, the answer was not simple or straightforward.

Despite the complexity of the issue, the emotional appeal of redress was a powerful force. Redress was an issue that dealt with sufferings of real, living people with whom many representatives and senators could identify. Heart-wrenching stories of Japanese American families, uprooted from their homes, having to sell all their worldly possessions for a few cents on the dollar, not knowing if they would ever return to the West Coast, could appeal to the lawmakers' sense of compassion. The record of the Nisei military units made an impact, especially among the many members of Congress who took pride in their own distinguished military records.

One example will illustrate the power of the personal appeal: the story of Rudy Tokiwa and Congressman Charles Bennett (D–Fla.). Bennett, the second-ranking member of the House Armed Services Committee, dean of the Florida congressional delegation, and a disabled veteran of World War II himself, was originally opposed to H.R. 442. When a group of Nisei veterans, including Rudy Tokiwa, a decorated and grievously wounded member of the 442d Regimental Combat Team, paid him a visit to persuade him to reconsider his position, Bennett reluctantly agreed to vote for the bill. Between the lobbying visit in July 1987 and the floor vote two months later, however, he returned to his original stand on the issue. But Tokiwa was present for the floor vote, and as Bennett walked into the House chamber, he spotted Tokiwa, wearing his army coat and hat, sitting in the handicapped spectators' section. Unable to vote against redress with Tokiwa there to remind him of the sacrifices of the 442d, Bennett, to the surprise of many, cast his vote in favor of redress. And because as head of the Florida delegation Bennett had told three other members of the House from Florida to follow his vote, the legislation gained four "yea" votes, in large part because Rudy Tokiwa had related his own wartime experiences on a short visit to a congressional office one summer afternoon.[1] Tokiwa's story, and his presence, had as much persuasive power as thousands of letters from constituents.

A Fortuitous Convergence

Its emotional nature enabled the redress bill to overcome the political odds and garner the votes necessary for passage. Just like electoral interest theory, however, the uniqueness of the redress issue cannot fully explain the redress victory alone. Another factor played an equally significant role: time. The special nature of the bill only created a situation in which representatives and senators *could be persuaded* to support redress on the basis of moral conviction. It did not guarantee that key players in Congress would fervently jump on the redress bandwagon or that the main grass-roots lobbyists supporting the bill would be able to mobilize the human, political, and financial resources that would be needed to pass it. Nor did it guarantee that the bill would survive the institutional barriers that prevent most legislation from ever reaching a vote of both chambers. Rather, the complexity and personal aspect of the redress issue ensured that the redress campaign would be long and arduous. It took the federal government over 40 years to redress its wartime actions. Even after the commission made its recommendations in 1983, Congress took another five years to pass the legislation. In good part, that delay can be attributed to the time needed to educate and make personal contact with individual members of Congress. Outside the West Coast, few people, including members of Congress, had full knowledge of what had happened to Japanese Americans during the war; a large proportion of the American population was not even aware of the internment. This widespread ignorance, as well as the deeply personal aspect of the issue, made talking one-on-one with senators and representatives the most effective way to gain the votes required to secure passage. But one-on-one contact takes a tremendous amount of time; redress did not succeed when the early redress bills were introduced in the first half of the 1980s because there had not been enough personal contact with individual members to secure passage.

Thus, the redress campaign must credit its success at least in part to timing. In the 100th Congress, all the necessary elements for success, both within Congress and within the Japanese American community, fell into place. Until then, institutional features of Congress made success unlikely, while internal divisions as well as lack of conviction within the Japanese American community made it impossible to launch an effective lobbying effort. But as the 100th Congress opened, those conditions coincidentally changed: the leadership in Congress jumped on the redress bandwagon, and after years of development, a coherent and workable lobbying strategy finally came to fruition for the Japanese American community. The next six chapters will examine the fortuitous convergence of these two factors, which culminated in the passage of the Civil Liberties Act. As Congressman Robert Matsui explained, the redress bill "became very ripe for passage in 1987,"[2] the year that the House initially passed H.R. 442.

The Commission on Wartime Relocation

Both in Congress and in the Japanese American community, the 1982 report of the Commission on Wartime Relocation and Internment of Civilians was an important catalyst that eventually led to successful redress legislation. In Congress, the commission report effectively educated members about the internment experience and the issue of redress, giving the bill credibility. In the Japanese American community, the commission helped to bring a silent and disjointed group together in support of the redress cause. The commission hearings gave Japanese Americans their first real opportunity to speak out about their wartime experiences. They resulted in an emotional outpouring among the 80,000 surviving former internees, providing the energy and spirit needed to galvanize the community and to bring the issue to its forefront. Just as important, the commission's findings and recommendations gave the Japanese American community hope and a renewed faith in the government—two things it had been lacking since that fateful day in 1942 when President Roosevelt signed Executive Order 9066. In other words, the commission was the much-needed spark that lit the fire under the campaign for redress.

Although the CWRIC played a pivotal role in the redress campaign, it had an unlikely beginning, and at the time of its creation its existence was a divisive issue in the Japanese American community. Prior to the commission's establishment in 1980, the debate among those who advocated that the federal government make restitution for its wartime actions focused ón what form that restitution should take, not whether the wartime relocation and internment warranted review or whether any type of redress was justified at all. Thus, it was surprising that the campaign for redress's first step into the congressional arena was the introduction of legislation creating a commission to study the issue.

The original goal of the Japanese American Citizens League, one of the principal interest groups working on strategies to get redress legislation passed, was to push for redress outright. JACL had first addressed the issue of redress at its 1970 biennial convention in Chicago, when it passed a nebulous resolution accepting redress as an issue of concern. Nearly a decade later, however, it had only a vague idea of how to approach the enormous hurdle of lobbying Congress to pass major civil-rights legislation. As John Tateishi, appointed chair of JACL's National Redress Committee in 1978, and his committee realized at a meeting in December 1978, they lacked experience on Capitol Hill and did not know what needed to be done strategically to get the legislation passed. Moreover, they did not know how four Japanese Americans who did have power in Washington—Senators Inouye and Matsunaga and Congressmen Mineta and Matsui—felt about the issue. As a result, Ron Ikejiri, JACL's Washington representative, set up a meeting between JACL leaders and the four Nikkei members of Congress in 1979.[3]

At this January 1979 meeting, the idea of a study commission first came to the forefront of the redress movement. To start the meeting, Tateishi presented three or four different proposals for possible draft legislation that the JACL committee had outlined. Matsunaga and Mineta responded positively, while Matsui, then a freshman congressman, said little. Inouye proposed the idea of a blue-ribbon congressional commission with the task of investigating the government's wartime actions and issuing a report on its findings. The advantages, he said, were that the commission would receive public exposure and that its report would become an official part of government records. Moreover, he expressed concern over the possible political backlash that the four would receive if they immediately came forward in support of direct redress, which could be perceived as special-interest legislation. Mineta agreed that public education was crucial. Though politically inexperienced, the JACL leaders knew that if redress legislation were to have any chance of succeeding, it needed the support of the Japanese American members of Congress. When they saw that the two senators and two congressmen were leaning toward the commission idea, they realized that this was the route they had to take.[4]

In February 1979, the National Redress Committee met to make its final decision on its legislative approach. Going into the meeting, the sentiments of the committee members were split. Two members, Ron Mamiya and Henry Miyatake, from the activist Seattle chapter strongly felt that direct appropriations was the only acceptable option. In a 5–2 vote, however, the commission proposal won. Ray Okamura, speaking for the majority, which also included Tateishi, Bill Marutani, Phil Shigekuni, and Min Yasui, gave the reasoning: in his heart he wanted to go for redress directly, and if he thought it was possible, he would go for it. But given the reality of Washington politics, which Inouye had appraised so astutely, a study commission had to be established if redress were to have a chance of passage.[5] Congress itself was relatively ignorant of the issue, and the public exposure the commission would receive and the public awareness it would raise were crucial to the success of any redress legislation.

Reaction to the decision was predictable. The Seattle contingent said the committee had sold out the community, and backlash against it from the Japanese American public was immediate. Many thought that it was obvious that a wrong had been committed and that it was insulting that former internees would have to go before a review board to prove that their rights had been denied. They saw the commission as a cop-out and a politically expedient step for the four Nikkei members of Congress who did not want their names to become closely associated with a controversial special-interest issue that was likely to fail. The response from Capitol Hill was favorable, however, and the offices of Inouye, Matsunaga, Mineta, and Matsui were all very supportive. On August 2, 1979, a bipartisan group of senators, headed by Inouye and Matsunaga,[6] introduced S. 1647, the Commission on Wartime Relocation and Internment of Civilians Act. Matsunaga had previously sponsored the Native Hawaiian Claims Commission Act, and it was used as the model for this bill.[7] Nine Democrats introduced the House companion bill, H.R. 5499, on September 28, with over 110 other representatives as cosponsors.[8]

In the meantime, a group of Seattle activists and others who opposed the commission route made its move into the congressional arena. On November 28, 1979, Congressman Mike Lowry (D–Wash.) introduced H.R. 5977, the World War II Japanese American Human Rights Violation

Redress Act, calling for individual monetary compensation of $15,000 for each internee plus $15 for each day spent in camp. This bill was based on the "Seattle Plan" developed in the early 1970s by Shosuke Sasaki, Mike Nakata, and Henry Miyatake of the Seattle Evacuation Redress Committee of the Seattle JACL chapter.[9] Support in Congress and in the Japanese American community at large was lacking, however, and the Lowry bill experienced a quick death as the House directed its attention to the commission bill. It was in response to the commission bill that the National Council for Japanese American Redress was formed by a group that had supported the Lowry bill.[10] Eventually NCJAR filed a class-action suit against the U.S. government on behalf of all former internees. NCJAR's efforts and impact on the passage of the redress legislation will be further discussed in Chapter Eleven.

On May 22, 1980, the Senate overwhelmingly passed S. 1647, with one significant amendment attached in the Senate Committee on Governmental Affairs. Approximately 1,000 Aleut Native Americans had been evacuated from villages in the Aleutian and Pribilof Islands during World War II and interned in inadequate facilities in southeastern Alaska. The military's decision to evacuate was based on the Japanese bombing of Dutch Harbor in the Aleutian chain and the Japanese invasion of Attu and Kiska Islands. Even though their situation was not directly related to that of the Japanese Americans and the Aleutians had no blood ties to Japan, they were included in the commission's study as a result of the persuasion of Senator Ted Stevens of Alaska, the ranking Republican on the Governmental Affairs Subcommittee on Civil Service, Post Office, and General Services. On July 21, 1980, the House easily passed H.R. 5499, with 297 yeas, 109 nays, and 45 not voting. By July 24, the two chambers had reached agreement on the differences in their bills and sent the Senate version to the White House. President Jimmy Carter signed the legislation into law on July 31, stating:

> It is with a great deal of pleasure I sign this legislation into law. The commission study is adequately funded. It is not designed as a witch hunt. It is designed to expose clearly what has happened in that period of war in our nation when many loyal American citizens of Japanese ancestry were embarrassed during a crucial time in our nation's history. I don't believe anyone would doubt that injustices were done and I don't think anyone would doubt that it is advisable now for us to have a clear understanding as Americans of this episode in the history of our country. . . . We also want to prevent any recurrence of this abuse of the basic human rights of

American citizens and also resident aliens who enjoy the privileges and protections of not only American law but of American principles and ideals.[11]

With this declaration and the president's signature, the Commission on Wartime Relocation and Internment of Civilians was created.[12]

Next came the task of selecting the people who were to make up the commission. The president, the House, and the Senate each appointed three members. President Carter appointed Dr. Arthur S. Flemming, chairman of the U.S. Commission on Civil Rights and Secretary of Health, Education, and Welfare under President Eisenhower; Joan Z. Bernstein, former general counsel of the Department of Health and Human Services; and Judge William Marutani of the Philadelphia court of common pleas and the only Japanese American on the commission. The Senate named Edward W. Brooke, former U.S. senator from Massachusetts, an African American Republican; Hugh B. Mitchell of Seattle, also a former U.S. senator and former U.S. congressman; and Father Ishmael Vincent Gromoff, a Russian Orthodox priest and former Aleutian internee. The House appointed Arthur J. Goldberg, former ambassador to the United Nations and former U.S. Supreme Court justice; Congressman Daniel Lungren of Long Beach, California, a Republican who asked to be named to the commission; and the Reverend Robert F. Drinan, a Jesuit priest, president of Americans for Democratic Action, and former U.S. congressman from Massachusetts. This distinguished list of members gave the commission credibility and ensured that it would be taken seriously.

Nonetheless, rocky times lay ahead. With work quickly piling up, the commission lacked the administrative capacity to function effectively and efficiently. Paul Bannai, the first Japanese American elected to the California legislature, was appointed executive director, responsible for all the commission's administrative duties, but overall, the small commission staff was overwhelmed. Hearings needed to be scheduled and organized, witness lists put together, and archival research coordinated and conducted.

The commission elected Joan Bernstein as chair. An astute Washington insider, she soon took control of and gave direction to the commission's activities. The commission's goal, according to Bernstein, was to

> seek to understand what happened, how, and why. We need to understand how it was that the nation's military and civilian leaders decided to evacuate and confine approximately 120,000 people for no other reason than their ancestry. We need to examine what protections the law offered, and

whether those protections need to be expanded. And finally, the commission must come to grips with the difficult, but crucial, question of redress.[13]

Personality conflicts led to a change in personnel, as Bannai was let go from the commission staff. By the time the commission arrived in Chicago for hearings in September 1981, Bernstein had picked attorney Angus Macbeth as Bannai's successor in the renamed position of special counsel. A Washington old-timer, Macbeth played an instrumental role in directing archival research and the commission's business.

From July to December 1981, the commission held twenty days of hearings in nine cities. It traveled from Washington, D.C., to Los Angeles, San Francisco, Seattle, Anchorage, Unalaska, Chicago, back to Washington, D.C., to New York, and then to Boston. Over 750 witnesses testified, ranging from former Japanese American and Aleutian internees to former government officials, public figures, academics and other professionals with relevant expertise, community leaders, and other interested people. From the start of the hearings until December 1982, the commission staff conducted extensive primary research, collecting materials from government and university archives and reviewing historical texts already written on the subject.[14]

In December 1982, the commission released its 467-page report entitled *Personal Justice Denied*. The findings were submitted to Congress in February 1983, with the unanimous backing of the commission members. The report gave an account of Japanese American history, the process involving the military's decision to evacuate and intern West Coast Japanese Americans, and a description of the evacuation and internment, along with an account of the experience of the Aleutian Islanders. In the report, the commission stated that Executive Order 9066

> was not justified by military necessity, and the decisions which followed from it—detention, ending detention, and ending exclusion—were not driven by analysis of military conditions. The broad historical causes which shaped these decisions were race prejudice, war hysteria and a failure of political leadership. Widespread ignorance of Japanese Americans contributed to a policy conceived and executed in an atmosphere of fear and anger at Japan. A grave injustice was done to American citizens and resident aliens of Japanese ancestry who, without individual review or any probative evidence against them, were excluded, removed and detained by the United States during World War II.[15]

Furthermore, in its analysis of the Aleuts' situation, the commission concluded that although their evacuation was justified by the area's status as a theater of war, "there was no justification for the manner in which the Aleuts were treated in the camps in southeastern Alaska, nor for failing to compensate them fully for their material losses."[16]

Six months later, in June 1983, the commission made public its recommendations for remedies as an act of national apology. Although it acknowledged that history could not be rewritten and that no amount of money could compensate for the former internees' losses and sufferings, it stressed its power to suggest remedies for violations of the nation's laws and principles. The federal government must provide some sort of redress, because "nations that forget or ignore injustices are more likely to repeat them."[17] The commission made five recommendations: (1) that Congress pass a joint resolution, to be signed by the president, acknowledging that a grave injustice had been done and offering a national apology; (2) that the president pardon those convicted of violating the curfew or exclusion orders; (3) that Congress direct executive agencies to which Japanese Americans may apply for restitution of position, status, or entitlements lost during the war to review such applications with liberality; (4) that Congress appropriate money to create an educational and humanitarian foundation; and (5) that Congress make individual compensation payments of $20,000 to each of the surviving evacuees and internees. The recommendations had the unanimous support of the commission members except for the one providing for individual payments, on which Congressman Lungren dissented.[18] In the case of the Aleuts, the commission recommended that Congress appropriate funds to rebuild churches damaged or destroyed in the Aleutian Islands during World War II; that Congress appropriate funds to the Army Corps of Engineers to clear away war debris around the populated areas of the Aleutian Islands; and that Congress declare Attu to be native land. With Congressman Lungren again the lone dissenter, the commission also recommended that Congress establish a $5 million fund for the beneficial use of the Aleuts and that it appropriate funds for direct payments of $5,000 to each of the few hundred surviving evacuated Aleuts.[19]

The Commission's Impact in Congress

Just as Senator Inouye had predicted in the February 1979 meeting, the establishment of the commission turned out to be the most prudent political move that the effort for redress could have made. JACL leadership had decided that it would take whatever recommendations the commission made and present them as legislation to Congress.[20] To JACL's good fortune, the commission responded with the basic recommendations that it was hoping to hear, especially the provisions for individual monetary compensation, and in 1983, the first redress bills were introduced in both houses of Congress. In the end, the commission, its findings, and its recommendations fulfilled three important functions on Capitol Hill: they gave the redress legislation credibility, an educational vehicle, and support.

First, the findings and recommendations provided the basis for legislation dealing directly with measures for redress and, more important, gave considerable credibility to such measures. Only one official government position had been taken before the commission report, and that was a tainted 1943 report by General DeWitt justifying all actions taken by the military. The commission report entered the annals of American history, with the conclusion that the evacuation and internment had not been justified or necessary and had been a great mistake. Thus, no longer did redress supporters have to raise the issue of whether internment was right or wrong; the issue now was solely whether Congress would commit the funds for redress. Moreover, the blue-ribbon commission had been created by the very governmental body that was soon to vote on redress—Congress. An individual senator or representative could hardly question the injustice of the military's wartime actions without running the risk of appearing ignorant or racist.

Second, the commission's report and recommendations helped in the process of educating both the public and senators and representatives on the historical facts and issues involved. Debate on and passage of the bill creating the commission brought the redress issue to the attention of members. Once the commission had released its findings, every member of Congress had a copy of the commission's report and recommendations, and even though it is doubtful that many had read all or even much of this documentation, they could no longer plead ignorance. Moreover, the commission, its hearings, and its report received wide media coverage. Every major national newspaper ran articles on the commission, and in cities in which hearings were held, the commission was front-page news.

The most important factor in the educational value of the commission was the separate release first of the report and then of the recommendations for redress. If the report and recommendations had been released together, all attention, both in the media and in Congress, would have focused on the recommendations for monetary payments and the $1.25 billion price tag. As it turned out, the delay in announcing the recommendations proved to be a great help to the subsequent lobbying effort undertaken by the redress campaign. The nation and its leadership needed to listen to the findings of the commission—the historical facts assembled and the conclusions that racism, war hysteria, and failed political leadership, not military necessity, had led to the evacuation and internment. Once the public and representatives and senators had been made aware of the historical facts and the commission's conclusions, it became much easier to persuade Congress to support all the provisions for redress.

Finally, the commission and its report created an environment in which it was politically easier for the four Japanese American members of Congress to come out in full support of the redress legislation. As they had realized when they first supported the idea of the commission, it might have been politically disastrous for them suddenly to begin lobbying for what might appear to be costly special-interest legislation from which they, their families, and their friends would benefit. But once a congressionally created independent panel had reviewed the facts and recommended legislation calling for monetary compensation, there was a more favorable political environment for the four men to lead the redress fight. Of course, it did not eliminate all the risk, especially for Congressmen Mineta and Matsui, who, unlike Senators Inouye and Matsunaga, had constituencies with negligible Asian American populations. But it did make it much easier than if there had been no commission, and just as important, the commission and its findings encouraged the four to believe that redress had a good chance of success and was worth the political risk they would run in leading the fight for passage.

Thus, the commission was a major factor in creating a more favorable institutional environment in Congress. Although it was not involved with lining up the necessary institutional leadership, it did an invaluable job in the educational process prerequisite to passage. It also brought together, with the exception of Senator Hayakawa, the Japanese American congressional delegation. Even though redress did not see victory until five years after the commission had completed its work, its report started the wheels turning in Congress and put the legislation on the road to success.

The Commission's Impact in the Japanese American Community

Not only did the commission have a strong impact on Capitol Hill, its significance was also great within the Japanese American community. Until the commission began its hearings, redress was not a pressing issue for most Japanese Americans outside the leadership of a few community groups. It had been over 35 years since the last internment camp had been closed; most former internees had put that time in their lives behind them. The few surviving Issei were in their seventies, eighties, and nineties, whereas the Nisei, many of them children during the war, had families of their own and had established themselves as farmers, teachers, doctors, and businessmen throughout the nation. Overall, Japanese Americans were doing quite well economically; their median family income in 1979 was $27,354, compared with the national figure of $19,917.[21] Japanese American unemployment ran about 3 percent, much lower than the national rate of 6.5 percent. Whereas 9.6 percent of the nation's population was below the poverty level, only 4.2 percent of Japanese Americans were.[22] The general feeling within the community was, "We're doing all right now. Why pour salt in old wounds? There's no reason to rock the boat." Not heavily engaged in national politics, the community was both apathetic and ambivalent about the cause. Even those who agreed with redress in principle had little hope that it would ever come to pass. But the commission—and more specifically its hearings—precipitated a major change in the Japanese American community. The hearings served as the catalyst for an outpouring of long-repressed feeling, which generated the commitment and energy needed for a successful redress campaign. The commission and its hearings brought the redress issue to the forefront of the Japanese American conscience and became a turning point in a campaign that was soon to make legislative history.

The mere establishment of the commission by Congress and the appointment of a notable panel gave the Japanese American community hope of some day obtaining a national apology and, more important, a reason to become involved in the redress movement. Japanese Americans had endured being stripped of their fundamental rights, rounded up, and hauled off to concentration camps in desolate lands by the U.S. government—not to mention alien land laws, laws barring the naturalization of Japanese immigrants, and other aspects of the nation's history of anti-Asian discrimination. They had little reason to put much faith in the government. They realized that the odds against such a small minority group successfully lobbying for major civil-liberties legislation were great. But the establishment of the commission showed them that redress was no longer just a pipe dream; Congress had originated, debated, and passed a piece of legislation creating a commission that included two former U.S. senators, a former U.S. Supreme Court justice, and a current U.S. representative to research their wartime experience. Four Japanese American members of Congress had showed enough faith in the issue to bring it to the attention of their colleagues. This showed the Japanese American community that the evacuation and internment were events about which Congress wanted to know more, events that raised important issues that Congress was preparing to confront.

The commission and the publicity it received also forced the Japanese American community to confront the redress issue. Before, it had been easy for Japanese Americans to dismiss the issue, saying that redress had no chance of success, so it was futile even to talk about it. But the establishment of the commission, the widespread media coverage it received, and its report and recommendations stimulated debate over redress within the Japanese American community itself. An unexpectedly high number of people, predominantly former internees, asked to testify at the hearings. Many of those who did not testify saw friends, relatives, or former campmates on the witness stand on the evening news or read their testimony in the next morning's newspaper, causing them to acknowledge their own feelings about their camp experience and what the government should now do in recompense. The Sansei, or third-generation Japanese Americans, began to take an interest in the redress issue. Although they had been aware that their parents and grandparents had endured the evacuation and internment, few knew details about life in camp or how their parents felt about the experience. They realized that a part of their history was missing—not only from the pages of history books and from general knowledge, but from their own lives as well. The desire to learn what had happened inspired their involvement in the redress campaign.

More than anything else, the commission hearings precipitated an emotional catharsis within the Japanese American community, with former internees for the first time giving voice to feelings they had kept buried for nearly 40 years. The despair, anger, frustration, and bitterness expressed by people who were usually reserved and reticent was astonishing. After the war, few internees talked about the experience, even with their children; they had been silenced by feelings of helplessness and shame. Consequently, the release triggered by the hearings had the quality of an explosion. Sansei saw their normally stoical Nisei fathers break down in tears in front of the commission, a remarkable scene for men brought up in a culture that stresses emotional restraint. Many witnesses relived the horror of the wartime experience, relating vivid pictures of squalid living conditions, stories of having to sell their homes and property hurriedly for negligible sums, and demands for government reparations.

Akiyo Deloyd's testimony about her wartime experience and its effect on her life since then was representative of many stories told to the commission:

There I was a girl of 19 years, native born American, declared a menace or a spy or a possible saboteur of her own country, without any legal process or a chance to defend myself. So I presumed the reason I was put away was because of my ancestry.

This experience has made me feel like a second-class citizen for 40 years, and I have suffered from this. Recently I had therapy to take care of this problem. I think this particular aspect of my experience is very important. Feeling like a second-class citizen affected all phases of my life, the inner and outer workings of a person.

This is difficult to understand, because you function well, as far as being self-supporting and being an adequate and contributing person. It is the inner quality of feeling, how it makes you feel. . . . It has affected us far more than we will ever realize.

The only belongings we could take were what we could carry. When we arrived in camp, what I saw was complete desolation. A camp in the middle of the desert; a barbed wire fence surrounding the entire camp with an armed sentry at each gate; no paved roads, only heat and dust storms. If this was not a complete prison-like atmosphere, I will leave it to members of the committee to tell me what they would consider it was if they were 19 years old.

We lived in a bare room, seven of us, five children and our parents. No separate partitions for my parents. Our bedding—we filled canvas bags with hay. I can remember how the hay pricked through the canvas as I slept. I felt this to be especially demeaning and degrading.

In addition, I was told that one member of the family had to work in the kitchen in order for the family to eat. This frightened me, so I did not hesitate for one second to work as a waitress. My monthly salary was $16 for eight hours a day, seven days a week.

My mother died in Poston, Arizona. She was a diabetic. I can remember the time that I went to the kitchen for milk. I was told the milk was for babies and small children. The diet of rice, macaroni, and potato was hardly a suitable diet for a diabetic. As far as that goes, it was not an adequate diet for anyone.

In a way, the stress of going into camp, poor diet, and worry hastened the death of my mother. She was 52 years old. She had to be cremated; there was no choice. My sorrow that I have to this day is that I could not put a fresh flower on her grave. All our flowers were made of Kleenex.

Using the bathrooms and the community showers was unpleasant. The toilets were partitioned, but no door in front, no privacy for the most intimate matters.

Putting Americans in concentration camps is against everything we stand for. For this it is only fitting and proper that the United States government give full apology and pay each person and their heirs a monetary compensation. Even this would not be enough to pay for all the suffering, psychologically, emotionally, and physically, that we Americans of Japanese ancestry were forced to experience, and to this day our suffering and feeling is a fact.[23]

At the Los Angeles hearings, Albert Kurihara, in a written statement read by his wife, told of his plight:

I remember I had to stay at the dirty horse stable at Santa Anita. I remember thinking, "Am I a human being? Why are we being treated like this?" Santa Anita stunk like hell. I had to do hard seasonal labor during that time, harvest and sugar beets work, which no one else wanted to do.

After camp I was treated like an enemy by the other Americans. They were hostile and I had a very hard time finding any job. I had to take so many different jobs that it made things very insecure. This was the treatment they give to American citizens.[24]

Some former internees expressed confusion about their experience and distress over what their government had done to them. According to Mary Sakaguchi Oda:

The most difficult problem for me to overcome as a result of the evacuation was the anger and bitterness which has gradually surfaced over the past 39 years. When the photographs of camp were shown at the Pasadena Art Museum some years ago, I burst into tears and could not stop the tears from flowing. All the pent-up emotion held back for so many years was released. The numbness of the evacuation was finally lifted, and because of the humiliation and shame, I could never tell my four children my true feelings about that event in 1942. I did not want my children to feel the burden of shame and feeling of rejection by their fellow Americans. I wanted them to feel that in spite of what was done to us, this was still the best place in the world to live.[25]

At the Los Angeles hearings, Amy Iwasaki Mass related the mental agony she encountered as a result of her childhood experience at the Heart Mountain internment camp in Wyoming:

As a clinician in the field of mental health, I tried to understand why so many Americans, Japanese and otherwise, were able to justify, rationalize, and deny the injustice and the destructiveness of the whole event....

I have come to the realization that we lulled ourselves into believing the propaganda of the 1940s so that we could maintain our idealized image of a benevolent, protective Uncle Sam. We were told that this was a patriotic sacrifice necessary for national security. The pain, trauma, and stress of the incarceration experience [were] so overwhelming [that] we used the psychological defense mechanism of repression, denial, and rationalization to keep us from facing the truth.

The truth was that the government we trusted, the country we loved, the nation to which we had pledged loyalty had betrayed us, had turned against us. Our natural human feelings of rage, fear, and helplessness were turned inward and buried. Experiencing and recognizing betrayal by a trusted source leads to a deep depression, a sense of shame, a sense there must be something wrong with me. We were ashamed and humiliated; it was too painful for us to see that the government was not helping us, but was, in fact, against us. . . .

[We experienced] the same psychological defense that beaten and abused children use. . . . Like the abused child who still wants his parents to love him and hopes that by acting right, he will be accepted, the Japanese Americans chose the cooperative, obedient, and quite American facade to cope with an overtly hostile, racist America.

By trying to prove that we were 100 percent super patriotic Americans, we hoped to be accepted. The problem is that acceptance by submission exacts a very high price. It is at the expense of an individual's sense of true self-worth. Although we may have been seen by others as model Americans, we have paid a tremendous psychological price for this acceptance. On the surface we do not look like former concentration camp victims, but we are still vulnerable. Our scars are permanent and deep.[26]

Anger stirred some of the witnesses to put forth a clear call for redress. William Hohri, chair of NCJAR, told the commission: "We want reparations for the deprivation of our civil and constitutional rights; for wrongful evacuation, detention, and imprisonment and the suspension of due process; for our loss of income, property, and education; for the degradation of internment and evacuation and for the psychological, social, and cultural damage inflicted by our government."[27] At the first hearing in Washington, D.C., Bert Nakano, national spokesperson for the National Coalition of Redress/Reparations, asked for at least $3 billion in reparations. He asked for a minimum of $25,000 for each Japanese American evacuated and interned as partial payment for loss of property, wages, and educational opportunities.[28] Min Yasui, one of the three men whose challenge to the legality of the military's orders had reached the U.S. Supreme Court in 1943, agreed, saying, "Whatever the sum may be . . . that's not enough."[29]

An explosion of emotion is the best description of the twenty days of testimony before the commission. But this release was not limited to the former internees who served as witnesses. The emotional outpouring spread throughout the Japanese American community. In interviews with local newspapers, on television talk shows, and in conversations with friends, family, and one another, Japanese Americans began to make public their thoughts and feelings. As one internee, still bitter, said on a television talk show, "We had been fooled, and I had been detained without cause and unjustly treated as an outcast. . . . I had been betrayed by my own government. All those years thinking I had done wrong."[30] The hearings, in effect, brought the redress issue home to all Japanese Americans.

Moreover, the hearings changed the tenor of the debate.[31] Redress was no longer an abstract issue of constitutional rights and wrongs, a debate for lawyers, scholars, and legislators. Rather, it had been moved to the personal: "We lost everything we owned, our children went hungry in camp, we lived in a horse stall." Once the debate reached that level, Japanese Americans began to feel an attachment to the redress bill; they saw how it applied to their own lives. Furthermore, they realized the enormity of their suffering and began to see redress as a just and necessary measure.

The result was the galvanizing of the Japanese American community and a surge of energy that fueled the campaign for redress for the years and battles to come. This marked a new beginning for the redress movement, and the creation of a true grass-roots campaign. Of course, in the long run, even broader support from religious, civil-rights, and minority groups would be required. But the first spark had to come from the Japanese American community, and the commission hearings made that possible. After all, if Japanese Americans did not care about the issue, why should anyone else? Thus, with the commission, redress was no longer just a JACL or NCRR or NCJAR issue; it was an issue for the whole community and, eventually, the whole nation.

CHAPTER SIX

The Institutional Setting in the 100th Congress

Even though the hearings of the Commission on Wartime Relocation and Internment of Civilians in the early 1980s marked the true start of a serious grass-roots effort, redress was anything but a sure bet. Even Senator Inouye, the originator of the commission idea, expressed apprehension about the chance of success, stating at the commission's first hearings in Washington, D.C., that it "may come to pass that a budget-conscious Congress will find itself unable to provide any significant form of monetary redress or reparations."[1] Despite the extensive public exposure that the commission's findings and recommendations received, many citizens, not to mention elected officials, were still not fully educated on the issue. Although the Japanese American community had finally come to life over the issue, it was still not unified and only a small group was actively involved. Most important, though the commission was the impetus for the redress campaign, the legislation still lacked a favorable institutional environment. After the commission legislation was passed in 1980, the political environment of Washington, D.C., changed dramatically. The presidential and congressional elections of 1980 marked the start of a new era in American politics, the Reagan era. With a conservative like Ronald Reagan at the Oval Office and the Republican party in control of the Senate, what appeared to be minority-rights issues had little chance of finding strong support on Capitol Hill. As a result, from 1980 to 1986, redress was essentially a dormant issue in Congress. It was not until the 100th Congress that the institutional structures of Congress gave redress a real chance for success. No matter how motivated and mobilized the Japanese American community and its lobbying effort may have been, it was going to take more than just writing letters to members of Congress and holding rallies. It was fortuitous that in 1988 the peak of the grass-roots lobbying effort and a propitious institutional structure in Congress converged.

The Democrats Recapture the Senate

President Jimmy Carter signed the bill creating the CWRIC in July 1980, about three months before he was to lose his reelection bid. In 1980, the executive branch and both chambers of the legislative branch were under Democratic control, a situation that does much to explain how the commission was created in the first place and, in theory, a situation more likely to secure passage of legislation like redress. But by 1983, when the commission had issued its findings and recommendations, the political landscape had been drastically altered. In 1980 a charismatic conservative defeated the incumbent president in one of the biggest landslides in American electoral history, marking the advent of a conservative tide that would prevail for much of the decade. On Ronald Reagan's coattails came Republican control of the Senate. Having gained thirteen seats in the 1958 elections, Democrats, and usually liberal Democrats, had overwhelmingly dominated the Senate for over twenty years. But from 1981 to 1986, Republicans gained a slight advantage in the upper house,[2] as well as control of the presidency, and as a result, the median voter swung to the right and a large amount of relatively conservative fiscal and social legislation was enacted into law. The period saw cuts in funding for federal social programs and increases in defense spending. With the budget deficit reaching all-time highs and the economy in a severe recession in the first few years of the Reagan Administration, a bill like redress had little chance of success.

But in 1986, the senators who had been swept into office in 1980 on Reagan's coattails were up for reelection for the first time. Running this time in a nonpresidential election year, these freshman senators had a difficult time, as the Democrats regained control of the Senate by a margin of 54–46. Although it refers only to the general environment in the Senate, this change in party power was significant for redress. First, although party affiliation was not an entirely relevant or powerful variable with regard to redress, it remains true that Democrats tend to be more liberal when it comes to the rights of minorities. With the change in the party in power, the median voter in the Senate shifted back to the left, creating a more propitious environment for the passage of a redress law. The concept of the median voter is important because the median voter on a particular issue ultimately decides a bill's fate, no matter how how far to the right or left the ideological extremes go. To illustrate this concept, suppose that the Democrats have control of the Senate 55–45. Suppose, too, that the 55 Democratic senators are more or less evenly distributed across the political spectrum from moderate to liberal to far left; none are conservative. On the other hand, the Republicans are concentrated on the right side of the spectrum, with few moderate conservatives. The mean, or average, ideological position on the political spectrum would be slightly to the right of center—and therefore it would appear that liberal legislation would have little chance of passage. Even if all the Republicans were ultraconservative, however, if the median—the 51st—voter were a left-of-center Democrat who supported the legislation, it would pass. Although in reality the ideological leanings and distribution of Senate Democrats and Republicans are not so clear-cut, the concept of the median voter remains relevant.

Second, with a shift in party control came a change in Senate leadership, and again the Democratic leaders were more inclined to be sympathetic toward redress. It helped that the positions of Majority Leader, Majority Whip, and Secretary for the Majority, as well as the chairs of the Committee on Governmental Affairs and its Subcommittee on Federal Services, Post Office, and Civil Service, were filled by Democratic senators. Senators in these positions held significant control over the legislative agenda, determining what legislation would make it to the floor for a vote by the whole Senate and on what issues hearings and debate would focus. Institutionally, they had the power to make or break a bill by setting procedures and rules. Although the fact that the senators in those positions were Democrats rather than Republicans in no way ensured passage of the redress law, it was a promising development.

The most significant changes in the leadership positions were the replacement of Alan Simpson of Wyoming by Alan Cranston of California as Majority Whip, the second-ranking Senate leader; the replacement of John Chafee of Rhode Island by Dan Inouye of Hawaii as Secretary of the Majority, the third-ranking position; and the replacement of William Roth (R–Del.) by John Glenn (D–Ohio) as chair of the Governmental Affairs Committee. Having Cranston in the number two position was important not only because he came from California, the state with the second-largest percentage of Japanese Americans and from which most internees were relocated, but also because he was an ardent liberal who had long been concerned with the wartime evacuation and internment. During World War II, Cranston had worked in the Office of Facts and Figures for the government. With the support of Eleanor Roosevelt, Archibald MacLeish, and then–attorney general Francis Biddle, he tried to dissuade President Roosevelt from authorizing the military's orders under Executive Order 9066. He also visited several of the internment camps during the war and saw firsthand what life was like for the internees.[3] He had long favored measures for redress, including monetary compensation, and as Majority Whip he was in a position to influence the bill's chances. Even more critical was the rise of Daniel Inouye to the position of Secretary of the Majority. As third in the leadership structure, Inouye—a 442d veteran and the most senior Japanese American elected official—was in a key position, and, as the next chapter will explore in more depth, Inouye played a crucial role at several points in the fight for passage and funding of the bill.

Finally, and arguably most important, was the replacement of Roth by Glenn as committee chair. Although redress was not one of Glenn's top priorities, the switch was significant because Roth was a staunch opponent of redress, whereas the former astronaut agreed with redress in principle and eventually cosponsored and voted for the legislation. As chair, Roth had blocked any chances for redress's success by preventing it from emerging from committee. As later chapters will show, redress had overwhelming support in the Senate among both Democrats and Republicans. By the 100th Congress, Senator Matsunaga had persuaded nearly three-fourths of his colleagues to cosponsor the legislation, and it is likely that Matsunaga would have been able to rally the necessary votes had the legislation made it to the floor at an earlier date. But, with Roth obstinately against redress, the legislation had no chance to survive the committee review process. Only with the switch from Roth to Glenn did redress finally have a chance in the Senate.

One should not, however, overstate the importance of the changes in Senate leadership. The switch in Majority Leader from Republican Robert Dole to Democrat Robert Byrd did not significantly enhance redress's chances, since Dole, although a moderate conservative, was an early supporter of redress, whereas Byrd generally agreed with redress but was not an especially active supporter. The switch from Ted Stevens (R–Alaska) to David Pryor (D–Ark.) as chair of the subcommittee with jurisdiction over the bill also did not mean much; Stevens was a staunch supporter of the bill because of its benefits for Aleutian Islanders,[4] whereas Pryor, a southern Democrat, had little interest in redress and hesitated before agreeing to cosponsor the legislation once hearings on it began. Although Pryor had no direct experience of the camps during the war, he was from Arkansas, where two of the ten internment camps were located, and thus was probably somewhat more attuned to the issue than other southern senators. Thus, although it was important that the general climate in the Senate had become more propitious, the changes in Senate leadership made a difference only in specific cases, the most important being the new positions of Cranston, Inouye, and Glenn. As we shall see, the changes in the House were even more significant.

A New Leadership in the House

Although there was no change in party control of the House in 1986 and no shift in the median voter, Speaker Tip O'Neill (D–Mass.) decided not to seek reelection, bringing about a major transformation in the House leadership. After O'Neill's departure, the new configuration included Jim Wright (D–Tex.) as Speaker, Thomas Foley (D–Wash.) as Majority Leader, and Tony Coelho (D–Calif.), an up-and-coming congressman who had turned the Democratic Congressional Campaign Committee (DCCC) into a successful fundraising machine, as Majority Whip. These three men were all strong supporters of redress. Both Foley and Coelho, who came from states from which internees had been evacuated and from districts with larger-than-average Japanese American populations, were educated on the subject and committed to redress. While to some extent it was politically shrewd of them to support redress, much of their commitment to the legislation arose from their own belief that the legislation was a necessary action that Congress had to take to redress the government's past injustice and that it was constitutionally and morally right. Although Wright was not from the West Coast or a district with a large Japanese American constituency, he was committed to redress as an issue for Congress to decide. After he returned from combat in the Pacific theater during World War II and learned about the evacuation and internment and the *Korematsu, Hirabayashi,* and *Yasui* Supreme Court decisions, he said that such injustices were not what he had been fighting for in defending the American flag. According to Congressman Mineta, Wright saw his war service as an affirmation of his commitment to and belief in the fundamental rights to be free from discrimination based on race or ethnicity, to be free to live and work where one chooses, and to be left alone by the government except for reasonable cause and with due process of law.[5] Moreover, Wright had a long-standing record of supporting redress. He was the original author of the bill that created the CWRIC, as well as the principal sponsor of the two redress bills introduced in the 98th and 99th Congresses. Collectively, the example of these three leaders—especially that of Jim Wright, who as a Texan had little to gain electorally—could be expected to have a substantial effect on the Democrats in the House.

Individually, the support of Wright, Foley, and Coelho was important in different ways. As Speaker, Wright was the Democrats' legislative leader of the House. As political scientist Nelson Polsby describes the office, "The Speaker, by tradition and practice the active leader of the majority party in the House, the 'elect of the elect,' second in succession to the Presidency, occupies an office of great prestige and importance in the Federal government."[6] Among the Speaker's powers are the ability to "speed a member's pet bill through the unanimous consent process or through suspension of the rules,"[7] to ask a member to preside over the House as the Committee of the Whole, and to assign bills to committee. Acting out of personal conviction, Wright used his institutional power as Speaker to redress's advantage, conferring with Congressmen Mineta and Matsui on the strategy and timing with which to bring H.R. 442 to the floor for vote by the full chamber.

Foley's contribution to the redress movement derived both from his powers as Majority Leader and from the respect in which his colleagues held him. The Majority Leader is the floor leader for the party: "He is the custodian of the weekly schedule; he makes *pro forma* motions from the floor, and, if he desires, he leads his party in debate on substantive issues. Off the floor he divides the duties and functions of leadership, negotiating with committee chairmen and the White House, informally persuading reluctant members to 'go along' with the Speaker."[8] As administrative manager for the Democrats, Foley was a valuable supporter. But even more important was his personal support. Although more recently Foley's leadership has been tarnished by the House Bank scandal, which surfaced during his tenure as Speaker of the 102d Congress, during the 1980s he was for the most part well respected by his colleagues. In a profile of Foley for the *New Yorker*, John Newhouse describes the former Majority Leader and present Speaker:

> Foley is an anomaly—a leader who not only stays above partisan strife but also seems immune from, certainly unaffected by, the febrile skir-

mishing on Capitol Hill. Many people there and elsewhere wonder how he succeeds so well in his job without making enemies or even stumbling occasionally. Congress is a colder and more unsentimental place than it was in the [1950s and 1960s], but Foley receives remarkably generous tributes from the sharp-eyed men and women there. . . . Foley seems to be a major player almost in spite of himself.[9]

According to then-Congressman Dick Cheney (R–Wyo.), who was the Minority Whip, "Tom Foley has enormous respect on both sides of the aisle,"[10] and because even his greatest critics do not suspect him of harboring a private agenda, Foley's reasons for supporting a piece of legislation, such as redress, are taken at face value. In addition, when Wright became Speaker of the House in the 100th Congress and therefore could no longer sponsor legislation, Majority Leader Foley took over principal authorship of H.R. 442 in its final introduction in the House.

In addition to Tony Coelho's institutional powers as Majority Whip—the party leader responsible for "whipping" in the vote and facilitating communication between rank-and-file members and the leadership—his success as a campaign fundraiser meant that many other House members owed their seats to him. Many people agreed that "his record-breaking fundraising efforts as chairman of the [DCCC] made the party so rich that he is fairly credited by many in Congress with the Democratic lock on the House."[11] Although many of the qualities that made him a top-notch fundraiser—his ability to use a mixture of "backslapping, arm twisting, and shakedown artistry"[12] to get whatever he wanted—eventually led to his downfall during the 101st Congress, when he was forced to resign from his seat under the cloud of ethical scrutiny, during the 100th Congress his roles as Majority Whip and leading fundraiser made him a great asset to the redress campaign.

When they worked as a team, the different personalities and styles of Wright, Foley, and Coelho "complement[ed] one another as well as or better than any recent predecessors and . . . provid[ed] stronger leadership than either chamber has seen since the heyday of Sam Rayburn in the House and Lyndon Johnson in the Senate."[13] Although critics of Wright and Coelho, both within Congress and in the nation at large, were many, and though both men have since relinquished their seats as a result of separate scandals over ethics, together the Wright-Foley-Coelho troika produced one of the most productive Congresses in recent history. With the support of such a team, it is not surprising that redress had its best chance, and did indeed succeed, in the 100th Congress.

While Wright, Foley, and Coelho provided the necessary leadership in the House as a whole, Congressman Barney Frank made the difference for redress in committee. In many cases, the chair of the subcommittee handling a specific piece of legislation has ultimate power over whether that bill has even a chance of passage, merely by deciding whether to hold hearings on it or to stall it in subcommittee. If the legislation is not on the chair's agenda, the bill may never emerge from subcommittee. This is what happened to the redress bill in the 98th and 99th Congresses. Although redress had the strong support of the Judiciary Committee's chair, Peter Rodino of New Jersey, in the 98th Congress, the chair of the committee's Subcommittee on Administrative Law and Governmental Relations was Sam Hall, a conservative Texan. Hall held hearings on the bill—but hearings that were skewed in a negative way. The hearings focused on the issue of the MAGIC cables, intercepted Japanese diplomatic messages that supposedly gave reason to doubt the loyalty of Japanese Americans during World War II. During the hearings, David Lowman, a former official of the National Security Agency, argued that intercepted MAGIC cables proved that there were subversive, disloyal elements within the Japanese American community and, hence, that the internment was justified. The debate never really came to the issue of whether incarcerating 120,000 people, including infants, the elderly, and the mentally ill, was justified even if a few Japanese Americans had been disloyal. As Congressman Mineta said, "We went into the hearings with the idea of talking about the evacuation," while Hall only wanted to talk about who spied for Japan.[14] With Hall as chair, H.R. 4110 had little chance of emerging from committee, much less succeeding on the floor.

Fortunately for redress, Hall resigned from the House when he was appointed to a federal judgeship during the 99th Congress. With his departure, Congressman Dan Glickman, a moderate Democrat from Wichita, Kansas, took over as chair of the Judiciary subcommittee. Although Glickman, with a considerably more liberal voting record than Hall, was much more sympathetic to redress than his predecessor, the legislation did not fare much better at his hands. Glickman agreed with the basic principles of redress, but he worried about his constituents back home in Kansas. Glickman was seriously considering making a run for either senator or governor. The risk entailed in helping pass legislation that authorized $1.25 billion to benefit a minority group not well represented in the state, at a time when federal budget deficits were huge and Wichita was hurting economically, was too high for Glickman to take at the time, although he did eventually vote for the bill. Moreover, Glickman probably thought that redress stood little chance of passage even if it made it to the floor of the House in the 99th Congress and saw no advantage in supporting a futile cause. The bill never made it out of committee.

With the start of the 100th Congress, the tide turned drastically. There was an opening on the Agriculture Committee, and Glickman, coming from a state with a large agricultural base, jumped at an offer to take that seat, while Barney Frank took over Glickman's old post. That change in personnel on the Judiciary subcommittee was critical. It opened a door that had been locked against redress for years and, for the first time, gave the bill a real chance of passage. From an electoral interest point of view, Frank had little reason to support redress: only 1 percent of the voters in the Fourth Congressional District in Massachusetts were Asian American. Frank, however, is not the typical politician; he took a number of personal and professional risks to become the gifted legislator he was at the time of the 100th Congress. As an ideological liberal, he is uncompromising when it comes to upholding the rights of minorities: for the 100th Congress, his ADA and ACLU ratings were both a perfect 100 percent, while his ACU rating was an unequivocal zero. Although Frank was the subject of an ethical probe concerning his handling of personal matters in 1989, leading to an official reprimand by his colleagues in 1990, his reputation as a legislator at the time was impeccable: "In an era of buttoned-up, blow-dried moderation, Frank was and is a viscerally committed liberal: agile, acerbic, and ferociously intelligent, the kind of Democrat who struck fear in the hearts of Republicans, conservatives, and hypocrites of all ideological persuasions."[15] Most important, Frank had always been firmly committed to civil-rights issues and effective in winning legislative support for them.

With the full support of Committee Chair Rodino, Frank was responsible for getting the bill out of committee. He used all his powers as subcommittee chair to redress's best advantage. Whereas Hall had opposed the legislation overall, and Glickman had been preoccupied by political worries, Frank made redress a priority during his tenure as subcommittee chair. When he first met with his subcommittee staff, according to assistant counsel Belle Cummins, he told them that getting H.R. 442 out of committee was an important item on his agenda, one that he was determined to see happen during his first term as chair.[16] With that kind of support, redress had its first real chance to make it to the floor for a full vote.

Moreover, with Frank as chair, the hearings held in April 1987 on the legislation were heavily skewed in favor of redress. With final say over who testified at subcommittee hearings, Frank stacked the panel of witnesses in favor of the outcome he desired.[17] The witnesses included Congressmen Mineta and Matsui; Congresswoman Pat Saiki and Congressman Daniel Akaka, both from Hawaii;[18] Congressman Don Young from Alaska; Grayce Uyehara, executive director of JACL's Legislative Education Committee; Angus Macbeth, former special counsel to the CWRIC; Mike Masaoka of the Go for Broke Nisei Veterans Association; Harry Kajihara, national president of JACL; William L. Robinson, representing the American Bar Association; and John C. Kirtland, of counsel to Bishop, Cook, Purcell & Reynolds—all of whom were advocates of redress. The only witness in opposition to the legislation was Richard K. Willard, assistant attorney general, Civil Division. In addition, Frank steered the discussion in the hearings toward the issue of whether the provisions in H.R. 442 were the best means of redressing the government's past wrongs. For Frank, the debate was not over whether the wartime evacuation and internment had been wrong and unjustified; that they were was absolutely clear in his mind. Rather, he wanted to ascertain from the hearings whether the proposal for monetary compensation, a national apology, and an educational fund was the right way to address a grave governmental mistake.[19] Frank knew that selling the idea of $20,000 payments to all surviving internees was going to be the greatest hurdle in getting the legislation out of committee and passed by the full chamber, and he focused much of the testimony on that point. Before Grayce Uyehara took the witness stand, Frank told her, "Now, Grayce, just one piece of advice. Don't go on [talking] about the injustice of what happened to the Japanese Americans. It was an injustice, and anyone with half a mind knows that. You better just spend your time talking about that payment."[20] That piece of advice clearly reflected Frank's commitment to H.R. 442 and his determination to make sure that it got out of committee unamended.

Frank's diplomatic skills were essential when the differing versions of H.R. 442 and S. 1009 were sent to conference committee for reconciliation.[21] There were three major differences between the two bills, and in conference committee, the potential for stalemate existed. First, the Senate bill included redress for Aleutian Islanders, which the House bill had eliminated. Second, the House version included a provision for vested right of payment; that is, a former internee would have the right to receive payment as of the date of the bill's enactment, so that if an eligible person died after that enactment but before receiving compensation, the internee's heirs would get the money. In the Senate version, conversely, only eligible persons who were still living at the time of payment could claim the money; if an individual died after the legislation was passed but before payments were distributed, heirs would have no right to receive the money. Finally, the two chambers disagreed on the issue of staggered payments and appropriation limits. The House bill originally called for payment over a ten-year period and had no restriction on the amount that could be appropriated in a given year. The Senate, on the other hand, set no time limit over which payments would be made and limited the money appropriated each year.[22] In settling these issues and creating the final report— in which the Aleuts were included, internees gained a vested right to payment at the time of enactment, and Congress had ten years to distribute all monetary payments and could appropriate no more than $500 million for redress in any given fiscal year—Frank tried to accommodate both houses. His greatest fear was a stalemate, so he did all he could to keep the middle ground intact.

H.R. 442 realized its first victory on September 17, 1987—the bicentennial of the U.S. Constitution—when the House voted 243–141 in favor of the legislation. In the Senate, the bill passed 69–27 on April 20, 1988. Although the changes in leadership structure were clearly essential to the bill's success, they do not explain why so many senators and representatives with no apparent electoral motivation to support the legislation voted in favor of it, or why many diverse interest groups lobbied Congress in support of redress. I take up that part of the story in the chapters that follow.

CHAPTER SEVEN

The Nikkei Members of Congress

Peer pressure is a powerful force in any interactive context, and the U.S. Congress is no exception. Just as peer pressure dictates fashion in junior high school or the newest dance moves at nightclubs, it affects how representatives and senators behave when voting on public policy. Because the atmosphere in Congress, especially in the Senate, is collegial, it is difficult for members of the House and Senate to vote against legislation that directly affects their colleagues; this is particularly true when the electoral costs of voting against the legislation are low. In the case of the Civil Liberties Act of 1988, lobbying by four Nikkei members of Congress—Senators Inouye and Matsunaga and Congressmen Mineta and Matsui—was a critical factor. It is not far-fetched to say that redress would not have succeeded, or at least not when it did, without their leadership. All four had personal ties to the legislation: both Mineta and Matsui were evacuated and interned as children, whereas Inouye and Matsunaga fought with the 442d Regimental Combat Team during the war. In addition, all four were respected by their colleagues and held positions of leadership and power within their respective chambers. Most important, although initially they had their doubts about redress, all four made concerted efforts to win passage of the bills; they personally and vigorously lobbied their colleagues, at some political risk to themselves.

The roles played by the four Japanese American members of Congress differed, but all were motivated by a feeling that the evacuation and internment had violated basic American values and that redress in the form of a national apology and monetary compensation was the appropriate way for the government to compensate for its horrible mistake. The end result of their varying efforts was essentially the same: they made their fellow senators and representatives "reluctant to vote against the legislation because it is very tough to vote against the interest of their respected colleagues."[1]

Leadership in the Senate

On the Senate side, Inouye and Matsunaga took on different roles in the redress battle. Senator Inouye took the lead early on, when JACL leadership approached the four members of Congress for advice in January 1979. As mentioned earlier, at that initial meeting, Inouye suggested the idea of lobbying for a congressional study commission that would issue a report on the factors behind the evacuation and internment, rather than push for monetary compensation from the start. Once the other three Japanese American members had agreed, Inouye took the lead in getting the commission bill passed. The bill establishing the commission was not very controversial, since it only authorized a study of wartime events without mandating that actual redress be made, but the commission's hearings and report were pivotal to the redress movement, both institutionally and externally. When it came to getting the Civil Liberties Act of 1988 passed, Inouye took a back-seat role, letting his fellow senator from Hawaii take the lead. Although Inouye did not actively lobby individual senators as Matsunaga did, his support was still important. He was one of the original key cosponsors of S. 1009, a fact that carried considerable weight with other senators.

Senator Inouye's presence as a high-ranking and respected senator made it difficult for his colleagues to vote against the legislation. As Hawaii's senior elected official, having been in office since Hawaii gained statehood in 1959, Inouye was known, both to his constituents and to his colleagues, as a loyal and determined statesman. During the 100th Congress, Inouye was secretary of the Senate Democratic Conference and the third-ranking member of the Senate leadership, and had recently risen to national prominence as chair of the Senate Select Committee on Secret Military Assistance to Iran and the Nicaraguan Opposition (commonly known as the Iran-Contra committee), as he sharply questioned Oliver North and other Reagan Administration officials in televised hearings on the biggest political crisis of the decade. He was also the fourth-ranking member of the powerful

Appropriations Committee and chair of the Select Committee on Indian Affairs. As a legislator, he was considered a shrewd politician as well as a dedicated public servant, qualities that led to his appointment as keynote speaker at the 1968 Democratic National Convention and as a member of the Watergate committee in 1973–74. Admittedly, Inouye has made some mistakes in his career on the Hill—such as when, in 1987, he inserted in an appropriations bill funds to construct schools in France for North African Jewish refugees, for which he publicly apologized and admitted failure of judgment—but overall, he is known for his conscientiousness and determination.

In the case of the redress legislation, one additional factor made Inouye's support significant: he had served with the all-Nisei 100th Battalion and 442d Regimental Combat Team, losing part of his right arm in combat. Thus, he represented the ideal of the true statesman and patriot. He had lost a limb for the nation that had incarcerated fellow Japanese Americans in concentration camps. He later became the first U.S. Representative from Hawaii. Veterans' groups provided some of the main opposition to the legislation, yet their arguments about the wartime sacrifices other soldiers had made crumbled against Inouye's military record and support for redress. In Chapter Twelve, we will also see the crucial role Inouye played, once the bill was passed, in getting it funded.

In the 100th Congress, when Congress considered H.R. 442 and S. 1009 for the final time, Senator Matsunaga led the effort for passage. Matsunaga's initiative gave the bill new life in the Senate. Many people, including the other Nikkei members of Congress, credited Matsunaga with almost single-handedly getting the legislation passed in the upper chamber. Although he worked on redress from the start of its congressional journey, it was not until the 100th Congress that he made it a top priority. Matsunaga personally lobbied all 99 other senators at least once, talking to many about the legislation two or three times.[2] Such sustained personal effort is rarely expended in the Senate, and then only on very special issues.[3] The energy and time that Matsunaga dedicated to redress was all the more impressive considering that throughout the 1980s he battled debilitating health problems.

Although peer pressure per se is a powerful tool in gaining support for a piece of legislation, Matsunaga's lobbying efforts were particularly persuasive for reasons specific to the situation. First, like Inouye, Matsunaga was a decorated veteran of the 100th Battalion and the 442d Regimental

Combat Team. Second, Matsunaga, who died on April 15, 1990, after a difficult bout with cancer, was a highly respected member of the upper chamber. Besides holding positions of power within the Senate—he was the second-ranking Democrat on the Finance Committee and chair of its International Trade Subcommittee, as well as the Chief Deputy Majority Whip—Matsunaga was reputed to be one of the hardest-working and most personable senators around. His habit of working into the early hours of the morning led the *Washington Post* to dub him the "senator who never sleeps,"[4] and colleagues as well as constituents knew that Matsunaga's commitment to certain issues—notably peace, energy, and space—was more than just hollow campaign rhetoric.[5] In addition to his convictions, Matsunaga's amiable personality made him one of the most well-liked senators in the collegial Senate; he was even named "most popular," along with Nancy Kassebaum (R–Kans.), in the "Lawmakers"[6] survey of all members of Congress in 1981. Finally, Matsunaga was not one to ask his colleagues for favors very frequently. This made his commitment to the issue all the more impressive and made it especially difficult for his colleagues to say no to Spark when he approached them.

Matsunaga's efforts cannot be overemphasized. His lobbying efforts were phenomenal in sheer quantity; it takes a good deal of time and energy to speak personally to every other senator. According to the late Mike Masaoka, a Japanese American lobbyist in Washington, D.C., and a personal friend of Matsunaga's, "No doubt many who personally did not favor this corrective and remedial measure joined in the co-sponsorship and final endorsement of this extraordinary congressional language because of their personal friendship and affection for the Hawaiian lawmaker."[7] Thanks to his effort, S. 1009 ultimately had 75 cosponsors, an unheard-of number for major civil-rights legislation. The high number of cosponsors assured passage in the Senate and, significantly, prevented a possible filibuster. With 75 cosponsors, well over the necessary 60, the senators in charge of the bill had the power to invoke cloture, a legislative device used in the Senate to block a filibuster. With this backing, the redress legislation was a sure winner, largely thanks to the junior senator from Hawaii.

A Tougher Road in the House

While Matsunaga supplied the manpower and Inouye the moral support in the Senate, Congressmen Norman Y. Mineta and Robert T. Matsui provided the necessary leadership in the House. Their efforts were even more important than their counterparts' in the Senate, because redress had a much rougher road to travel in the House. Members of the House, who have smaller, more homogeneous electorates than senators do and are up for election every two years, are more apt to yield to constituency pressure in policy decisions. Thus, Mineta and Matsui had a much tougher job of lobbying their colleagues than did their Senate counterparts and had to be more vigilant in securing the votes needed for passage. They did so at greater political risk than Inouye and Matsunaga, too, since they had very small numbers of Asian Americans in their districts and thus faced a potentially devastating electoral backlash for their efforts.

It took some time for Mineta and Matsui to jump wholeheartedly onto the redress bandwagon. When community leaders first approached them about redress in the late 1970s, neither seemed enthusiastic about spearheading the fight. Coming from predominantly non-Asian congressional districts, both had avoided being branded "Japanese American congressmen" and were to varying degrees hesitant to throw themselves behind an issue that had little chance for success. From one perspective, they almost seemed relieved when the commission was suggested, as a way of pushing the issue of redress payments aside for a while. At the commission's first hearing in Washington, D.C., in July 1981, neither bothered to appear in person; rather, they sent a joint statement that made no mention of redress, but simply apologized for not being present and stated the importance of the commission's review of historical events.[8] Once the commission released its report and recommendations and the grass-roots campaign began to gain momentum, Mineta and Matsui gave their strong support to the legislation.

When JACL asked the four Japanese American members of Congress in 1979 for advice, Mineta was in his third term representing the Thirteenth Congressional District of California. At that meeting, Mineta agreed with Senator Inouye that lobbying for a study commission was the best route to take. He stated that public education was crucial if redress in the form of monetary compensation and a national apology were to win approval. As the legislation establishing the commission was taking form, his legislative office and staff were helpful. Once the commission had issued its report and recommendations and the first redress legislation was introduced in the 98th Congress, Mineta's commitment to redress was solid. Although the commission was originally Inouye's idea, its condemnation of the government's wartime actions and explicit recommendations for redress made it possible for Mineta to devote himself to the issue. The Thirteenth District encompasses part of San Jose in the booming Silicon Valley area of northern California and, except for returning Mineta to office by considerable margins, the district tends to be relatively conservative. Although the district has an above-average percentage of Asian Americans, Japanese Americans in particular, Asian Americans still make up only 6 percent of the electorate. Thus, for Mineta to stick his neck out and use up his chits with other representatives for this piece of legislation took a certain amount of courage as well as commitment to the redress issue. He had to risk appearing, to both his constituents and his colleagues, as if he supported special-interest legislation from which he, as a former internee, would personally benefit. Consequently, the strong backing of the CWRIC, created by Congress and the president and consisting of highly respected members, was crucial. With the commission report in hand, he could make the case that redress was not a Japanese American issue, but an American issue, and that a vote in favor was a vote for upholding fundamental American ideals, not a vote to give Norm Mineta $20,000.

From the start, Mineta's office was the operational headquarters on the Hill for redress. Mineta's staff—especially Glenn Roberts, his legislative director from 1983 to 1987, and Carol Stroebel, who took Roberts's place when he departed—played a key role in formulating the legislation, working with Barney Frank's subcommittee staff and the conference committee staff, keeping in touch with the other key senatorial and congressional offices and the House leadership, and coordinating letter-writing and lobbying efforts with Japanese American interest groups. Even more important, however, were Mineta's personal lobbying efforts. With Congressman Matsui, Mineta went after every colleague who might possibly be persuaded to support redress. He used his personal contacts and called in favors that others owed him. For example, when the commission bill was still being formulated, Mineta first convinced Jim Wright, who at the time served on the Public Works and Transportation Committee with him, to join the redress bandwagon; he also persuaded Wright, then Majority Leader, to be the principal sponsor of the commission bill in 1979 and then of H.R. 4110 and H.R. 442 when they were first introduced. As the previous chapter explained, Wright's leadership was crucial later in the redress fight.

Mineta was present and testified at every hearing held on the redress bills in the House. It is not uncommon for members of Congress to testify at committee hearings, but Mineta's lobbying efforts and testimony were especially poignant, not only because he was a respected member with some seniority, but also because he was himself, at age ten, evacuated with his family and interned for the duration of the war. These two aspects of Mineta's personal history brought the issue home to the other members of the House. In his twelve years in Congress, Mineta had made many friends and had become a respected colleague. During the 100th Congress, he was a Deputy Majority Whip, as well as the third-ranking member on the Committee on Public Works and Transportation. As the chair of the Sub-committee on Aviation, he has been one of the chief policy-makers on aviation issues. If a Nisei woman recounting how her family was forced to sell its house for one-tenth its value and leave all other possessions behind could convince a representative with no political reason to support the legislation to do so, the testimony of Norm Mineta could be that much more persuasive. Whereas a representative could be touched by the woman's testimony and still oppose the legislation on political grounds, it became much more difficult for the same representative to say no to Mineta. It was not just anyone saying, "I must confess that this is a moment of great emotion for me. Today we will resolve, if we can finally lift the unjust burden of shame which 120,000 Americans have carried for 45 painful years. It is a day that I will remember for the rest of my life."[9] The speech Mineta gave on the floor of Congress in front of the full chamber, as well as his testimony in the various committee hearings and the private talks he had with other members, laid bare the pain that even a highly successful man felt over this issue and made it clear that redress was a matter of principle, not personal gain.

Like Mineta, Congressman Matsui was present and testified at all the committee hearings, and he called in numerous favors from colleagues to help get the votes needed for passage. Born in 1941 to second-generation American parents, Matsui was interned as an infant with his family during the war. Even more than Mineta, however, Matsui hesitated before agreeing to lead the fight on the Hill. When JACL first approached the four Nikkei members of Congress, the idea of spearheading an uphill battle over a potentially controversial bill must have been daunting to Matsui. At that first meeting, while Mineta, Inouye, and Matsunaga gave their views on strategy, Matsui said little—and with good reason. In 1979, Matsui was a freshman congressman from the Third Congressional District of California, representing most of the city of Sacramento and some of its surrounding suburbs. Even though the district was about 6 percent Asian American and included a relatively active Japanese American community, whites still made up the vast majority of its population, and the electoral risks of sponsoring legislation related to redress, even the bill creating the commission, seemed great for Matsui in his first year in office. Although the district tended to vote resoundingly and consistently Democratic, owing to the high percentage of civil servants in the state capital and the presence of a staunchly Democratic McClatchy newspaper, in 1978 Matsui had narrowly won a tough primary fight over four other Democratic candidates and then election over a Republican, Sacramento County Supervisor Sandy Smoley, for the seat left vacant by the retirement of 26-year incumbent John Moss. The district was becoming more conservative; the city that had voted against Ronald Reagan for governor would give him a majority for president in 1980 and 1984. The increasing strength of the private sector, growing affluence, and immigration from other areas led to increased Republican strength in the district. Thus, a commitment to redress might cost Matsui his seat. Whereas Mineta had already established himself both within Congress and among his constituents by the time the redress campaign began on the Hill, Matsui had just arrived in Washington and was trying to learn his way around the Hill, both literally and figuratively. Thus, the last thing he wanted to do at that point was to lead the fight for a controversial bill that could have disastrous political consequences.

Once Matsui had established himself both as an elected representative from Sacramento and as a competent legislator, he dedicated himself to redress. When H.R. 442 first passed in the House in September 1987, Matsui was in his sixth term and had learned the ropes within the Beltway. In the 100th Congress, Matsui was an Assistant Majority Whip At Large. As a member of the powerful Ways and Means Committee, Matsui in 1985 and 1986 was a strong supporter of rate-lowering, preference-cutting tax reform. Besides serving the interests of his constituents in particular and California in general, Matsui proved to be an effective politician and a dynamic public speaker. His sense of humor and congenial personality had brought him many friends within the chamber.

As in Mineta's case, Matsui's position as a respected member of Congress together with his personal history of internment became his greatest assets once he began to lobby his peers. When Matsui, on the floor of the House chamber, explained "what it was like to be an American citizen in

1942 if you happened to be of Japanese ancestry,"[10] he was talking from experience. And when he said that

> we have a responsibility to die for our country, but I tell you one thing that in a democracy, this democracy, with our Constitution, a citizen does not have a responsibility to do: every one of us does not have a responsibility to be incarcerated by our own government without charges, without trial, merely because of our race. That is what our constitutional fathers meant 200 years ago when they wrote the Bill of Rights. That is not a responsibility and an inconvenience of a democracy,[11]

other House members knew that to vote against H.R. 442 meant to vote against a respected friend and colleague.

The combined efforts of Mineta and Matsui were indispensable, especially in getting the bill out of committee. Even though Barney Frank as subcommittee chair was doing everything in his power to get the bill to the floor, there were many conservative members of the subcommittee and its parent Judiciary Committee who were not comfortable with supporting the bill. They questioned the premise that the internment was the result of racism, war hysteria, and failed public leadership, and had a strong disinclination to "rewrite history" 40 years after the fact. Intimidated by the presence of Mineta and Matsui at the bill's final mark-up, however, representatives like E. Clay Shaw (R–Fla.), the ranking minority member, eventually voted for the bill in committee. Roger Fleming, the minority counsel for the Subcommittee on Administrative Law and Governmental Relations, credited the tenacity of Mineta and Matsui with persuading the Republican subcommittee members to vote for the legislation.[12] Committee members that he had reason to believe were personally opposed to the legislation surprisingly voted for it, apparently because of Mineta and Matsui.

The Power of Peer Pressure

Generally speaking, senators and representatives prefer not to vote against legislation to which a colleague is personally committed, for a number of reasons. Each chamber of Congress, especially the Senate, is like a family; everyone knows everyone else and feels a common bond with fellow members of one of the most powerful legislative bodies in the world. Voting against a colleague is almost like voting against a sibling. Moreover, Congress is a place where no one can get a piece of legislation passed without the help of others; favors and bargaining are integral to the legislative process. Favors are reciprocal, and just as Congressman A may ask for Congresswoman B's vote on one piece of legislation, Congresswoman B may need Congressman A's support on another. Similarly, it seems advisable to avoid making enemies, because any member can cause a colleague grief or embarrassment. Peer pressure is especially important in cases where the legislation at issue is essentially a free vote for the member, as the redress legislation was for most members. Among the choices available were to vote according to one's own preference, to follow the party leadership, or to follow the lead of another member for political or personal reasons.

The peer pressure aspect was intensified for the redress legislation, however. Inouye, Matsunaga, Mineta, and Matsui were not just speaking for their constituents, as they might be in asking for new Air Force bases or housing projects for their districts; when they lobbied other members, they were speaking for themselves and the injustices they had personally endured. To vote against colleagues who had been sent as children to concentration camps or who had fought in the U.S. armed forces even as their fellow Japanese Americans were behind barbed wire might have seemed gratuitously disrespectful.

In a sense, then, the passage of the redress legislation is a tribute to these men—a tribute not only to their dedication to this issue, but to their sacrifices during the war and to their previous work as respected legislators. They brought the redress movement crucial inside connections, which they were willing to use to redress's benefit. This is not to say that redress would not have passed had these men not been in office, had they not had been the respected and powerful members that they were, or had they not been so committed to the cause. The road to passage would have been much more turbulent without their efforts, however, and it is unlikely that the legislation would have passed at the time or in the form that it did.

CHAPTER EIGHT

Strange Bedfellows:
Redress for Aleutian Islanders

Although the Civil Liberties Act of 1988 is usually thought of as the Japanese American redress bill, in fact it also deals with another, completely unrelated issue that arose out of World War II: the issue of compensation to Aleutian Islanders who had been mistreated by the U.S. government during the war. Originally, the House wanted the two cases to be addressed by two separate bills. In the Senate, however—with Republican Senator Ted Stevens of Alaska in the pivotal position of ranking minority member of the Governmental Affairs subcommittee responsible for the Japanese American legislation—the two issues were kept together so that the smaller issue of Aleutian Islander redress could ride on the coattails of the more widely publicized and larger issue of Japanese American redress.

At first glance, the addition of a second set of claimants might appear to have been a hindrance to the Japanese American redress issue. Aleutian Islanders make up an even less significant proportion of the American population than Japanese Americans, and their influence is restricted to Alaska, one of the most sparsely populated states in the nation. Thus, electorally it seems that the inclusion of the Aleutian Islanders would have been extra baggage for the already burdened campaign for Japanese American redress. Yet its inclusion actually contributed to the bill's success, especially given Senator Stevens's strategic seat on the Governmental Affairs Subcommittee on Federal Services, Post Office, and Civil Service. However small its positive impact institutionally, it did not make the struggle for the bill's passage any more arduous. In essence, the combination of the two issues of redress in the Civil Liberties Act of 1988 proved to be a successful marriage of political convenience.

Evacuation and Internment of Aleutian Islanders

The Aleutian Islands comprise a chain of small islands nearly 900 miles long, from the Alaska Peninsula to the island of Attu, which is 300 miles from the Kamchatka Peninsula of the former Soviet Union. The islands are treeless, coated with fog, and blanketed with tundra. During the war between Japan and the United States, the islands were strategically critical to both nations. Three months after Japan bombed Pearl Harbor and the United States declared war on Japan, U.S. military intelligence began to warn defense commanders in Alaska that Japan was likely to invade the Aleutian chain at any moment. In June 1942, this prediction came true, as Japan bombed Unalaska, invaded two other islands, and captured Aleut villagers on Attu.[1] As a result, American military officials in Alaska ordered the immediate evacuation of Aleuts on the remaining islands to areas of southeast Alaska. The islands of Attu and Kiska remained in Japanese hands until the summer of 1943. The evacuated Aleuts were shipped to primitive camps and housed in atrocious conditions until the United States regained control of the islands and allowed them to return to their homes in 1944 and 1945.

Although the military had anticipated a possible Japanese attack for some time before June 1942, the preparations for evacuation were minimal. Since Alaska was at the time a territory of the United States rather than a state, the measures to be taken for the Aleuts' security were at the discretion of civilians who reported to the Secretary of the Interior—the Office of Indian Affairs, the Fish and Game Wildlife Service, and the territorial governor. Unable to agree on whether to evacuate and relocate the Aleuts to avoid the risks of war or to leave them on the islands on the grounds that staying would disrupt Aleut life less than relocation, they had no concrete plan ready when the Japanese attacked. Hence, once Japan invaded the islands, military officials hurriedly formulated plans and began the evacuation. On June 3, 1942, Japan bombed the strategic American base at Dutch Harbor in the Aleutians. In response, a U.S. ship evacuated most of the island of Atka, burning the entire Aleut village to prevent its use by Japanese troops. Navy planes picked up the rest of the islanders a few days later.

In early June, the Pribilof Islands were also evacuated as a precautionary measure. In a sweep eastward from Atka to Akutan, by mid-July residents were removed from the Aleut villages of Mikolski on Umnak Island, Makushin, Biorka, Chernofski, Kashega, and Unalaska on Unalaska Island, and Akutan on Akutan Island. At that point, the Navy decided that no further evacuations were necessary. Over 870 Aleuts had been removed from villages west of Unimak Island, and except for Unalaska, the entire population of each village, including at least 30 non-Aleuts, was evacuated. Nearly all the Aleuts were moved to southeastern Alaska; 50 others were either evacuated to the Seattle area or hospitalized in an Indian hospital in Tacoma, Washington.[2]

The evacuation of the Aleuts from their home villages was a reasonable move to ensure their safety in wartime. In contrast to the Japanese American case, racism did not determine who was to be evacuated from the islands; total evacuation meant that white teachers and government employees on the islands were removed along with the Aleuts, the only exceptions being people directly employed in war-related work. The Aleuts' treatment after evacuation, however, was another matter. The conditions in which the Aleuts were forced to live were utterly deplorable— lacking in safe food and water facilities, proper bedding or heat, and essential medical services. The conditions were more despicable than those in the internment camps to which the Japanese Americans were sent. Typically, housing for the Aleuts consisted of abandoned gold miners' shacks or fish cannery buildings. The miserable housing together with almost nonexistent medical care created a situation in which disease and death were rampant.[3]

The conditions at the Funter Bay cannery in southeastern Alaska, where 300 Aleuts from St. Paul and 180 from St. George in the Pribilofs were relocated, were typical of the Aleut relocation camps. The cannery buildings in which 300 of the Aleuts were housed had been unoccupied for over a decade and as a result were hardly adequate living spaces, especially during an Alaskan winter. Family ties were strained as most Aleuts were forced to live in two dormitory-style buildings where groups of between six and thirteen people slept in areas nine or ten feet square. Lumber to build walls was in short supply, so some families strung up blankets or sheets as partitions to create a semblance of privacy. At the beginning, the camp was so overcrowded that people had to sleep in shifts. Lack of facilities and crowded conditions were only part of the problem for the Aleuts staying at Funter Bay, however; the buildings were also very run-down and impossible to keep clean. The camp lacked even the materials—such as mops, brooms, and soap—to attempt cleanliness. A single toilet on the beach just above the low-water mark served 90 percent of the evacuees. In another part of the Funter Bay camp, almost 200 evacuees were housed at the Funter Bay Mine, which had also been out of operation for years. The conditions here were similar to those at the cannery: most families lived in unpartitioned buildings, with common mess halls and lavatory facilities nearby. The military officials overseeing the camps realized how inadequate living conditions were, but cookstoves, plumbing fixtures, water tanks, and other equipment were difficult to obtain.[4]

At Funter Bay in the fall of 1942, only one white nurse and one Aleut nurse attended to the medical needs of all Aleuts at the camp. Doctors were occasionally assigned to the camp, but only for a few days at a time. Medical supplies were virtually nonexistent. Under the crowded, unsanitary conditions, disease ran rampant in the camps, from influenza and measles to pneumonia and tuberculosis. At least 40 people died at Funter Bay alone during the internment. In addition, the education of Aleut children almost ceased, as a shortage of books, school supplies, and teachers made holding regular classes nearly impossible.

The indifference displayed in the evacuation and relocation of the Aleuts was again evident in the efforts to return the Aleuts to their native islands. Those from the Pribilof Islands were allowed to return home by the summer of 1944, nine months after the U.S. armed forces had driven the Japanese out of the area. Evacuees from the Aleutian Islands had to wait another year before being allowed to return home. Although the reasons remain unclear, some Aleuts were never able to return to their home villages; the Attuans were offered transportation to Atka Island, and even today have not returned to their ancestral homeland. Like the interned Japanese Americans, the Aleuts returned to homes and communities that had been ransacked, vandalized, and, in essence, destroyed. The government gave them scant support, monetary or otherwise, to help them rebuild their homes, communities, and lives. At most, while Aleut villages attempted to salvage weather-beaten and war-torn buildings, the government provided free groceries. Although the material losses were considerable, they hardly compare to the cultural and symbolic losses that the Aleuts suffered. As devout adherents of the Russian Orthodox faith, Aleuts treasured the religious icons from czarist Russia and other family heirlooms that were lost forever during the evacuation. For both their material and personal losses, they received little compensation.

The Legislative History of Redress for Aleuts

Clearly, despite superficial similarities, the wartime experiences of the Aleutian Islanders and the Japanese Americans were very different, and the issues of redress require separate evaluations. As the Commission on Wartime Relocation and Internment of Civilians concluded, both groups suffered violations of their basic constitutional rights at the hands of a body that was supposedly protecting those rights, the federal government. In the case of Japanese Americans, however, the question revolved around whether military necessity was a reasonable rationale for evacuating and interning a group of Americans, en masse, solely on the basis of ancestry. For the Aleutian and Pribilof Islanders, the need for evacuation was not at issue; clearly, their homelands had become military battlegrounds. Given the circumstances, evacuation was a "reasonable precaution taken to ensure [Aleuts'] safety."[5] But the way the military evacuated the Aleuts, the conditions in which they were forced to live, and their treatment after the war were almost criminal. In this case, then, the question was whether the government had taken the proper steps to ensure their safe evacuation and survival in the relocation camps.

For the purposes of this study, the important point is that despite the differences between the two issues, they are both integral parts of the Civil Liberties Act of 1988, as passed by Congress and signed by the president in August of that year. Although the portions of the act pertaining to redress for Japanese Americans were predominant and more highly publicized, the inclusion of redress for the Aleuts played a role throughout the legislative history of H.R. 442. Not only was Aleut redress part of the final bill, it was included in the CWRIC study and was argued over in congressional committee hearings as well.

The idea of including redress for other groups who had suffered during World War II in legislation addressing Japanese American redress first came up as part of the Seattle Plan in the 1970s. Seattle JACL members who were among the first to call publicly for redress, headed by Henry Miyatake and Shosuke Sasaki, thought that including others would give any legislation a better chance for passage since it would widen the base of support and keep redress from becoming a "special-interest Japanese American" issue.[6] With the vocal support of Alaska senator Ted Stevens, the Aleutian Islanders' wartime experience became a substantive part of the commission legislation. Besides researching the circumstances surrounding the relocation and incarceration of Japanese Americans, the commission was responsible for reviewing "directives of United States military forces requiring the relocation and, in some cases, detention in internment camps of American citizens, including Aleut civilians, and permanent resident aliens of the Aleutian and Pribilof Islands."[7] Consequently, one of the commissioners nominated by the Senate was Father Ishmael Vincent Gromoff, a Russian Orthodox priest and a former Aleut evacuee. In addition to visiting cities with large Japanese American communities, the commission held hearings in Anchorage and Unalaska, listening to the testimony of former Aleut evacuees and military officials involved with their evacuation. In *Personal Justice Denied,* the detailed report of its findings, the commission devoted almost 50 pages to the wartime situation in the Aleutian and Pribilof islands. As we have seen, in its recommendations, the commission proposed five remedies for the injustices Aleuts suffered during the war.

The five recommendations, with slight modifications—the most important being an increase from $5,000 to $12,000 for individual payments—were ultimately passed as part of the Civil Liberties Act of 1988. In the Senate, the two issues were always kept together; Senator Stevens insisted on it. In the House, however, they were viewed as distinct from one another; although H.R. 442 originally consisted of all the recommendations of the commission, another bill, H.R. 1631, or the Aleutian and Pribilof Island Restitution Act, was introduced. In the 100th Congress, the Judiciary Committee's Subcommittee on Administrative Law and Governmental Relations held hearings on H.R. 442 and H.R. 1631 together. The legislation that the full House initially passed in September 1987, however, contained only the measures for Japanese American redress; the parts related to the Aleuts had been removed from the bill. After the Senate had passed H.R. 442 amended to adopt the language of S. 1009, which included the Aleut legislation, in April 1988, Senate members of the conference committee insisted on retaining the Aleut portion, and the House conceded. Thus, the passage of the Civil Liberties Act of 1988 marked an important juncture in Aleut, as well as Japanese American, history.

The Impact of Aleutian Islander Redress on H.R. 442

According to electoral interest theory, the inclusion of Aleut redress should have had little impact on the passage of H.R. 442. Aleuts make up a minuscule proportion of Alaska's population, to say nothing of the American population overall, and thus electorally have little power. Only a few hundred Aleuts could benefit from the legislation, and as an organized interest group they had little leverage. Moreover, very few people, even members of Congress, knew much about the situation in the Aleutian Islands during World War II, and for that reason public sentiment had little impact, one way or the other, on the Aleut portion of the bill.

Inclusion of redress for the Aleuts did play a supporting role in making the road to the president's desk a little less bumpy, however. By adding provisions that benefited Alaskans, the legislation gained the support of the three members of Congress from Alaska and that of other members of Congress whom they could influence. Although the Alaskan congressional delegation is small, the wholehearted support of its members was important for two reasons. First, all three—Senators Stevens and Frank Murkowski and Congressman Don Young—were Republicans, who without the inclusion of Aleut redress might not have voted for the legislation. Alaska has an insignificant Asian American population, and without the Aleut portion, the three as conservatives would have been more likely to oppose the bill on fiscal or other grounds. As Republicans, the three used their influence to round up additional votes among their colleagues, some of whom might otherwise have opposed the bill. Second, the support of Alaskan members was significant because Senator Stevens was the ranking minority member of the Governmental Affairs subcommittee to which the bill was assigned, which gave the legislation a strong proponent in a key institutional position. Even though the redress legislation never made it out of committee in the 98th or 99th Congresses, when the Republicans held control of the Senate, Senator Stevens as subcommittee chair kept the bill alive when support for it was minimal. In the 100th Congress, when the bill finally succeeded, Stevens was pivotal in scheduling hearings and getting the legislation to the floor expeditiously. He also helped see that the bill made it to the full Senate for a vote in its original state, without any major amendments.

The inclusion of the provisions for Aleut redress was also critical in an institutional sense. The Aleuts' wartime treatment fell under the jurisdiction of the Department of Defense and the Department of the Interior, whereas redressing Japanese Americans for loss of constitutional rights was under the jurisdiction of the Department of Justice. The addition of the Aleut section to the Japanese American redress legislation made S. 1009 eligible for referral to the Governmental Affairs Committee, rather than the Judiciary Committee. Although at first glance this may seem to be an insignificant matter, in fact the committee to which a particular piece of legislation is assigned can make all the difference for its success. At the time of the 100th Congress, the Governmental Affairs Committee provided a much more favorable environment for the redress legislation than the Judiciary Committee would have. First, Senator Stevens was the second-ranking minority member of the Governmental Affairs Committee and the ranking minority member of the relevant subcommittee, whereas no senator from a state with special interest in the legislation—California, Oregon, Washington, Hawaii, or Alaska—was on the Judiciary Committee at the time. Moreover, the Republican members of the Judiciary Committee were extremely conservative: the ranking minority member was Strom Thurmond (R–S.C.), and other minority members included Orrin Hatch (R–Utah), Charles Grassley (R–Iowa), and Gordon Humphrey (R–N.H.)—whereas on the Governmental Affairs Committee, the Republican members, though still conservative, were less ideologically right-wing and had a better record on civil-rights issues. Furthermore, support for the legislation on that committee did not come from a notably liberal senator. Stevens was a conservative, and the moderate subcommittee chair, Senator David Pryor (D–Ark.), eventually supported the legislation but did not personally consider it a priority issue. Had the legislation gone to the Judiciary Committee, it is likely that Senator Ted Kennedy (D–Mass.) would have been a leading spokesperson for passage, which might have triggered conservative opposition. Because Pryor and Stevens were not known as civil-rights crusaders, their support gave the bill the appearance of broader support; it was not seen as just a "liberal," special-interest issue, as it might have been had a liberal stalwart such as Kennedy led the fight.

Although it was only a small, overshadowed portion of the legislation, the inclusion of redress for Aleuts worked in favor of passage of the Civil Liberties Act of 1988. One should not, however, overstate its role. Aleut redress was not a major issue in the debates surrounding the legislation, and, unlike redress for Japanese Americans, which hit the television networks and the major news wire services with considerable power, the Aleuts attracted little media attention. Moreover, the bill affected only 400 or so surviving Aleut evacuees, as compared to 80,000 surviving Japanese American internees, and the amount of government funds involved was significantly smaller. It is doubtful that by itself the Aleutian Islander issue had the support or organization either in Congress or in the electorate at large to succeed; thus, it had a much greater chance for passage as an attachment to the Japanese American redress legislation. Would Japanese American redress have passed without the provisions for the Aleuts? Probably, but not necessarily at the time it did or with the ease it did. Thus, redress for the Aleutian Islanders did not hurt the larger cause of Japanese American redress at all; it contributed to an already complex and intricate combination of factors that made the 100th Congress the setting for a favorable response to H.R. 442.

CHAPTER NINE

A Community Comes to Terms with Its Past

Institutional factors alone can hardly explain why representatives and senators are inclined to vote for a piece of legislation; they merely determine whether a bill has any *procedural* chance to succeed, not whether it will actually do so. They only play a role in creating an institutional setting that is or is not conducive to a particular bill. An institutional factor's greatest power is negative; it has the ability to prevent a bill from becoming law, but it can never ensure one's successful passage. It is only once a bill surmounts institutional barriers that electoral interest politics come into play. Thus, in the case of the Civil Liberties Act of 1988, the favorable environment within Congress only partially explains the bill's success. True, the four Japanese American members of Congress were indispensable in garnering votes for H.R. 442. But they did not commit themselves to redress without taking a risk, and institutional structure does not explain what motivated them to do so. Moreover, although their efforts were great, it takes more than a few men lobbying their colleagues to pass extraordinary legislation. Although the fight for redress was in large part an insiders' game, it is simplistic to view it solely as an "inside-the-Beltway" battle. What is so far missing from this explanation of the legislation's success and what helps explain their dedication to the cause is the subject to which this study now turns: the Japanese American community.[1]

Five decades have passed since that fateful day of February 19, 1942, when President Franklin Delano Roosevelt signed Executive Order 9066. Since then, the United States and the world have witnessed remarkable social, political, and economic changes. For the Japanese American community, both internal and external changes affected the redress campaign. Redress could not have happened without the support and commitment of a large part of the Japanese American community; the leadership and the organizational skills of a core group of men and women were invaluable in seeing redress to its historic end. Their leadership, with the backing of the community, motivated Senators Inouye and Matsunaga and Congressmen Mineta and Matsui to take an active role in the campaign. But the development of a supportive Japanese American community did not come quickly or easily. It was only during the 100th Congress, over 40 years after the last internee had been released from camp, that grass-roots mobilization reached its peak, when the community was economically, socially, and politically in a position to take a strong stand on the issue. The internment experience had left deep scars, and the healing process was slow. It took Japanese Americans many years to begin to come to terms with their wartime experience, and even then they did so only with great reluctance and pain. Moreover, it took a great deal of time for an organized and politically astute lobbying mechanism to develop within the community. Cultural barriers as well as personal conflicts had to be overcome for an effective grass-roots campaign to unfold. Although these tasks seemed difficult, and indeed they were, they had to take place for redress to have a chance in the halls of Congress.

Forty Years Later: A Community Coalesces

Why did it take 40 years for the Japanese American community to organize and fight for recompense for the loss of constitutional rights? Why didn't Japanese Americans take action sooner? Wouldn't the period just after the war have been a more appropriate time to press their case? The answers to these questions are complicated, and one must take into account the social, political, and economic conditions both after the war and in the late 1980s. It is not hard to understand why the redress movement got off the ground in the 1980s. The immediate postwar period did not provide former internees with circumstances favorable to a full-scale campaign for redress, and it was not until the 1980s that redress was a politically viable issue or that Japanese Americans as a whole were in a position to fight for redress.

After the war, anti-Japanese sentiment was still strong on the West Coast. Although Japan had surrendered unconditionally to the Allies, the attitudes that had led to the Japanese Americans' evacuation and incarceration persisted. In many cases, friends and neighbors welcomed internees home, but in others Japanese Americans faced acts of violence and pressure groups that wanted them out permanently. Many restaurants, gas stations, grocery stores, and other businesses refused to serve Japanese Americans. And outside the West Coast, there still existed a great deal of ignorance about the internment episode. After the war, the government was not eager for knowledge of the internment to spread, and most Americans were too preoccupied with rebuilding their own lives to care. In this environment of continuing hostility on the one hand and ignorance on the other, any effort to seek redress was unlikely to have a favorable reception. The same legislators who had successfully lobbied for the evacuation would have prevented any redress measures from even being proposed. Even if redress had had some supporters on principle in Congress, it is doubtful that many of them would have been willing to stick their necks out for legislation that held many more risks than benefits.

By the 1980s, however, the political climate had changed dramatically. The stereotype of the "sneaky Asian" had dissipated, and, more important, the nation had come to a new sensitivity over civil-rights issues during the 1950s and 1960s. Minority groups had begun to fight for their rightful place in society and had learned to use the political process to achieve that goal. The concept of equality of opportunity had taken on an entirely new meaning with such Supreme Court decisions as *Brown v. Topeka Board of Education*, the landmark case overturning the "separate but equal" doctrine and calling for integrated public schools, as well as such legislation as the Civil Rights Act of 1964 and the Voting Rights Act of 1965. Equal opportunity no longer meant equal opportunity only for white Americans, but equal opportunity for all, regardless of race, creed, or ethnicity. That is not to say that racism, specifically anti-Asian racism, ceased to exist after the 1960s; indeed it persists even today, as Japan-bashing, with its roots in U.S.-Japan trade tensions, reaches new heights. But de jure discrimination—that is, blatant discrimination sanctioned by law—was no longer acceptable. And what could be a better example of singling out one group solely on the basis of ethnic background than the internment of Japanese Americans during World War II? It was in this environment of increasing social consciousness and tolerance that redress finally had a chance to succeed.

Second, right after the war Japanese Americans were in no position to take on such a large and consequential project as redress. After 1945, as former internees returned to the communities from which they had been evacuated, they were faced with the predicament of having to rebuild their lives, literally and figuratively. According to the report of the Commission on Wartime Relocation and Internment of Civilians, at the time of evacuation,

> owners and operators of farms and businesses either sold their income-producing assets under distress-sale circumstances on very short notice or attempted, with or without government help, to place their property in the custody of people remaining on the West Coast. . . . Homes had to be sold or left without the personal attention that owners would devote to them. Businesses lost their good will, their reputation, and their customers. Professionals had their careers disrupted.[2]

After the war, many returned to find the homes they had left behind ransacked; others lost any land they had held to squatters. Internees had made little income in the camps; thus, they returned home with little or no savings and no job, and in many cases were faced with the task of finding a new place to live. For the first-generation Issei, their entire lives' earnings and hard work were lost, and they were too old to start rebuilding their fortunes. According to the 1970 U.S. census, about 20 percent of the surviving Issei were below the poverty level. Many of their children, the second-generation Nisei, could not afford to complete their college educations because they had to support their families.

In these circumstances, Japanese Americans had scant hope of obtaining redress. Lobbying representatives and senators for redress was not a high priority; survival was. But by the 1970s, Japanese Americans overall were doing well. In 1979 the median income for a Japanese American family was nearly $7,500 above the national average; the poverty rate for Japanese American families was less than half the national rate; and Japanese Americans on average had completed more schooling than Americans had overall.[3] Financially secure, the community now had (1) the monetary resources necessary for a lobbying campaign, and (2) the time, mental energy, and assurance to devote to redress.

Although by the 1970s Japanese Americans were economically in a position to fight for redress, the community still lacked the emotional commitment to launch such a campaign—possibly the most essential ingredient. The internment experience left a deep emotional scar on the Japanese American community. Even though their only crime was being born to parents of Japanese ancestry, former internees felt ashamed of what had happened; their self-esteem was shattered. Like victims of rape, internees needed many years to confront their feelings of anger, pain, betrayal, confusion, and sadness. It would be difficult for anyone to come to terms with being taken from one's home and sent off to concentration camps by one's own government, but cultural factors made it all the more difficult for Japanese Americans. Traditional Japanese culture encourages self-restraint and deference to authority and discourages displays of emotion and attention-getting behavior. In addition, there is the matter of pride; to "lose face," as evacuees did during the war, was a great disgrace for individuals, families, and the community as a whole. As one internee explained:

> We felt we were raped by our own country—raped of our freedom, raped of our human dignity, and raped of our civil liberties.
>
> A rape victim feels guilt and shame. A victim of rape feels violated, unclean. And so it is with us.
>
> We felt that somehow we were party to this act of defilement, that we had somehow helped to bring it on. We, innocent victims, felt guilt and shame about it all. And if you know anything about Japanese culture, you know that guilt and shame are strong influences upon us.
>
> . . . We had internalized a lot of our feelings for a long time. We had repressed these feelings and we began to feel that we were in touch with some of our feelings. And, so we were able to get out some of these feelings—feelings of frustration, of anger, and even of rage.
>
> We have come to the realization that the camp experience had a very negative psychological effect on us. It has profoundly affected our sense of ethnic identity, and thereby our sense of self-worth. One internee said, "I felt terribly ashamed and guilty about being Japanese." Think of the self-hatred this kind of mentality fosters in people. Our self-esteem, our self-regard were shattered.[4]

As a result, it took decades for many internees even to begin to talk about their experience and to show any degree of emotion about it. Many Sansei and Yonsei (third- and fourth-generation Japanese Americans) have grown up without knowing what happened to the Issei and Nisei during the war, because their parents, grandparents, and great-grandparents never talked about it and because their textbooks and libraries were virtually silent on the subject. In many families, internment was not an acceptable topic for dinner conversation; it was a black mark on their history, something on which they looked back with shame and disgust, a topic best left alone.

One of the first occasions on which the community began to come together and explore the many different feelings about the internment was one of the first "Day of Remembrance" programs in November 1978. Covered by local media and ABC's "20 / 20," the event included a six-mile caravan of 200 cars and 2,000 people to the former Puyallup, Washington, assembly center, called Camp Harmony. The purpose was to give the community a chance to reflect on the evacuation and internment and to demonstrate for redress. According to Cherry Kinoshita, a former internee from Seattle, the Day of Remembrance "was the most moving thing I had seen in a long time. . . . It was the first time that people really thought about that experience. The emotion had been buried for a long time."[5] In a sense, that event represented the broad realization that a great injustice had been done by the U.S. government to its own citizens; until that time internees had always tried to suppress their feelings, and to some extent blamed themselves for what had happened. The positive reaction that the Puyallup event received from the community and the emotional outpouring that it prompted triggered many similar Day of Remembrance events up and down the West Coast, and today many local Japanese American communities, from Los Angeles to San Jose to Portland, hold annual Day of Remembrance programs. The event thus became a catalyst for the community, bringing it together and allowing it to come to terms with its emotions.

Most important, as we have seen, were the hearings of the CWRIC in the early 1980s. The forum that the hearings created, the opportunity they offered finally to confront the issue, had an impact that was not limited to the hearings themselves; they stimulated discussion throughout the community. The commission and its hearings forced the community to confront the redress issue; it had been relatively easy for former internees to put the experience behind them, but the hearings brought the evacuation, the internment, the issue of redress, and long-suppressed feelings about them to the forefront of Japanese American consciousness. The hearings provided a much-needed emotional catharsis; intense feelings of betrayal, shame, and disgust suddenly poured forth.

Time itself was a crucial factor, for it really took the coming of age of the Nisei and Sansei to get the redress movement going. The younger Nisei, especially Nisei women, were the backbone of the redress campaign, and without them redress would probably never have been passed. The Issei and the older Nisei had lost the most during the war, both economically and emotionally. Having established themselves as businessmen, farmers, and the like, they lost everything. They could no longer support their families—a disgrace by the terms of Japanese culture. Many of the older Nisei were in college when the war broke out and had to leave their studies to enter the camps. Many never returned to college, since they were needed to help support their families just after the war; it can hardly be doubted that many of them keenly resented the loss of opportunity. Because they were children during the internment and personally had less to lose materially and psychologically,[6] the younger Nisei had a much easier time, once they matured, coming to terms with the experience as one involving principles of justice, not personal disgrace. It was their energy, determination, and feistiness, as we shall soon see, that launched a massive grass-roots lobbying organization and gave redress a chance. In addition, though the Sansei played a smaller role in the redress battle, they prodded and questioned their parents and grandparents about the internment. Having grown up in an environment in which such a significant episode in their history was taboo, Sansei became involved in the movement as a way of filling in a hole in their past. Finding that the most important episode in their family's history was unaccounted for, they began to question their elders and piece together what had happened. These children of the 1960s and 1970s, having grown up in an environment stressing equal opportunity for all, quickly saw the experience as an injustice that had to be addressed.

Finally, it took years for the Japanese American community to be convinced that the redress movement had a realistic chance of succeeding. Besides the wartime internment, America's past is marked by a long-standing tradition of anti-Asian, in particular anti-Japanese, sentiments, from alien land laws to laws forbidding intermarriage with whites. Trust in government does not come easily. For Japanese Americans willingly to invest their time, energy, and money in fighting for redress, they had to feel relatively secure that the government would not again strip them of their fundamental rights. One way in which they regained confidence in the system was by establishing themselves as productive members of society. That meant finding stable, respectable jobs, educating their children, sending them to college, and in general being good citizens. Gaining economic, political, and social strength did not guarantee that redress would succeed, but it did assure the community of a fair hearing, which was all it asked. Moreover, President Gerald Ford made an effort to set the record straight, when on February 19, 1976, he formally rescinded Executive Order 9066 by signing Presidential Proclamation no. 4417. Although President Harry S Truman had lifted the order in 1946, no formal proclamation of termination had ever been issued. Ford's act was a mere formality, but it was significant in that the president of the United States was admitting that "we now know what we should have known then—not only was that evacuation wrong, but Japanese Americans were and are loyal Americans."[7] Furthermore, he called "upon the American people to affirm with me this American Promise—that we have learned from the tragedy of that long-ago experience forever to treasure liberty and justice for each individual American, and resolve that this kind of action shall never again be repeated."[8] The most concrete reassurance was provided by the establishment of the commission, the appointment of an esteemed panel of members, and the respect that it was given. These developments proved that the government was now willing to hear the Japanese Americans' story and to reconsider the actions it had taken 40 years before.

Once the Japanese American community began to believe in the redress campaign and to marshal the resources and energy that a major legislative battle required, they had enormous personal assets on which to draw: a mental toughness that had survived the devastating blow of the wartime internment. The same "go for broke" attitude that motivated young Japanese American internees in the camps to volunteer for the armed services in order to prove themselves as Americans and to fight with valor for their country was now marshaled in support of redress. The underlying values are difficult to explain in Anglo-American terms. They can best be described as a combination of *oyakoko*, a Japanese term meaning obligation to parents, and *bushido*, an unwritten Samurai code rooted in Confucianism that roughly translates as "the way of the warrior." Once redress became a priority for the community, the combination of familial obligation and fighting spirit was mobilized to see redress to a victorious end. Winning was the only way to redeem shame with honor.

A Lobbying Structure Evolves

As we have seen, certain conditions had to be met before major portions of the Japanese American community were willing and able to commit themselves to the redress effort—namely, financial independence, emotional release, and a sense of all-around security—and it was not until the late 1970s and early 1980s that they were. Along with these developments came the emergence of an organized lobbying structure and an understanding of political realities. No longer politically naive, key community members realized that success on Capitol Hill required much more than a just cause and heightened sensitivity to the issue. Community mobilization, commitment, money, and connections on the Hill are critical factors for an interest group hoping to influence congressional policymaking. When redress first entered the congressional arena in 1979, the campaign to varying degrees lacked all these assets. In Chapter Three, I reviewed several factors that made it difficult for Japanese Americans to mobilize as a political force, such as the small size and regional distribution of the population, values that discourage political activism, the lack of mobilization by either political party, and financial and emotional insecurity. Given their lack of faith in the American system and long-standing avoidance of politics, most Japanese Americans were unwilling to commit their time, energy, thought, or money to a risky campaign with a dubious outcome. Most Nisei grew up during the Great Depression of the 1930s as the children of immigrants and thus were habitually frugal. Redress hardly looked like a winning proposition, and many former internees saw little reason to throw money away on its support. With respect to connections on the Hill, the community was in a strong position, in that Senators Inouye and Matsunaga and Congressmen Mineta and Matsui were in office, but as we saw in Chapters Five and Seven, they were still not wholeheartedly behind redress when the commission bill was introduced. Indeed, it took much of the 1980s for all critical factors—mobilization, commitment, money, and connections—to develop, and it was at the time of the 100th Congress that they all peaked. Even at that time, the community was not completely unified; although by the end of the 1980s an overwhelming majority of the community supported the various redress efforts to varying degrees, factions existed and conflicts in strategy, ideology, and personality ensued. Within all the turmoil, however, an organized grass-roots campaign developed on two levels. Fortunately for the redress movement, the lobbying campaign reached its high point at the same time that the institutional setting in Congress became most favorable.

Although the redress movement established itself in the 1980s, its roots go back much farther. The idea has floated through the Japanese American community since the time of the evacuation and internment. According to William Hohri, early stirrings for redress began both with individuals who escaped the evacuation orders and in the camps themselves.[9] As Bill Hosokawa, a noted Japanese American writer, explained, redress was "an issue that had been simmering under the surface of JACL for years. Even while the Evacuation was under way in 1942 there had been talk of seeking compensation for material losses from the federal government after the emergency ended. 'Reparations' had been discussed in the first post-war JACL convention in 1946, and the subject kept cropping up sporadically after that."[10]

Even some people outside the Japanese American community advocated compensation for material and constitutional losses by internees, including Norman Thomas, a five-time Socialist Party candidate for president, in a 1942 pamphlet distributed by the Post War World Council. The pamphlet outlined nine recommendations for rectifying the situation. One advocated that the federal government compensate Japanese Americans for their material and constitutional losses: "The sound American principle that compensation should be paid to an individual when for a public purpose his rights are impaired or his property taken, ought to be applied retroactively to the Japanese. Unquestionably the losses of the evacuees are hard to measure individually in terms of dollars and cents, but when that can be done the government should make individual compensation."[11]

The organization that eventually got the redress movement off the ground was the same one that had advised the community to enter the camps peacefully—the Japanese American Citizens League. Even though JACL has been much criticized for having "sold out the community" during the war, for caving in to the white establishment, and for being relatively conservative in ideology and nature, it was the only community organization that had the reputation of being a long-established, legitimate group representing Japanese Americans. It has been the only truly national organization representing Americans of Japanese ancestry, and whatever its shortcomings, it was the only organization with the membership, resources, and connections on Capitol Hill to give the redress campaign the momentum and credibility it needed.

One might say that the redress movement officially started at the 1970 JACL national convention in Chicago. At the urging of Edison Uno and Ray Okamura, two feisty Nisei, the national convention passed a resolution that called for JACL to take action to rectify the "worst mistake of World War II."[12] Little came of it, however, as the resolution merely accepted redress as an issue of concern for JACL, without specifying any action to be taken. At the 1972 convention another resolution was passed, this time making redress an issue of priority for the organization. In 1974 in Portland, the national convention reiterated its declaration that redress was a priority issue, and in a volatile meeting created a special task force to deal with redress, named the National Redress Committee. The battle over the creation of the National Redress Committee split JACL into two groups: those who were adamant that JACL should make a vigorous effort to fight for redress (this group was headed by the activist Seattle chapter), and those who wanted to tread lightly and not make waves (this group tended to include many of the older Nisei). At the 1976 convention in

Sacramento, JACL again declared redress a priority issue; this time, however, the session was much less stormy, because some of the JACL old-timers had begun to warm to the idea of taking a more active role in fighting for redress.[13] These early years of the redress movement were frustrating for many of its ardent supporters, like Uno, a lecturer at San Francisco State University, who complained about the unwillingness of the organization's leaders to make a concerted fight for redress. Much of the impetus for redress at this point came from individuals at the local level, while portions of the organization's old guard at the national level tended to display considerably more reluctance.

Although JACL was beginning to tackle the issue of redress, discussion of the issue was limited to a relatively small inner circle. Only a small percentage of Japanese Americans was actively involved in JACL, and as we saw earlier in this chapter, redress still was not a common topic for discussion in the community. The views varied among those who were informed (see Chapter Three): some wholeheartedly supported measures to obtain redress, including monetary compensation, for loss of constitutional rights; others supported the idea of a national apology but found "the thought of setting a price on the priceless sacrifice of freedom . . . distasteful . . . [and] disturbing."[14] Others thought redress was a pipe dream and that any campaign would be a waste of time and effort. In general, redress was not widely discussed and, other than among a few people, did not arouse much passion on either side.

The 1978 convention was a turning point of sorts for JACL and redress. Prior to the meeting in Salt Lake City, John Tateishi, redress chair for the Northern California–Western Nevada–Pacific District, suggested to Clifford Uyeda, JACL national chair, that the National Redress Committee meet to draft guidelines to serve as JACL's position on redress, which would be presented at the convention for adoption. In an April 1978 meeting at JACL's San Francisco headquarters, representatives from all eight JACL regional districts met to hammer out the guidelines to be proposed. After tossing around different amounts, the group finally agreed on the relatively arbitrary sum of $25,000 in monetary compensation for each of the 120,000 former internees or their survivors, for a total of $3 billion. The guidelines also called for an equal amount of money to be set aside in a trust fund to be administered for the benefit of Japanese Americans by a commission of Japanese Americans nominated by Japanese Americans. Other demands included reimbursement for losses, reinstatement in jobs, and an acknowledgment of wrongdoing and apology from the U.S. government. The proposal was presented to the 1978 convention and, after considerable debate, was unanimously accepted as a guideline for the National Redress Committee and JACL.[15] In addition, the 1978 convention earmarked $12,000 in JACL money to fund the committee for the next two years and approved Tateishi, a teacher at the City College of San Francisco, as chair of the National Redress Committee.

The Campaign Gets Under Way

Under the direction of Tateishi, JACL's first concerted effort in quest of redress was finally under way. As chair, Tateishi established two primary goals for the committee to achieve within the next two years: a public education campaign and the drafting of proposed legislation to present to Congress. Tateishi selected the rest of his committee quickly—Ron Mamiya and Henry Miyatake from Seattle; Ray Okamura, a longtime advocate of redress; Min Yasui, one of the men whose wartime challenge of the curfew restrictions went to the Supreme Court and a staunch JACL activist from prewar times; and Phil Shigekuni from Los Angeles. In choosing the members, Tateishi concentrated on people from the western region of the country, picking people who were active in the redress movement and who could make significant contributions to the two goals he had set. As a relative newcomer to JACL, Tateishi disregarded the established organizational hierarchy, and his actions were taken as a breach of protocol and criticized by JACL veterans. Tateishi maintained, however, that only with such an assortment of people could the committee be effective.[16]

Tateishi first focused on the educational goal, but starting with the 1978 convention, the committee found itself in difficulty. Ironically, at the end of the Salt Lake City meeting, one day after the national organization had made a firm commitment to redress, Republican Senator S. I. Hayakawa was the featured speaker at the Sayonara dinner. In his talk, the senator expressed his open opposition to redress, reprimanding Japanese Americans for dwelling on the past. After the program, Hayakawa gave an interview to local reporters, and the next morning some shocking comments appeared in the *Salt Lake City Tribune*. The story, which was distributed nationally by wire services, opened as follows: "The Japanese American Citizens League has no right to ask the U.S. government for reparations for Japanese American citizens placed in relocation camps during World War II, according to Sen. S. I. Hayakawa. . . . 'Everybody lost out during the war, not just Japanese Americans,' and JACL asking for $25,000 in redress for each Japanese American placed in relocation camps was 'ridiculous.'"[17] After that rocky start, Tateishi focused heavily on the media. He decided that JACL would respond immediately to any newspaper article, letter, or statement regarding redress, most of which could be expected to be negative. He realized that what the movement needed was a full-scale public-relations campaign, and he exploited any press or television opportunity available. He convinced Bernard Goldberg, a CBS evening news correspondent in San Francisco whom he had met through mutual friends, to do a segment on the Tule Lake internment camp for the national network; both ABC and NBC soon followed with comparable pieces. Tateishi started to make guest appearances on a number of radio and TV talk shows.[18]

A December 1978 committee meeting provided JACL with important insights about the campaign. First, Frank Chin, a prominent Chinese American playwright whom Tateishi had invited, suggested that the key to success lay in creating an illusion that there existed a grand union of all Japanese Americans across the nation that supported JACL's stand on redress, even though the community was severely fragmented on the issue. Fortunately, Tateishi had the results of a survey he and Clifford Uyeda had conducted when Tateishi was the regional redress chair that indicated strong support for redress. Over 85 percent of the 4,000 responses collected throughout the Northern California–Western Nevada–Pacific District via numerous church, cultural, and community organizations agreed with the proposition that the government should apologize for its wartime actions and financially compensate those who had been affected. Although Tateishi realized that these results were skewed and not indicative of community sentiment as a whole (especially among Japanese Americans outside California), he used those results to present a rosy picture of a unified community to the media.[19]

At the December 1978 meeting, JACL leaders came to a second realization: they had little idea how to reach their second goal, namely, to get legislation introduced into Congress, or how the Japanese American members of Congress felt about the issue. It was at this point that Ron Ikejiri, JACL's Washington, D.C., representative, scheduled the January 1979 meeting with the four Japanese American members of Congress at which Senator Inouye proposed a blue-ribbon study commission. Shortly after, in a sensitive meeting the committee decided to follow Inouye's advice and lobby for a commission. And with that, as we have seen, redress entered the congressional arena.

With the establishment of the commission, the divergent views within the Japanese American community soon became very evident. The National Council for Japanese American Redress was created in opposition to JACL's decision to lobby first for a commission and opted to fight for redress through the courts. The National Coalition for Redress/Reparations was another group that emerged in the early 1980s. Self-described as a coalition of progressive-minded grass-roots organizations that evolved from the 1960s, emphasizing community organizing efforts and alliances with Third World causes, NCRR was created at a 1980 convention in Los Angeles attended by over 500 people. It brought together a number of Japanese American organizations that tended to be to the left of JACL on the political spectrum. As opposed to JACL, which has traditionally been led by Nisei, NCRR's membership included a high percentage of Sansei, many of whom were disgruntled with JACL's old-boy network and conservative stance. Representatives of NCJAR attended the 1980 conference, but soon broke off from NCRR to concentrate on court action. With coalition members in Los Angeles, San Francisco, San Jose, New York, Chicago, and Seattle, NCRR took a more media-focused, high-visibility approach to redress than JACL. Driven by the edict that "when the bottom moves, everything moves on top," NCRR was committed to such grass-roots activities as letter-writing drives and rallies.[20]

The divisions within the community were not simply between organizations. Infighting over control of JACL's redress efforts developed between two factions within JACL's leadership. In 1982, the organization's leadership created the Legislative Education Committee (JACL-LEC) as an independent lobbying arm of JACL out of concern that the Internal Revenue Service was looking into JACL's redress operation and that JACL might lose its nonprofit IRS status; but it was not until 1985 that JACL-LEC became operational. Min Yasui became JACL-LEC's first chair. According to Tateishi, who was by this time a paid JACL staff member responsible for running the redress campaign, JACL-LEC's primary function was to build up funds for the lobbying operation, but direction of the operation was still in the hands of JACL's leaders. But then personality conflicts and internal problems arose between Tateishi—who had been running the politics of the campaign behind the scenes, staying in close contact with the Washington office and Capitol Hill—and Yasui, who was in charge of public affairs and had become a highly visible spokesperson for JACL. When in 1985 the JACL board of directors stripped Yasui of power and gave control to Tateishi, tensions increased. According to Tateishi, word that JACL-LEC was being activated and taking over the redress campaign, with Yasui as chair, began to spread. Personal barbs began to fly between the two groups, with one side led by Tateishi, Frank Sato (1984–86 JACL national president), and Ron Wakabayashi (1981–88 JACL national director) and the other by Yasui, Grant Ujifusa (JACL-LEC strategy chair), and Harry Kajihara (1986–88 JACL national president). According to Ujifusa, the opposing group was selling out by not seriously pursuing redress and pushing JACL into conflicting issues, notably U.S.-Japan trade issues. Supporting Japanese companies would have discredited JACL and undercut the redress campaign, Ujifusa said.[21] According to Tateishi, such accusations were ludicrous; it would have been a mistake for JACL to become a single-issue organization; its integrity and credibility depended on its supporting the entire Asian American community and civil-rights issues in general. Furthermore, Tateishi contended, dealing with the Japanese trade issue did not necessarily harm the community, as the issue logically affects all Japanese Americans, for they are often the targets of hostility arising out of tense U.S.-Japan trade relations.[22]

No matter which side one takes, the end result was increasing tension within JACL and the rise of JACL-LEC. By late 1985, with the power struggle taking an emotional toll on him and his family, Tateishi, the focus of much of the infighting, quit his JACL staff position. Although he "wanted to stay on until the end because [he] thought it would be nice to be around"[23] when the campaign finally triumphed, Tateishi was pressured to leave JACL and went into private business.

In October 1985, Grayce Uyehara, a Nisei woman from Philadelphia, took the helm of JACL-LEC as its first executive director. A recently retired social worker, Uyehara, who had been JACL's Eastern District redress coordinator, took charge of the grass-roots campaign, giving JACL-LEC full-time leadership. Uyehara was well suited to running the grass-roots campaign. A longtime active JACL member, Uyehara was relatively well known and well liked in the Japanese American community. She had contacts throughout the country, as well as connections with many other social-service, religious, veterans', labor, and minority organizations. Working out of her house, Uyehara undertook the arduous commute between her home outside Philadelphia and Washington, D.C. Overall, Uyehara had the personality, drive, connections, and time needed to steer the grass-roots campaign.

Uyehara and the other redress leaders knew little about the politics of the legislative process, however, and they lacked the inside connections that often decide the fate of legislation. While searching for someone to spearhead the lobbying efforts, Mike Masaoka and Min Yasui came across the name of Grant Ujifusa, coauthor of the *Almanac of American Politics*, the bible of Washington politics. Yasui knew Ujifusa and thought well of him, whereas Masaoka was acquainted with Ujifusa's parents and had years earlier been the neighbor of Michael Barone, Ujifusa's co-author on the *Almanac*. Unlike Uyehara, Ujifusa was not well known in the Japanese American community, but he had the great virtue of being a Washington insider. As the *Almanac's* coauthor, Ujifusa had access to congressional offices, contacts on congressional staffs, and a keen sense of how congressional politics operates. Through his work on the *Almanac* and with members of Congress on books they had written, Ujifusa had established friendships all over the Hill. In addition, he understood how the legislative process worked—the politicking, arm-twisting, and favor-trading that would be required. Ujifusa's Republican connections were important, since the four supportive Nikkei members of Congress were Democrats, and since the signature of President Reagan was needed on the bill. For the last leg of the fight, Ujifusa laid out much of the strategy and tactics that would give the redress legislation the best chance in Congress.

At that point, JACL-LEC had full control over the redress operation, and the internal power struggle subsided—but did not end. Personality conflicts as well as disagreements regarding strategy persisted. The abrupt Ujifusa often put off some of the less politically astute, more community-oriented members of the population by focusing solely on the necessary political maneuvering inside the Beltway. Many JACL activists on the local level felt ignored by JACL national leaders and left out of the important decision-making. After years of laying the groundwork for a legislative battle, however, an organized lobbying structure had developed. With its years of nurturing relationships with key power players in Washington and its development of a coordinated grass-roots pressure–inside lobbying structure, JACL-LEC differed significantly in structure, strategy, and status from the other community groups campaigning for redress.

At the same time, NCRR had been gaining strength as a grass-roots organization. Its membership had grown considerably, especially on the

West Coast, and it had set into place mechanisms for massive letter-writing and phone-calling campaigns. The organization did not have the Washington connections and lobbying sophistication of JACL-LEC, but its efforts were important for raising awareness, both within the Japanese American community and with the public at large, and for rounding up community support. Although the two groups did not work closely together, the different strengths of JACL-LEC and NCRR were to some extent complementary. Although NCRR was more politically naive, its community mobilization efforts were impressive. Moreover, it gave community members who felt frustrated by the old guard running JACL a mechanism to become involved in the movement. JACL-LEC, on the other hand, as the strategic arm of the most established national Japanese American organization, had the reputation, credibility, and inside connections needed to make redress a reality, and as a result, its efforts are much more closely chronicled in this study.

Serious philosophical and strategic conflicts still existed, and JACL and NCRR worked together only reluctantly. Outside the two organizations, the community at large was still divided over the issue. Some people were ambivalent about redress, and many of those who did support it did not participate in the effort to secure it. The internal conflicts and infighting were less significant, however, because by then, the major battle had to be waged within the corridors of Congress. The CWRIC had already released its report and recommendations, and the public-relations campaign had been going strong for a few years. By that time, Sam Hall, the House Judiciary subcommittee chair who had prevented the redress bill from getting out of committee, had been appointed to a federal judgeship, so a major institutional barrier had been lifted. The Japanese American members of Congress, as well as other important congressional leaders such as Barney Frank, Jim Wright, Tom Foley, and Tony Coelho, were firmly committed to redress. The community had been aroused, supporters were in key positions in Congress, and JACL, whatever its problems, had developed a rather sophisticated but straightforward legislative strategy that would turn these strengths into victory.

CHAPTER TEN

Strategy for Victory

As we saw in Chapter Three, Japanese Americans are hardly the ideal organized interest group. Their numbers are too small, and concentrated in too few congressional districts, for them to have much chance of becoming an effective force in national politics. Cultural and social factors have also worked to discourage political mobilization. The result has been a generally apolitical Japanese American community. Hence, in formulating a strategy for the redress movement, community leaders realized that redress could not be won by Japanese Americans alone; they were going to need the help not only of the greater Asian American community, but of other Americans as well. Two important strategic questions confronted them. First, how should they frame their argument in support of redress? And second, what lobbying strategy was best to implement? The issue needed to be framed in terms that would attract broad support. One option was to get groups outside the Asian American community to participate in grass-roots lobbying. Even with a broadened base of grass-roots support, however, straight electoral interest pressure was probably not going to be enough to get the legislation passed. Another angle was needed from which to approach representatives and senators in a way that took into account the prevailing conservative climate.

On the surface, the Japanese American redress bill might appear to be typical special-interest, minority-group legislation—after all, it authorizes monetary payments from federal government funds to two specific minority groups—and as such, liberal Democrats would seem most likely to support it. Although Democrats span the political spectrum, in general they tend to be more liberal than Republicans, particularly with respect to racial and social issues. Not surprisingly, liberal Democrats like Congressmen Barney Frank and Ron Dellums and Senators Ted Kennedy and Paul Simon supported redress from the start. It is far more difficult to explain, then, why ultraconservatives who traditionally oppose any social measures that appear to benefit specific minority groups—men like Newt Gingrich and Jack Kemp—supported passage of H.R. 442. Four factors contributed to the building of a broad proredress coalition: the changing role of Asian Americans in American politics, the absence of effective opposition, the specific merits of the legislation and a strategy that made them appeal to a wide range of people, and the way in which the movement drew in a broad coalition of other organized interest groups.

Asian Americans and American Politics

By 1988, both Republicans and Democrats were bidding for the Asian American vote. Unlike the African American population, which votes 90 percent Democratic, Asian Americans were viewed "as a voting bloc that nobody has captured."[1] Although at one time neither party had much to gain or lose by vying for Asian American support, the situation has changed dramatically in the past decade. Although they are still relatively small in number, in percentage terms Asian Americans are the fastest-growing minority in the United States. In 1985 they made up about 2.1 percent of the nation's population, and demographic estimates have predicted that the proportion could grow to nearly 5 percent by the turn of the century. Following the 1990 U.S. census, California gained seven electoral college and congressional seats, for a total of 52. As a result, especially considering the winner-take-all aspect of electoral-college voting, votes from California, which has more Asian Americans than any other state except Hawaii, are increasingly critical in the national political scene. Moreover, Asian Americans have financial strengths disproportionate to their numbers, making them attractive targets for campaign fundraisers. According to a fundraiser for S. B. Woo, a Chinese American who in 1988 was the Democratic challenger of Delaware senator William Roth, "Asian Americans are ideal [for campaign financing]. They are cost-effective. They have more. With other minority groups, it's like pulling teeth. You fight over two-digit numbers. With Asians, it's four-digit numbers. And they demand less. So they don't become a political liability."[2] In California, it is now widely believed that Asian Americans are second only to the Jewish community in campaign contributions. During the 1988 presidential campaign, the Democratic Victory Fund hosted one predominantly Asian American event in Boston that raised over $1 million and collected another $200,000 from 40 Chinese Americans one evening in Los Angeles.[3] Republicans, too, have a good chance of attracting Asian American contributors. Indeed, traditional Confucian values, which attach great importance to family, education, respect for authority, and reliance on one's own efforts, have much in common with American conservative values. Thus, in many respects Republicans are more in tune with the Asian American community, a fact reflected in the roughly equal percentages of Democrats and Republicans among Asian Americans.

Moreover, 1988—the year in which H.R. 442 was enacted into law—was both a presidential and a congressional election year. California's Republican senator, Pete Wilson, fearing that he might have to run for reelection against Bob Matsui, came out in strong support of redress in April 1988 after numerous occasions on which he had declined to commit himself on the issue. In addition, realizing that winning California, with its large number of electoral votes, was crucial to his election as president, George Bush announced his support for redress just before California's June primary. As a result, for representatives and senators with increasing Asian American electorates, redress became a potentially pivotal electoral issue. And even for members of Congress with very small numbers of Asian Americans among their constituents, the issue was important in terms of fundraising, strengthening their party, and affecting presidential elections.

By the time the redress movement had shifted into high gear, Asian American activists had gained political clout in other arenas. They pressured several major universities to revise admissions policies that seemed to put a cap on the number of Asian Americans admitted. And the Asian American community took the lead in the battle to defeat Congressman Dan Lungren's 1987 nomination as California state treasurer after the incumbent, Jesse Unruh, died. Although Lungren's confirmation seemed a safe bet, the Asian American community, led by Japanese American activists who could not forget Lungren's vocal opposition to the monetary compensation provisions of redress as a member both of the CWRIC and of Congress, mounted a successful campaign to deny Lungren confirmation in February 1988, by examining and publicizing his ultraconservative voting record. The community proved that it had learned to play political hardball, and that it was a force with which both parties would have to reckon.

Assessing the Opposition

Mobilization of grass-roots support for redress was all the more important given the failure of an effective opposition to emerge. There were two main sources of opposition: the Lillian Baker group, Americans for Historical Accuracy, and the veterans' organizations. The first group made the most active efforts to block the legislation's passage: it conducted letter-writing campaigns, held political rallies, and submitted testimony for inclusion in committee hearing records. Led by historian Lillian Baker, the group lacked substantial numbers but had a strong commitment to the goal of stopping redress. Baker, however, came across as an embittered woman engaged in a personal vendetta. She had little credibility as an expert on the legislation; her writings on the internment and her testimony to Congress displayed racist feelings and scant respect for Congress. For example, she depicted the redress legislation as essentially asking members of Congress to partake in "historical revisionism" and asking Americans to subscribe to denigration of the United States. Moreover, she contended that *Personal Justice Denied*, the final report of the CWRIC, contained "predetermined conclusions published in various ethnic newspapers months before a single witness was called or hearing held."[4] She also stated that the commission's conclusion that the evacuation and internment were in part the result of racism was wholly incorrect since the U.S. Supreme Court had upheld the constitutionality of the curfew and evacuation orders in its *Korematsu*, *Hirabayashi*, and *Yasui* decisions—decisions that exemplify the very wartime hysteria and racism that the legislation sought to redress. As a result, AFHA's lobbying efforts were not taken very seriously on Capitol Hill. In fact, according to Congressman Mineta, Baker pushed people "into our camp" because after hearing her arguments, "they would realize what a kook she is."[5] Overall, AFHA did not provide insurmountable opposition, but it succeeded in throwing a few obstacles in redress's way.

Veterans' groups, too, posed a potential threat. The two largest and most organized groups, the American Legion and the Veterans of Foreign Wars, had a combined membership of over five million and in sheer numbers could have been formidable opponents. But they never lived up to that potential. Although some local chapters of veterans' groups came out against the legislation and lobbied members of Congress, the national organizations of the American Legion and the VFW never officially opposed H.R. 442. Indeed, both passed general resolutions in support of redress at their national conventions, though neither actively lobbied Congress on the bill's behalf. As mentioned in Chapter Three, the reason for these groups' quiescence was primarily the distinguished record of the Japanese American veterans of World War II. Japanese American veterans, led by the Nisei, convinced the national VFW, American Legion, and other veterans' groups not to oppose redress. They attended national conventions and kept in close touch with leaders of various veterans' groups in order to prevent any official stand against redress. In 1984, a resolution drafted by the Chicago Nisei Post 1183 was adopted by the 1st Division and the Department of Illinois and presented at the National American Legion convention at Salt Lake City. As a result of the Illinois delegates' lobbying effort, the national organization adopted Resolution 318, which recognized the injustice of the internment of Japanese Americans and the patriotism they had displayed during the war. The 1984 convention of the VFW in Chicago adopted a similar resolution, presented by the Nisei VFW 14-Post Coalition of California. On the local level, Japanese American veterans also kept individual chapters to which they belonged from officially opposing redress. Invoking the remarkable record of the 442d Regimental Combat Team, the 100th Infantry Battalion, and the Military Intelligence Service, Japanese American veterans argued that they had fought bravely in World War II, risking their lives in defense of this nation while their families and friends were behind barbed wire. They were just as American as their Caucasian counterparts and had given just as much for their country. Although during the war 442d members had been mocked by Japanese American dissidents who felt betrayed by the U.S. government, in the end their valor proved a great asset to the cause of redress.

Thus, no organized opposition group made a case persuasive to the majority of reelection-minded members of the House and Senate. Neither the Lillian Baker group nor any veterans' organizations convincingly made the argument that to vote for the legislation would be politically or electorally hazardous. In individual cases, effective opposition materialized, and the mail in many congressional offices ran decidedly against the legislation. Persuaded by a combination of this opposition and a fiscally difficult political environment, some members of Congress voted against redress. Organized opposition was not equally persuasive across the country, however. In this situation, with limited opposition, supporters of redress were able to concentrate on the benefits of voting for the legislation. Thus, it was now up to the redress movement to make a convincing case. The fate of the redress legislation was in the hands of the redress campaign itself—it had to frame the argument in a way that would appeal to a broad coalition of members and to lobby this position effectively to the diverse members of Congress.

Framing the Issue: Redress and Apple Pie '

On its surface, the redress bill appealed readily to most liberals and members with larger-than-average Asian American constituencies. It had the support of most Democrats outside the South; given the connections that the Nikkei members of Congress had with their fellow Democrats, focus shifted to Republican office-holders. Redress lobbyists needed to appeal to Republicans, especially conservative Republicans like the occupant of the White House, Ronald Reagan. The issue had to be framed in a way that conservative Republicans would accept as consistent with their principles. It was important, therefore, not to define the bill as a piece of traditional civil-rights, special-interest legislation, but rather as an issue of principle that was consistent with the most conservative, even original-intent, reading of the Constitution. The argument, however, had to be consistent with liberal values as well, because they could not "sell redress as a piece of liberal Democratic civil rights legislation to get it through Congress, and turn around and sell it another way to the White House. For Reagan, the liberal Democrats, not to speak of people farther left, are the bad guys, and chances are, if the bad guys are for it, he's going to be against it."[6] As Ujifusa put it, "The ultimate coalition that had to be constructed was one of liberal Democrats and conservative Republicans—a coalition of Barney Frank and Ronald Reagan."[7]

Such a coalition is not so surprising when one considers what drives both liberals like Frank and conservatives like Reagan: ideology. For both, it is principle, not interest, that is paramount when making policy decisions. The principle on which conservatives and liberals would unite, redress strategists concluded, was equal opportunity. Although conservatives and liberals differ on how to achieve it, equality of opportunity, as guaranteed by specifically enumerated rights in the Constitution, underlies the broad consensus one finds throughout American life. And equality of opportunity is exactly what Japanese Americans were denied in 1942. During the war, Japanese Americans asked for nothing more than the right to live with their families, raise their strawberries—and sell them at market, not subsidized, prices—and send their children to medical school. What redress sought, supporters contended, was not welfare payments or affirmative action;

Japanese Americans "just wanted to sit in [their] house and go to work like anyone else. But you can't do that and enjoy the fundamental freedom that everyone expects in this country if you're thrown into a camp."[8]

Framed in such a way, the issue was consistent with conservative as well as liberal beliefs in the right espoused by Thomas Jefferson to be left alone by one's government. To disagree with this argument was to appear racist. The principles the legislation represented were as American as motherhood and apple pie. First, redress dealt with government, not private-party, discrimination, and government discrimination violates the basic Jeffersonian ideals of limited government. Second, in the American system, crimes, even those perpetrated by the federal government, must be punished; to be consistent with this idea of justice, the government had to be held accountable for the arbitrary incarceration of 120,000 men, women, and children. Every member of Congress had a copy of the CWRIC report maintaining that the evacuation and internment resulted from racism, war hysteria, and failed political leadership. To disagree with these conclusions would have been to invite the stigma of racism, a sensitive issue for the Republican party, straining to overcome the public perception that it was insensitive to the concerns of minority groups. This framing of the issue also made it very difficult for a representative or senator to oppose the monetary provisions on fiscal grounds, because to do so would be to say that money is more important than our most fundamental values. As Grayce Uyehara put it, "When you come down to simple justice, to just say 'I'm sorry' places [Japanese Americans] back in second-class citizenship status because in this country, when you have been wronged and you have lost your possessions and your job and everything else when you are falsely imprisoned, then there is payment. That's the way our system works."[9]

Although some Japanese Americans would question this line of reasoning, redress supporters needed to approach members of Congress with an argument that conservatives could buy. Thus, redress had to be presented as a constitutional issue, not a racial issue, and the appeal couched in terms of bedrock American values. In the football metaphor Ujifusa likes to use, everyone in America accepts the proposition that ten yards make a first down—nothing more, nothing less. Japanese Americans were not asking for special privileges in 1942, like "eight yards make a first down"; they were willing to play the game by the rules, with no exceptions. But once they were locked up in concentration camps, it did not matter how many yards they ran. Behind barbed wire, they could never make a first down.

To play up the image of redress as a constitutional, all-American issue, redress leaders seized every opportunity to emphasize the relevance of the legislation to all Americans. Fortuitously, the peak of the lobbying campaign and the favorable institutional turn in the 100th Congress converged, in 1987, with the bicentennial of the U.S. Constitution. Congressman Mineta arranged with Speaker Wright that H.R. 442 would come before and be voted on by the full House on September 17, 1987, the exact bicentennial date. In discussing only that one piece of legislation on the 200th anniversary of the Constitution, the House made a symbolic statement that redress was not simply a Japanese American issue, but an American issue, because when one group is deprived of its constitutional rights, the freedom of all Americans is threatened. What better way to celebrate the Constitution than by reaffirming the rights it guarantees? The passage of H.R. 442 that day underlined the relationship between the bicentennial and redress.

In addition, JACL-LEC organizers used the very words of well-known conservatives to argue their point. According to Uyehara, they reviewed speeches by President Reagan and William Bradford Reynolds, former assistant attorney general for the Civil Rights Division, and incorporated in their publicity quotations about individual rights, freedom, and the principles that make the United States great. Presenting clips of Reagan speaking at the Geneva summit conference and before the United Nations, decrying communism and advocating freedom for all, the lobbyists showed conservative members of Congress that the values on which redress was based were completely consistent with the words of Mr. Conservative himself. Packaging the argument for redress in such ideological terms enabled redress strategists to gain the support of right-wing conservatives like Representative Newt Gingrich. They were less effective, however, in winning over moderate Republicans, who were more likely to be concerned with the impact of the financial provisions on the budget deficit.

Building the Coalition

The linchpin of the strategy to win passage of H.R. 442 was the effort to broaden the base of support to congressional districts all across the nation. It is one thing to frame an argument so that it appeals to various members of Congress; it is quite another to have members bombarded with that argument from as many directions as possible. The grass-roots campaign for redress succeeded because it had a core group of highly dedicated leaders who had a strategy and a planned order of lobbying, who engaged a significant portion of the Japanese American community in strategic grass-roots activity, and who, finally, built a coalition with other organized interest groups.

JACL's strategy for lobbying members of Congress was straightforward and logical. The first ones to approach, of course, were the Japanese American members, which JACL did in 1979. Next, it was rational to approach the other likeliest supporters, i.e., members who appeared to have some political reason to support redress or who tended to be sympathetic on civil-rights issues. This group included members of the House and Senate from the West Coast as well as liberal Democrats. After that, it was important to gain the support of the leadership in both houses, as well as members of the relevant committees and subcommittees. Once these key supporters were lined up, the campaign took whatever support it could get in whatever way possible, whether through personal favors or constituent pressure.[10]

Certain groups, of course, were easier to persuade than others. After the CWRIC was established in 1979 and its investigation was under way, Senators Inouye and Matsunaga and Congressmen Mineta and Matsui to varying degrees were supportive of the redress legislation. Fortunately, both Mineta's and Matsunaga's offices had unusual continuity in a setting notorious for high turnover, and as a result, specific members of their staffs became key members of the lobbying campaign. It did not take much persuading—maybe just a talk with Mineta or Matsunaga—to gain the support of some members, especially those from the West Coast and ideological liberals.

An example of the importance of personal contact was the case of Senator Alan Simpson (R–Wyo.). Simpson had first met Congressman Norman Mineta when they were Cub Scouts—Simpson a child growing up in Wyoming and Mineta an internee at the Heart Mountain internment camp in Wyoming.[11] In addition, Simpson remembered watching Grant Ujifusa play football against his high school's team years ago. It was because of his friendship with and respect for Mineta and Ujifusa that Simpson made the decision to support redress early and openly. As a conservative Republican senator from a state with a minute Asian American population and as Senate Minority Whip, Simpson became pivotal in persuading other Republicans to support the legislation and President Reagan to commit to signing the bill.[12] Simpson thus risked upsetting his electorate, according to a legislative assistant; his mail ran against the legislation.[13] Although Simpson voted in favor of the amendments to eliminate the monetary provisions of the bill—his record as a fiscal conservative and pressure from constituents at a time of critical budget decisions played a role here—he did ultimately vote in favor of H.R. 442, unamended, and his early support was crucial in persuading other Republicans to follow suit, especially because of the leadership role he often played in immigration and civil-rights issues as a member of the Judiciary Committee.

There is no concise way to explain how redress supporters managed to convince the dozens of representatives and senators with no evident reason to support H.R. 442 and S. 1009 to do so. Some votes were won by personal connections, others by the calling in of favors by Mineta or Matsunaga or Matsui, still others by ideological principle. Throughout the fight, the lobbying campaign relied on personal lobbying, either by former internees or by the Nikkei members of Congress, combined with strategic letter-writing and grass-roots pressure. Each of the 115 JACL chapters had a redress chair, who in coordination with Uyehara enlisted other Japanese Americans and their friends to contact members of the legislative and executive branches by phone or in writing.

Redress leaders recognized that redress could not be won with the support of Japanese Americans alone; the base of support had to be broadened to include the rest of the Asian American community, as well as other interest groups. As Uyehara explained, "We don't have enough Japanese Americans in this country to carry the redress issue by ourselves, and it is going to depend on all of us doing outreach to other human and civil rights organizations in the community."[14] The redress movement had the support of hundreds of different organizations throughout the nation (see Appendix A), and although many of them merely passed resolutions endorsing redress without actively lobbying in its behalf, a number of respected national organizations took an active role in the movement. What evolved was a coalition of interest groups, each of which used its own leverage on Capitol Hill and grass-roots lobbying.

The benefits of such outside support are obvious. First, it exponentially expanded the grass-roots capability of the movement. It opened the floodgates for constituent letters from across the nation. Uyehara said she wrote out a list of 1,700 people across the country, in places such as Mississippi and Iowa where there are few Japanese Americans. In such places, she would locate "surrogate Nikkei"—for example, someone who had fought alongside Japanese American soldiers during the war and knew what Japanese Americans had gone through.[15] Their letters showed members of Congress that redress was not simply a Japanese American issue, but an issue about which a wide range of Americans cared, an *American* issue. Outside support also brought the campaign a number of additional contacts on Capitol Hill and the help of some of the most effective lobbyists in Washington—people with considerable knowledge of the policy-making process who could make a difference in the necessary political maneuverings. Ralph Neas, executive director of the Leadership Conference on Civil Rights, considered a model lobbyist by many, donated his expertise and resources. Probably the most dedicated and helpful was David Brody, former director of the Anti-Defamation League of B'nai B'rith's Washington, D.C., office, who had been involved with redress since the commission bill was introduced. A longtime Washington lobbyist, Brody had many connections on the Hill and used those to aid the cause of redress. In addition to testifying on behalf of H.R. 442 and S. 1009 in committee hearings, for example, Brody talked to Congressman Howard Coble (R–N.C.), a member of the relevant Judiciary subcommittee who opposed the monetary aspect of the legislation. Although Brody knew he could not persuade Coble to support the bill, he did convince him to agree to mute his opposition to it; Coble voted nay when it came to the floor, but he did not lobby his colleagues against it.

Many of the outside groups supporting redress activated their own national networks of contacts in letter-writing and lobbying campaigns. Organizations like the American Civil Liberties Union inserted articles about redress in their regular newsletters, asking members to write letters in support of redress to their elected representatives and senators in Washington, D.C. Some groups also sent representatives to testify at congressional committee hearings, thus making their support of redress an official part of the congressional record. Again, their active support demonstrated that redress was an American issue and not a special-interest issue. It showed that a diverse cross-section of Americans agreed that the government should make restitution for its wartime mistakes and that they were willing to help pay for it.

Although it is not surprising that redress organizers reached outside the Japanese American community for help, the diversity of groups joining the coalition was noteworthy; they ranged from other minority-interest groups like the Anti-Defamation League of B'nai B'rith (ADL) and the National Association for the Advancement of Colored People (NAACP) to the National Education Association (NEA) to the American Bar Association (ABA). It is relatively easy to see why civil-rights organizations like the ACLU and the Leadership Conference on Civil Rights, a coalition of 300 smaller organizations, committed their resources in support of redress; the arbitrary exercise of government against a harmless minority was a threat to all minority groups. It is less obvious why mainstream groups such as the ABA, the NEA, a number of labor unions, and a host of Protestant church groups also actively supported redress.

The ABA apparently thought important legal principles were at stake. Representatives of the ABA testified in both Senate and House subcommittee hearings and wrote letters in support of the legislation. In his written testimony before the Senate Subcommittee on Federal Services, Post Office, and Civil Service, Committee on Governmental Affairs, William L. Robinson, an officer of the ABA Section on Individual Rights and Responsibilities, invoked the recently vacated convictions of Fred Korematsu, Min Yasui, and Gordon Hirabayashi, the three men whose cases challenging the wartime curfew and evacuation orders had reached the U.S. Supreme Court (see Chapter Eleven). "As attorneys and officers of the court," Robinson said,

> members of the American Bar Association feel a special duty to ensure the integrity and strength of our basic freedoms. This obligation is even stronger when a Congressional Commission has found a grave injustice was committed, and the Federal Judiciary has found that the government intentionally manipulated the evidence to facilitate that injustice. Accordingly, the American Bar Association urges the Congress of the United States to support legislation which would provide appropriate recognition for Japanese Americans.[16]

But how does one explain the commitment of other groups, like the NEA? They might have firmly believed in the merits of the bill, but by itself that hardly explains why they were willing to call on their memberships to contact their representatives in support of redress. The most tenable explanation for their support, and that of many other groups, is that they believed a moral wrong had been committed and wanted to erase this black mark on American history. The issue was not just about repaying a minority group for poor treatment; it was about repairing a huge abscission in the Constitution, about making the nation whole again. In a sense, by fighting for redress, these individuals and groups were doing what was necessary to clear their own consciences, and in doing so, the conscience of the entire nation. Thus, church groups with a strong social-justice agenda, the sole voice of moral outrage in 1942, were again heard from in

1987. However unsatisfactory the conclusion may seem to the hard-nosed political scientist, the most compelling reason for their support was the emotional, ideological, and moral imperative of the cause.

Lobbying by Letter and in Person

With an army of dedicated people ready to go to work, the key to the effectiveness of letter-writing and personal lobbying efforts was coordinating them with each other. Uyehara and Ujifusa, keeping in close contact with each other and with Matsunaga's and Mineta's offices, coordinated letter-writing with personal visits so that a particular representative or senator would be bombarded from all directions at the same time. For example, if Mineta planned to talk to a particular colleague soon, Uyehara would call the redress chair in the representative's district and ask her to deluge the representative's office with letters and mailgrams in support of redress. Or if a group of former internees was planning a personal visit to a member in a district office, Uyehara would make sure a blizzard of letters from constituents coincided with their visit. The combined effort was far more effective than either writing or personal lobbying would have been alone. Uyehara realized that meeting with representatives and senators personally was not always necessary; in some cases, it was enough to persuade a legislative aide of the bill's merits, and the aide in turn would convince the member. To the grass-roots organizers around the country she sent out "Redress Alerts" whenever a crucial juncture was imminent—for example, when the House subcommittee was about to take up the bill, she sent out a request for letters to members of the subcommittee.

Rather than sending random letters to various representatives and senators, Uyehara used every available connection she could unearth, no matter how obscure, to put pressure on particular members. One example involves Democratic Congressman E. (Kika) de la Garza, representing the Fifteenth Congressional District in Texas. Typically liberal on economic issues and hawkish on foreign policy, since 1981 Garza had been chair of the House Agriculture Committee—not the most powerful committee in the House, but a position that earned him respect from his peers. Representing a district that was 66 percent Hispanic and less than 1 percent Asian American, Garza had little electoral reason to support H.R. 442. He was a close friend, however, of a Japanese American couple in the Rio Grande Valley; moreover, Garza's wife was originally from Uyehara's hometown and was a friend of Uyehara's sister. When Uyehara found an opportunity to talk to Garza about redress, he agreed to support the legis-lation, primarily because of his regard for his Japanese American friends.[17]

Personal contacts and a little bit of luck were the keys to another rep-resentative, who in turn helped gain others' support. Through the grass-roots network, Uyehara came into contact with Gene Doi, a Japanese American woman employed as a deputy county clerk in DeKalb County, Georgia, who was enthusiastic about redress. By pestering Georgia's repre-sentatives and using personal contacts of her own, she persuaded a num-ber of representatives around Atlanta to support redress. Most signifi-cantly, she won the support of Pat Swindall, a born-again Christian and conservative Republican who was a member of the relevant House sub-committee.[18] The all-American, constitutional-rights argument worked with Swindall, who as an ideological conservative supported the principles of limited government and due process. In addition to adding his vote to the yea column, Swindall's endorsement was especially important because he helped persuade other conservatives on the committee to follow suit, and because he, along with Jack Kemp (R–N.Y.), Henry Hyde (R–Ill.), and Newt Gingrich (R–Ga.), sent a "Dear Colleague" letter urging other repre-sentatives to vote for the conference report. Citing the Fourth and Fifth Amendments to the Constitution, the four declared that "we, as Ameri-cans, are enlightened enough to learn from our mistakes and courageous enough to admit it. We will never again allow our Constitution and our individual rights to be undermined. . . . If our Constitution is truly our guiding document both in letter and in spirit, then this redress must be made. Please join us in supporting H.R. 442."[19] This endorsement of re-dress as a matter of constitutional principle was in no small part due to the determined efforts of one Japanese American.

The entire congressional delegation from the state of Washington was won over to redress in a textbook example of effective lobbying. The Seattle chapter of JACL-LEC took on the responsibility of persuading the two senators and eight representatives from Washington to support the redress legislation; remarkably, they won over every one of them. To be sure, Washington has a larger than average Japanese American population, and Japanese Americans were evacuated from the state during the war. Only one congressional district in the state of Washington has an Asian Ameri-can electorate of over 3 percent, however; most have electorates of only 1 or 2 percent. Thus, electoral interest pressure was not an important factor. Rather, the group ran a highly effective campaign, making multiple visits and phone calls to each member. According to Cherry Kinoshita, a leader of the Seattle group, the key to successful lobbying was persistence: "We kept at them and never let them go."[20]

Persistence helped persuade Al Swift, of Washington's Second Congressional District. The effort to win Swift's support began in 1983, at which time he had an unusual objection to the legislation: although he agreed that the internment was wrong, he did not think the individual compensation was enough to be meaningful. It did not, he said, address the grievance from the perpetrator's point of view, but from the victim's. The payments were too small to have a chastening effect on the majority. Although JACL-LEC members thought this was a strange position to take, they were sure that Swift could eventually be won over. So they made a series of visits to him in his district office, and on the fourth visit they brought along the local president of the American Jewish Congress, who was an old schoolmate and friend of Swift's, as an excuse to see him. At this point, Swift finally let it be known that he had come around to JACL-LEC's position, and that he would vote for the legislation, including the provisions for individual compensation.

In lobbying Swift, the Seattle group realized the value of repeated personal visits; once the member knew the lobbyist as a human being, the arguments in favor of the legislation were more persuasive. During the third meeting with Swift, Kinoshita became extremely upset with him because of his insistence on his unusual argument, and he could hear the irritation in her voice. Not wanting to leave Swift angry with her, Kinoshita sent him a plant at Easter. In response, she received a thank-you note from Swift, and although he did not explicitly say so, the tone of the note suggested that his position was softening. Although it is unlikely that sending a plant to the representative at Easter in itself changed his mind, the fact that Kinoshita had appealed to him as a compassionate human being probably helped soften his previous stance.[21] Similar stories can be told about the lobbying of the rest of the state's delegation, every one of whom, Democrat and Republican alike, voted for the legislation.

A still more improbable example of JACL-LEC's grass-roots activity in action involved Congressman Harley Staggers, Jr. (D–W.Va.). Uyehara and Ujifusa had no problem convincing Staggers that redress was just and necessary, but he had not heard from his constituents on the issue and was not in a position politically to come out in favor of the legislation. He told them if they wanted his vote, they would have to enable him to justify it to his constituents. It thus fell to Uyehara to find a few constituents in West Virginia's Second District to send letters to their representative. When she failed to locate a single Japanese American resident of the district, she searched for the next best thing, a "surrogate Nikkei." After ascertaining that Staggers is a Methodist, she located a JACL member who was an active Methodist and whose minister was originally from West Virginia. After she approached the JACL member, he asked his minister to approach other Methodist ministers in West Virginia and ask them to write to Staggers. She also talked to a Nisei veteran she knew who had contacts with West Virginia veterans, and he asked them to write to Staggers. Finally, she located a federal judge from West Virginia who had graduated from Harvard, Staggers's alma mater, who knew Staggers personally and who agreed to write to him. Although Uyehara could manage only a few letters from constituents, they were enough for Staggers to justify his position in support of redress and come out publicly on the issue.[22]

The foregoing are just a few examples of how JACL-LEC's lobbying network gathered support for H.R. 442. The reasons for supporting the legislation varied from member to member. Sometimes it was the ideological argument that won the vote, sometimes repeated personal contacts, other times an exchange of favors with the Japanese American members of Congress. But in the final push for redress, the lobbying machine, managed by community leaders and fueled by thousands of Japanese Americans and other redress supporters across the nation, was invaluable in persuading 243 House members and 69 senators to vote for the redress legislation.

Lobbying the Executive Branch

The final arena in which lobbying made a difference was the executive branch. From the outset, redress leaders knew that even if they were able to round up the votes for passage in the House and Senate, they would have one more hurdle to surmount before the legislation would become law—the president. If the legislation were to be vetoed by the president, it was unlikely to have the two-thirds support in each house needed to override a veto. Thus, securing the president's support became another strategic goal. As Ujifusa outlined the situation in an October 3, 1985, strategy memo, "For a variety of political reasons, we are unlikely to get open and public support for the bill [from the White House]. The goal is to get neutrality."[23]

When the legislation was first introduced in Congress, the Justice Department released an opinion opposing H.R. 442, which was taken to be the Administration's stand on the issue, even though it never officially came from the White House. Richard Willard, assistant attorney general for the Civil Division, reiterated that position at all committee hearings on the legislation. The Justice Department's arguments against the bill included (1) opposition to the concept of paying reparations to a specific group affected during World War II, since many suffer in time of war; (2) the claim that mistakes of this nature are best rectified by "historical comment," not by congressional efforts to rewrite history; (3) the claim that the conclusions of the CWRIC were a debatable interpretation; (4) the claim that fiscal constraints made the authorization of $1.25 billion in monetary compensation unacceptable; and (5) the claim that the government has no legal obligation to undertake such a program.[24] At the same time, the Office of Management and Budget (OMB) indicated that it, too, would recommend that the president veto the legislation. One day after the House first passed H.R. 442 in September 1987, the *Los Angeles Times* reported that OMB opposed the legislation on fiscal grounds.

Several factors contributed to ensuring that Reagan would sign H.R. 442 when it reached his desk in August 1988. Because 1988 was a presidential election year and the Republican candidate, George Bush, had committed his support to redress in hopes of securing California's Asian American vote, it would have been politically messy for Reagan to oppose his potential successor on this issue. In this sense, there was some political pressure on him to sign the bill. More important, just as it took time to educate members of Congress and convince them of the merits of the legislation, gaining Reagan's support required a gradual process of informing and pressuring him. During his term as JACL national president from 1984 to 1986, Frank Sato began supplying top White House aides with information about the redress legislation. As inspector general for the Veterans' Administration, Sato had direct access to the White House and had developed relationships with top administration officials, including John A. "Jack" Svahn, Reagan's chief domestic policy adviser. Sato asked the JACL national staff to put together packets of materials about the internment, the CWRIC's findings and recommendations, and arguments supporting the legislation, which he gave to Svahn and his colleagues.[25] The materials included articles that mentioned a story about a young actor named Reagan who participated in a 1945 ceremony awarding the Distinguished Service Cross to the family of Kazuo Masuda, a Nisei veteran of the 442d Regimental Combat Team who had died in combat. The community of Santa Ana, California, would not allow Masuda to be buried in the local cemetery. To assuage the town's opposition to Masuda's burial, General "Vinegar Joe" Stilwell flew out to California to preside, along with a few local personalities—including Reagan—over the award ceremony.[26]

Moreover, when Ujifusa became JACL-LEC strategy chair, he was assigned to lobby the White House, to which he had the best connections as one of the few Republicans in the redress leadership. Although he never spoke with Reagan personally, Ujifusa continued the process of trying to influence the president's decision. He was frequently in touch with Reagan advisers, and to offset the Justice Department's opposition, he persuaded then–Secretary of Education William J. Bennett, whom he had known since they were both students at Harvard, and Gary L. Bauer, former assistant to the president for domestic policy development and an extremely conservative born-again Christian, to support the legislation.[27] Congressman Matsui talked with Kenneth Duberstein, Reagan's deputy chief of staff, and also asked the Times Mirror Company's Washington representative, Patrick Butler, to ask his former boss and Reagan's chief of staff, Howard Baker, to speak with Reagan about redress.[28]

Finally, Ujifusa asked then–New Jersey Governor Thomas Kean (a Republican whose book, *The Politics of Inclusion*, Ujifusa had edited for publication by Macmillan) to talk to Reagan about redress the next time he saw him. For the first 35 minutes of a one-hour meeting in October 1987, when he could have been discussing the needs of his own state, Kean made his pitch, urging Reagan to support the legislation and reminding him of the Kaz Masuda story. Later, Ujifusa made sure that a letter from Masuda's sister and a photograph of the ceremony were sent to Reagan to stimulate his memory. As Carol Stroebel, Mineta's legislative director, explained, Reagan is a man who lives by anecdotes, and once he heard vivid stories of the internment experience and was reminded of his own participation in the Masuda ceremony, he climbed on the redress bandwagon.[29] Once Reagan seemed inclined to sign the bill if it reached his desk, Ujifusa got confirmation from Assistant Attorney General Willard that he would not send his staff to either the House or the Senate to lobby against the bill, and that if the legislation reached the White House, he would not contact the president to recommend a veto.[30] Willard made good on both promises. Thus, personal contacts and persuasive lobbying again played a pivotal role—this time in obtaining the president's support.

High Visibility: The NCRR Approach

While JACL-LEC was gathering support for H.R. 442, NCRR was contributing in a different way. NCRR, as a much younger and a much less structured organization, lacked the Washington connections and political know-how of JACL-LEC. Its membership was relatively small and concentrated on the West Coast. On Capitol Hill, it did not have the standing of JACL as the national representative of the Japanese American community, and it lacked the funds and fundraising capabilities of JACL-LEC. Moreover, the more progressive philosophy driving the coalition emphasized high visibility and media-focused activities, rather than behind-the-scene politicking. NCRR thus played a smaller role in the redress campaign.

One should not completely dismiss the efforts of NCRR, however. Its member organizations wrote tens of thousands of letters to representatives and senators across the country—a flood that surely had some effect on those members on the receiving end. In addition, NCRR sent two delegations to Washington in 1984 and 1987 to lobby Congress. Although the first trip included only a few people, the 1987 delegation of 127 made quite an impression on the Hill as the largest Asian American contingent ever to hit the halls of Congress. Rather than professional lobbyists, the group consisted primarily of Nisei and some Sansei and included veterans and internees, notably Fred Korematsu. Fanning out in groups of four or five, the lobbyists met with numerous representatives and senators, telling them about their own experiences and traumas.[31] NCRR also contributed greatly to the movement's educational goal. Its rallies often received coverage in newspapers and on television, and whenever an advance was made in Washington—i.e., more cosponsors joined in supporting the legislation—they immediately held a press conference or made a public statement.

To a greater extent than JACL-LEC, NCRR rallied the Japanese American community behind redress and made people feel they had an important role to play. NCRR drew a large number of people into the movement by sponsoring the lobbying teams, by going out into the community to enlist people to write letters, and by holding rallies in cities up and down the West Coast. Although the rallies themselves had little direct impact on Congress, together with the media attention NCRR attracted, they brought the movement home to Japanese Americans and got the community excited about what was happening—probably NCRR's greatest contribution to the redress movement. After all, if the Japanese American community had not cared about the issue, would Inouye, Matsunaga, Mineta, and Matsui have taken the lead, and would countless other members of Congress, lobbyists, and other interest groups have devoted time, energy, money, and emotion to the cause of redress? Without the community support generated by both NCRR and JACL-LEC, the redress campaign could not have capitalized on the favorable institutional environment in Congress leading to its 1987–88 triumph.

CHAPTER ELEVEN

The Impact of Other Redress Efforts

Although this study specifically examines the passage of the Civil Liberties Act of 1988, the legislative route was just one of several paths to redress traveled by the Japanese American community in the 1980s. Others contributed, in various ways, to the passage of H.R. 442. While the legislative battle was being fought in the halls of Congress, two attempts to correct the government's wartime injustices were being pursued in the courts. The first was the historic reopening of the *Korematsu*, *Hirabayashi*, and *Yasui* cases (in which the U.S. Supreme Court had upheld the constitutionality of the military's wartime orders) by means of a little-used legal mechanism, the petition for writ of error *coram nobis*. The second redress effort through the courts was an unsuccessful class-action suit filed by the National Council for Japanese American Redress against the U.S. government in 1983. The class-action suit, filed on behalf of all former evacuees and internees, listed 22 causes of action and 15 violations of constitutional rights. After a long, tortuous journey through the courts, the suit finally died in 1988, when the U.S. Supreme Court declined to grant certiorari on the case.

Both legal battles, although separate from the campaign for legislative redress, made the arguments in support of the redress legislation more compelling. They contributed to the effort to educate Congress and the public, and they drew media and public attention to the movement and to the experience of Japanese Americans during the war. In addition to the *coram nobis* cases and the class-action suit, H.R. 442's course through the legislative process was aided by a sympathetic media that intently and compassionately covered all aspects of the Japanese American redress battle, from the commission hearings to the court cases to all phases of the legislative fight, both educating the nation and establishing a national climate of regret and disgust over the government's wartime actions and of sympathy for the former internees. Other public events focused sympathetic attention on the redress movement. From a featured exhibit at the Museum of American History at the Smithsonian Institution in Washington, D.C., to an Oscar-nominated documentary on the *coram nobis* cases, Americans were provided with numerous opportunities to learn about the wartime episode, and the more they knew, the more sympathetic they were and the more favorable the political climate became for passage of the historic legislation.

The *Coram Nobis* Cases

The story of how three ordinary Japanese Americans—Fred Korematsu, Gordon Hirabayashi, and Minoru Yasui—were transformed into American heroes begins with General John L. DeWitt's curfew and evacuation orders, which followed President Roosevelt's issuance of Executive Order 9066 in 1942, as outlined in Chapter One. It was under these orders that these three men were arrested by local police and convicted in the federal courts. DeWitt's curfew and evacuation orders put Japanese Americans in a no-win situation. Compliance inevitably led to internment, first in "assembly centers" and then in "relocation centers," many of them in distant states. Resistance, too, led to internment, sometimes preceded by a stay in jail. At least those who followed the government's orders could stay with their families. Faced with this predicament, it is not surprising that only a courageous few defied the orders. Of the small group of challengers, Yasui, Hirabayashi, and Korematsu were the ones whose cases went all the way to the U.S. Supreme Court.[1]

Their Stories

Minoru Yasui was the first Japanese American to challenge the legality of DeWitt's orders. At midnight on March 28, 1942, Japanese Americans on the West Coast became subject to criminal penalties for violation of the curfew that DeWitt had placed on all persons of Japanese ancestry. At 11 o'clock that evening, five hours after the curfew went into effect, Yasui walked into a Portland, Oregon, police station and demanded that he be arrested for violating the curfew. As an army officer, a lawyer, a Japanese consulate employee, and a JACL leader, Yasui felt that he could not passively watch the government evacuate and intern his family and friends without putting up a fight.[2] Knowing that evacuation orders were imminent, he decided to resist as soon as the curfew orders went into effect. Yasui had no quarrel with the curfew on general principle or with a curfew applied only to aliens. But when Public Proclamation no. 3 applied to all residents of Japanese ancestry, regardless of citizenship, the articulate and acerbic Yasui felt he had to take a stand: "There the general is wrong, because it makes distinctions between citizens on the basis of ancestry. That order infringed on my rights as a citizen."[3] Yasui served nine months in solitary confinement, but he never regretted his decision to challenge the government. Compelled by devotion to what he saw as basic constitutional principles, Yasui's act of resistance was deliberate.

Whereas Yasui challenged the orders on legal grounds, Gordon Hirabayashi purposely violated the military orders on May 16, 1942, on moral grounds. The product of a Quaker upbringing, the 24-year-old University of Washington senior turned himself in to the FBI office in Seattle for failing on May 11 to register for evacuation, as required by Civilian Exclusion Order no. 57.[4] With local lawyer Arthur Barnett at his side, Hirabayashi submitted a four-page, typed statement explaining "why I refused to register for evacuation."[5] His statement clearly reflected his pacifist, Quaker beliefs:

> This order for the mass evacuation of all persons of Japanese-American descent denies them the right to live. It forces thousands of energetic, law-abiding individuals to exist in a miserable psychological and a horrible physical atmosphere. This order limits to almost full extent the creative expression of those subjected. It kills the desire for a higher life. Hope for the future is exterminated. Human personalities are poisoned. . . . If I were to register and cooperate under those circumstances, I would be giving helpless consent to the denial of practically all of the things which give me incentive to live. I must maintain my Christian principles. I consider it my duty to maintain the democratic standards for which this nation lives. Therefore, I must refuse this order for evacuation.[6]

Unlike Yasui, Hirabayashi had no legal background and was therefore delighted when the American Civil Liberties Union offered to use his arrest as a test case. Hirabayashi was ultimately convicted of two offenses under Public Law no. 503, violation of curfew and failure to report for evacuation.

Fred Korematsu, by contrast, was not inspired to violate military orders by high-minded principle. A shipyard welder in the San Francisco Bay area, Korematsu had no intention of becoming a test case of the constitutionality of DeWitt's wartime orders—much less the subject of a celebrated

Supreme Court decision. His reason was love. While the rest of his family duly reported to the Tanforan assembly center on May 9, 1942, Korematsu stayed behind with his girlfriend, Ida Boitano, who was of Italian descent. Korematsu was picked up on a street corner near his house in San Leandro on May 30, after the police received a tip from a local merchant. About a month before the evacuation orders were issued, he had undergone plastic surgery to make him look less Asian, hoping that it might be possible once he had saved enough money for him and Ida to go to Arizona and be married without anyone realizing he was a Japanese American. Although Korematsu's original motivations were not grounded in principle, he shared with Yasui and Hirabayashi a strong conviction of his rights as an American citizen. And when Ernest Besig of the ACLU approached Korematsu to propose that he become a test case, he willingly agreed to challenge the laws that sent him first to jail and later to the Tanforan race track.[7]

The cases of all three men arrived before the U.S. Supreme Court in the mid-1940s, and in each case the Court upheld the conviction and the constitutionality of the orders, citing the need to defer to the military in time of war. In June 1943, in *Hirabayashi v. United States*[8] and its companion case, *Yasui v. United States*,[9] the Court unanimously upheld the constitutionality of the curfew restrictions, stating that military necessity warranted the measures at the time they were imposed. The purpose of Executive Order 9066 and General DeWitt's military orders, Chief Justice Harlan F. Stone wrote for the majority, "was the protection of our war resources against espionage and sabotage."[10] Giving great leeway to the military, the Court furthermore stated:

> The military commander's appraisal of facts in the light of the authorized standard, and the inferences which he drew from those facts, involved the exercise of his judgment. But, as we have seen, those facts, and the inferences that could be rationally drawn from them, support the judgment of the military commander, that the danger of espionage and sabotage to our military resources was imminent, and that the curfew order was an appropriate measure to meet it.[11]

One and a half years later, in December 1944, the Court handed down its well-known ruling in *Korematsu v. United States*.[12] Justice Hugo Black delivered the majority opinion, joined by Chief Justice Stone and Justices Stanley F. Reed, William O. Douglas, and Wiley B. Rutledge. Reaffirming the principles set forth in *Hirabayashi*, the Court held the exclusion of "a single racial group"[13] to be within the war power of Congress and of the

president. The "pressing public necessity"[14] rested on the military judgment that immediate segregation of the disloyal from the loyal was not
possible. In turn, reliance on the military to decide the best course of action
was acceptable because Congress had declared war. The Court, however,
limited its ruling to the constitutionality of the exclusion order and avoided
the issue of internment.

Unlike *Hirabayashi* and *Yasui*, *Korematsu* inspired three stinging dissents, by Justices Owen J. Roberts, Frank Murphy, and Robert H. Jackson.
Justice Roberts could not accept the majority's ruling that the principles
enunciated in the *Hirabayashi* decision applied to Korematsu's situation—
"that exclusion from a given area of danger, while somewhat more sweeping than a curfew regulation, is of the same nature—a temporary expedient made necessary by a sudden emergency."[15] Rather, he viewed the
issue as one of "convicting a citizen as punishment for not submitting to
imprisonment in a concentration camp, based on his ancestry, and solely
because of his ancestry, without evidence or inquiry concerning his loyalty
and good disposition towards the United States."[16] Justice Jackson saw
great danger in validating the constitutionality of government action directed against individuals by virtue of their membership in "a race from
which there is no way to resign."[17] In the most biting opinion, Justice
Murphy dissented "from this legalization of racism."[18] Contending that
"no reasonable relation to an 'immediate, imminent, and impending' public danger is evident to support this racial restriction which is one of the
most sweeping and complete deprivations of constitutional rights in the
history of this nation in the absence of martial law,"[19] Murphy harshly
criticized the military orders:

> The main reasons relied upon by those responsible for the forced evacua-
> tion, therefore, do not prove a reasonable relation between the group
> characteristics of Japanese Americans and the dangers of invasion, sabo-
> tage and espionage. The reasons appear, instead, to be largely an accumu-
> lation of much of the misinformation, half-truths and insinuations that
> for years have been directed against Japanese Americans by people with
> racial and economic prejudices—the same people who have been among
> the foremost advocates of the evacuation.[20]

These dissents would be frequently cited in the ensuing debates.

Despite the wide debate that the three decisions engendered in legal
circles, *Korematsu*, *Hirabayashi*, and *Yasui* remained on the books as law.
But, in an unprecedented move, in 1983 the three men, with a legal team
headed by Peter Irons, professor of political science at the University of

California, San Diego, and San Francisco attorney Dale Minami, filed petitions to have their cases reopened. In 1981, under the Freedom of Information Act, Irons and Aiko Herzig-Yoshinaga, a researcher for the CWRIC and an NCJAR supporter, uncovered crucial Justice Department documents on the three cases that included internal complaints by government lawyers in 1943–44 and evidence that Justice Department and military officials had suppressed, omitted, and destroyed documents that proved there was no threat of espionage or sabotage by the West Coast Japanese American population and that directly refuted General DeWitt's claims of Japanese American disloyalty. The legal procedure they used to reopen the cases was the little-used petition for writ of error *coram nobis*, which can only be invoked in cases of fundamental error or manifest injustice. As opposed to habeas corpus, *coram nobis* is used when the convicted defendant has already served the assigned punishment. Claiming that the failure of the government to produce the newly uncovered documents in the original cases caused the lower courts' convictions as well as the Supreme Court's affirmations to be fundamentally unjust, the men demanded that their convictions be vacated by the trial courts in which their cases originated. Their petition rested on five main charges: (1) that officials of the War Department had altered and destroyed evidence and withheld knowledge of this evidence from the Department of Justice and the Supreme Court; (2) that War Department and Justice Department officials had suppressed evidence relative to the loyalty of Japanese Americans and to their alleged commission of acts of espionage; (3) that government officials had failed to advise the Supreme Court of the falsity of the allegations in the Final Report of General DeWitt; (4) that the government's abuse of the doctrine of judicial notice and the manipulation of amicus briefs constituted a fraud upon the courts; and (5) that the three men were entitled to relief on the ground that their convictions were based on governmental orders that violate current constitutional standards.

A string of decisions in federal district courts in San Francisco, Portland, and Seattle between November 1983 and January 1988 made these cases legal landmarks. In November 1983, U.S. District Court Judge Marilyn Patel granted Fred Korematsu's petition for a writ of error *coram nobis*, vacating his 40-year-old convictions. At a highly publicized and emotionally charged hearing in San Francisco, Judge Patel declared that the Court's 1944 opinion stood as a constant reminder that in times of war, our institutions must be vigilant in protecting the rights and freedoms guaranteed by the Constitution.[21] Although she admitted that she had no power to erase the original *Korematsu* decision from the record books, she felt there was compelling evidence that "the government deliberately omitted relevant information and provided misleading information in papers before the court."[22] Furthermore, she found that "the judicial process is seriously impaired when the government's law enforcement officers violate their ethical obligations to the court."[23]

In January 1984 in Portland, however, Judge Robert C. Belloni granted a motion by the government to vacate Min Yasui's conviction but dismiss his petition. In declining to hold hearings on the case, Judge Belloni refused to make any findings of government misconduct that deprived Yasui of his Fifth Amendment rights. Yasui appealed the dismissal of his petition to the Ninth Circuit Court of Appeals, but in November 1986, before the court ruled on his appeal, Yasui died, and the appeal became moot. After his death, as a tribute to Yasui's spirit, his family asked the Supreme Court to review his case, but in 1987 the Court refused to grant certiorari.[24]

Finally, Gordon Hirabayashi's case, unlike the other two, went to a full evidentiary hearing in Seattle in June 1985. The two-week hearing provided emotion and drama, as Victor Stone, a Justice Department lawyer from the Criminal Division in Washington, D.C., called central figures in the internment program—namely, Edward Ennis, formerly of the Justice Department, former assistant secretary of war John J. McCloy, and Colonel Karl Bendetsen—to the witness stand in an attempt to discredit the findings of the CWRIC. In his February 10, 1986, decision, Judge Donald Voorhees ruled that the suppression of evidence by the War Department "was an error of the most fundamental character"[25] and vacated Hirabayashi's exclusion order conviction. He found the curfew imposed on Japanese Americans to be a relatively mild burden, however, and decided that the curfew conviction was not affected by the government's misconduct. On appeal, the Ninth Circuit Court of Appeals reversed Judge Voorhees on the curfew conviction and remanded the case to him with orders to vacate both convictions. On January 12, 1988, Judge Voorhees set aside Hirabayashi's curfew conviction. The government was given 60 days to ask for a review of the order, but government attorneys decided against further litigation.[26] Thus ended 40 years of struggle in the judicial system.

Their Impact

The impact of the vacated convictions on the legislative efforts for redress was twofold. Their educational value and the media exposure they received were critical. This was the first time in American history that an effort had even been launched to overturn convictions in cases adjudicated by the Supreme Court. That the effort succeeded was all the more remarkable, and it is not surprising that the cases received considerable media attention. When the decisions were handed down, the courtrooms were packed with reporters, with television news cameras and photojournalists crowding the hallways. Major newspapers across the nation ran front-page stories on the decisions. A third-generation Japanese American, Steven Okazaki, made a film in 1985, after Judge Patel had handed down the *Korematsu* decision and while the *Yasui* and *Hirabayashi* cases were still pending, documenting the history of the cases; in addition to being added to the video collections of schools, libraries, and public television, "Unfinished Business" was nominated for an Academy Award in the "best feature documentary" category, and as a result garnered additional exposure. Thus the cases served to enlighten and educate and hence to gain public sympathy for the redress cause.

Even more important, the decision vacating the convictions swept away the last remnant of legal justification for the evacuation and internment, making the argument to correct the government's wartime mistakes all the more compelling. The cases brought to light documents that revealed government and military officials to have purposely suppressed information proving the loyalty of Japanese Americans and disputing the need to evacuate them from the West Coast. These government documents themselves gave legitimacy to the redress cause. Further, the vacated convictions wiped away any legal basis for a nay vote on the redress legislation on the grounds that there had been at least some military necessity for the orders.[27] A lobbyist for redress could use the courts' written decisions to persuade legislators to vote for redress. Like the report of the CWRIC, the *coram nobis* decisions became an effective lobbying tool.

The *coram nobis* cases also galvanized the Japanese American community. Like the CWRIC hearings, findings, and recommendations, the cases brought the community together and gave Japanese Americans both renewed faith in their government and a reason to become involved in the lobbying campaign—an attitude that was imperative if the community was going to put forth the energy, resources, and time that a successful redress movement demanded. The *coram nobis* cases also signified a change in the climate of public sentiment. In the 1940s, political, economic, and social conditions—notably wartime hysteria, racism, and economic fear of Japanese Americans on the West Coast—allowed the evacuation and internment to take place. But about 40 years later, after the civil-rights movement of the 1960s and as the United States developed into a more racially and ethnically diverse society, general feeling toward the evacuation and internment had become a mixture of regret, embarrassment, and revulsion. The time had come for the nation to make a formal apology to the former internees—not only as a way to compensate for what had been done to them, but also as a way to rid the nation's conscience of guilt. For the legislative redress movement, the court decisions that vacated the convictions of Korematsu, Hirabayashi, and Yasui—three men whose names are indelibly etched in the minds of legal scholars and Japanese Americans alike—provided a symbolic turning point in the transformation of the American conscience.

The Class-Action Suit

While the *coram nobis* cases sought to overturn three specific convictions of the 1940s, the National Council for Japanese American Redress was seeking redress for all 120,000 former internees in federal court. Led by William Hohri of Chicago, NCJAR in 1983 filed a class-action lawsuit, *Hohri et al. v. United States*,[28] against the United States on behalf of all former evacuated and interned Japanese Americans. Convinced that in 1979 JACL had betrayed the Japanese American community by working for the establishment of the CWRIC rather than for redress itself, NCJAR concluded that the legislative route to redress was a lost cause and opted for the judicial process as the only hope. While the commission was conducting its hearings, a core group of NCJAR supporters was organized to lead the courtroom fight. Aiko Herzig-Yoshinaga, a researcher for the commission and a former internee, and her husband Jack Herzig, a retired lieutenant colonel who had served in Army counterintelligence, joined forces with Hohri. Hohri secured the services of a Washington, D.C., law firm, Landis, Cohen, Singman, and Rauh, in 1981, and, under the direction of attorneys Ellen Godbey Carson and Benjamin Zelenko, the suit began to take form.

The History of the Suit

On March 16, 1983, NCJAR filed a class-action suit in the U.S. District Court for the District of Columbia, stating 22 causes of action, including 15 violations of constitutional rights. To represent the 120,000 Japanese Americans affected by the evacuation and internment during the war, NCJAR selected 25 people to be explicitly named as plaintiffs. In a geographically diverse cross-section of affected Japanese Americans, the plaintiffs included Issei, Nisei, and Sansei; veterans, dissidents, draft resisters, and the disabled; men, women, and children. The complaint named the United States of America as the defendant and sought $27 billion in damages. The plaintiffs reached this sum by asking for $10,000 (the legal limit for a single claim) for each count for each individual represented by the suit.

Most of the counts against the government were straightforward; others were more subtle. The first fifteen were constitutional in nature. The first concerned the Fifth Amendment right to due process and pointed out that what Japanese Americans had experienced during the war was "without individual hearings or the opportunity to be heard, in violation of the Fifth Amendment's guarantee that individuals shall not be deprived of life, liberty, or property without due process of law,"[29] whereas the second stated that the Fourteenth Amendment's Equal Protection Clause was violated because the defendant's actions were based "solely on . . . race and national ancestry."[30] The third count was entitled "Unjust Taking" and, under the Fifth Amendment, contended that the government unjustly took Japanese Americans' "real and personal property, commercial interests, livelihood, reputation, liberty, and other property rights" and "failed to compensate or has provided grossly inadequate compensation for plaintiffs' losses of property rights."[31] The fourth count concerned the Fourth Amendment's protection against unreasonable searches and seizures, while the fifth was based on the Fourteenth Amendment's privileges and immunities clause. The sixth count was based on the Sixth Amendment's right to counsel and representation, the seventh on the Eighth Amendment's protection against cruel and unusual punishment, and the eighth through eleventh on the First Amendment rights to freedom of religion, freedom of speech and the press, freedom of association, and freedom to petition for redress of grievances. The twelfth count dealt with the right to privacy and protection against confinement, and the thirteenth referred to the Thirteenth Amendment, dealing with inadequate compensation for labor. The fourteenth count cited a series of presidential proclamations and orders and public laws as bills of attainder and ex post facto laws. The final constitutional count was the fifteenth, citing the denial of habeas corpus.

Although not based on constitutional rights, the sixteenth through nineteenth counts were coherent and pointed: conspiracy to deprive Japanese Americans of their civil rights, assault and battery, false arrest and imprisonment, and abuse of process and malicious intent. The twentieth count stated that the government "failed to exercise reasonable care to protect plaintiffs' property from loss, destruction, and vandalism during plaintiffs' exclusion and imprisonment. Defendant negligently failed to feed, house, and otherwise care for plaintiffs adequately during their incarceration in the prison camps."[32] The twenty-first count contended that the government broke its contract with the internees in that they peacefully evacuated their homes with the understanding (1) that they "would be free to relocate to inland communities, and there pursue normal life, work, and schooling; (2) that defendant would protect plaintiffs and their property during relocation; (3) that plaintiffs would be permitted to return to their homes as soon as the alleged temporary military emergency subsided; (4) and that plaintiffs would not be deprived of their constitutional rights."[33] The final count, "breach of fiduciary duty," was not part of the original complaint, but was added on August 8, 1983, in order to take advantage of the Supreme Court's ruling in June 1983 in *United States v. Mitchell.*[34]

On May 16, 1983, the Department of Justice, as anticipated, filed a motion to dismiss the class-action suit. The brief contained three major arguments for dismissal: (1) the statute of limitations for filing such a suit against the government—six years—had run out; (2) the Japanese American Evacuation Claims Act of 1948 already remedied losses suffered by evacuees and internees; and (3) the doctrine of sovereign immunity, which states that one cannot sue the government without the government's consent, was applicable. On July 15, 1983, NCJAR filed a rebuttal to the government's motion to dismiss, attacking all three arguments. The Department of Justice filed its reply to NCJAR's opposition, and both sides made oral arguments to Judge Louis F. Oberdorfer. In his May 17, 1984, decision, Judge Oberdorfer in essence dismissed the entire suit on the grounds of sovereign immunity and the statute of limitations. First, Oberdorfer accepted the government's contention that it had not consented to be sued on the fifteen constitutional issues, except for the count on unjust takings. Thus, the fifteen constitutional counts were reduced to a mere one. On the Evacuation Claims Act issue, the judge ruled for the plaintiffs, stating that the "Act does not bar this Court from jurisdiction over all plaintiffs' claims."[35] On the final issue, however, that of the statute of limitations, the judge ruled wholly on the side of the defendant, stating that the unjust takings had occurred during World War II and that plaintiff had only six years starting from that time to file a complaint. With that, Judge Oberdorfer dismissed NCJAR's complaint entirely.

NCJAR appealed the decision, and a three-judge panel of the U.S. Court of Appeals for the District of Columbia Circuit heard the case. In a two-to-one decision, Judge Skelly Wright wrote the majority opinion, ruling in favor of NCJAR on the statute of limitations and reversing Judge Oberdorfer's decision. Judge Wright ruled that the period to which the statute of limitations applied did not commence until the establishment of the CWRIC in July 1980, because it was only then that the federal government began to question the validity of the military necessity argument, thus making it possible for the plaintiffs to file a complaint. The appeals court remanded the case to the trial court. In response, the Department of Justice requested a rehearing *en banc*, in which a panel of Court of Appeals judges would review the three-judge decision. The request was denied in May 1986 by a six-to-five vote.

The appeals court decision was only a partial victory for NCJAR, however. Although Wright's decision reversed the statute of limitations part of Oberdorfer's decision, the sovereign immunity ruling remained intact. NCJAR's suit was thus remanded to the trial court with its original 22 causes of action reduced to one. NCJAR leaders fervently believed that the evacuation and internment involved many constitutional issues other than simply the taking of property. Consequently, they decided to appeal the case to the U.S. Supreme Court. On August 26, 1986, NCJAR filed a petition for writ of certiorari, with friends-of-the-court briefs filed by a host of other organizations, from JACL-LEC to the Board of Church and Society of the United Methodist Church. In his response brief, the solicitor general of the United States raised two issues. The first was a question of jurisdiction; owing to changes in federal law, it was unclear whether the case had been filed in the proper court. In 1982, Congress had enacted the Federal Courts Improvement Act, which consolidated appellate decisions on federal, as opposed to state or regional, issues by establishing a Federal Circuit Appeals Court. Though the first fifteen causes of action in the class-action suit fell within the newly created jurisdiction, the other causes of action fell within the jurisdiction of the regional appeals court. The solicitor general's second point was again the issue of the statute of limitations. On April 20, 1987, the Supreme Court heard the appeal of *United States v. Hohri et al.*, and on June 1, 1987, the Court handed down its much-awaited answer. In a unanimous decision written by Justice Lewis Powell, the Court agreed with the government's jurisdictional argument, vacated the D.C. Court of Appeals' decision, and remanded the district court appeal to be reheard by the U.S. Court of Appeals for the Federal Circuit.[36] The federal circuit court ruled in favor of the government. Thus, the last chance for Hohri and all other Japanese Americans was another shot at the Supreme Court. After the petition for writ of certiorari had been filed, however, Congress passed and President Reagan signed H.R. 442. As a result, the Court declined to hear the case, implying that Congress had resolved the matter. The class-action suit had finally met its unsuccessful end.[37]

The Impact of the Suit

Like the *coram nobis* cases, the Hohri class-action suit had both a general and a specific impact on the redress legislation. Again, media coverage was extensive and contributed to the educational effort that was so critical to the redress law's chances. Television crews and newspaper articles directed the nation's attention to the case, educating the country on both the facts of the wartime internment and the issues involved. Besides the usual media attention that a major court case brings, Bill Hohri himself contributed greatly to the education campaign by issuing press releases, making speeches, and writing articles.

On the negative side, NCJAR's efforts further divided an already fragmented Japanese American community. In addition to the conflicts between JACL and NCRR, relations between NCJAR and the other groups were sometimes rocky, if not contentious. JACL supported the class-action suit by sending an amicus brief on its behalf, but NCRR never openly supported the case. NCRR also accused NCJAR of siphoning off limited funds in the Japanese American community for a hopeless cause.[38]

The class-action suit also had more specific effects on the redress legislation. While the suit was before the courts, members of Congress had a rationale for ducking the issue. But soon after the case's appearance before the Supreme Court in April 1987, the redress bill suddenly began to move in Congress. With the case remanded to the U.S. Court of Appeals for the Federal Circuit, which further delayed the judicial settlement of the issue for an indeterminate length of time, and where the plaintiffs' chances of winning anything were very slim, Congress could no longer pass the buck. As one NCJAR supporter said, passing the redress legislation was "a way for Congress to settle the [class-action] suit out of court."[39] Thus, the long and rocky route of Hohri's case in the end forced members of Congress to deal with the issue themselves.

Finally, the class-action suit made H.R. 442 appear to be a relatively inexpensive form of redress. The suit demanded in excess of $27 billion. With the possibility that NCJAR could ultimately win in court, if not with this suit, then with another at some future date, the settlement in the legislation looked reasonable; it seemed prudent to pay the smaller sum now rather than risk a much larger sum later. Thus, the class-action suit may have given representatives and senators an incentive to vote for H.R. 442.

Other Factors Affecting the Passage of H.R. 442

Although the *coram nobis* cases and the class-action suit were concrete events that had specific impacts on the redress legislation, other more general factors collectively contributed to a favorable climate of opinion. The first was a sympathetic media. In general, reporters held a relatively sympathetic view toward the issue of redress. Throughout the commission hearings, the court cases, the Day of Remembrance programs, and the legislative battles, the media tended to side with the former internees, running poignant stories that highlighted the plight of old Nisei women, small children, and Japanese American families who were abruptly uprooted from their homes and sent to desolate camps, and of young soldiers going off to fight in Europe to defend the very government that had put their families and friends behind barbed wire. Local television and radio talk shows featured former internees and veterans as guests, letting them tell their own stories. Newspapers across the nation covered the events of the redress movement with front-page stories, often highlighting the stories of former internees in the local area. Although an occasional editorial or letter to the editor opposed the redress efforts on racist, fiscal, or constitutional grounds, the majority of the press coverage on the issue was supportive. Even the negative pieces benefited the movement to a certain extent, in that they contributed to public awareness of the issue.

Other specific media-related factors had an impact on the overall national climate. Individually, their impact was limited; collectively, they had a significant effect on public opinion. I cannot list every television show, photo exhibition, and commemorative ceremony that took place, but it is important to highlight some of the larger events. For example, during the legislative battle, the CBS show "60 Minutes," the most widely watched news show on television, ran a segment on the internment and redress, relating the stories and issues involved to millions of households across America. A large exhibit that featured the men, victories, defeats, and awards of the 442d Regimental Combat Team and the 100th Infantry Battalion in Europe, entitled "Go for Broke," the slogan of the Nikkei veterans, traveled throughout the country in 1984. Another circulating exhibit that opened in 1984 was "Yankee Samurai," which detailed the story of the Japanese American members of the Military Intelligence Service in the Pacific theater. An exhibition of photos of Manzanar, one of the relocation camps, by Ansel Adams, the famed nature photographer, opened in October 1984. On small screens and large ones, the story behind redress was being depicted for the American public. As mentioned earlier, Steven Okazaki, a Sansei filmmaker on the West Coast, whose other works include "Living on Tokyo Time," created the documentary "Unfinished Business" in 1985, which traced the cases of Korematsu, Hirabayashi, and Yasui. The film was shown in schools, at libraries, and at public showings. Nominated in 1986 for an Academy Award in the "best feature documentary" category, "Unfinished Business" lost to another film about a civil-rights issue, "Broken Rainbow," about the recent removal of Navajos from their native land, but the nomination brought the film many additional viewers. Television specials such as an adaptation of Jeanne Wakatsuki Houston's novel, *Farewell to Manzanar*, in 1976 and the 1986 PBS documentary on the evacuation from Bainbridge Island, Washington, entitled "Visible Target," also brought the issue into many American living rooms.

Possibly the most significant media-related event was the exhibit "A More Perfect Union," at the National Museum of American History at the Smithsonian Institution in Washington, D.C. The event, which featured the entire Japanese American experience, from immigration to prewar anti-Japanese hostility on the West Coast to the evacuation and internment to the Americans of Japanese ancestry in the military to Japanese Americans today, in an eye-catching and easy-to-understand format, was *the* exhibit with which the Smithsonian decided to celebrate the bicentennial of the U.S. Constitution in 1987. The Institution could have picked any of a host of issues that would highlight the triumph of the Constitution as a governing document; partly at the urging of Congressman Mineta, a Smithsonian regent, it chose instead to shed light on an episode in which constitutional protections failed, thus emphasizing that the Constitution is a living document that requires active nurturance to survive. The exposure that evacuation, internment, and redress gained from that one exhibit, in a museum through which thousands of American and overseas visitors pass daily, was tremendous. Through that exhibit, adults who were alive during the war became more informed about a portion of American history they may not have known about or remembered; younger adults and children expressed astonishment that such an episode could happen in the United States, the nation that their school textbooks had told them upholds the individual's rights to freedom, justice, and equality. Moreover, the exhibit signified that the nation was finally coming to grips with a sordid episode in its past, that national sentiment had shifted momentously since the 1940s. In a way, the exhibit forecast the victory of redress in Congress; it was an issue whose time had come.

CHAPTER TWELVE

The Battle for Appropriations

The story of redressing Japanese Americans for their wartime loss of constitutional rights did not end with the bill's passage on August 10, 1988; the president's signature marked one major high point in a long and complicated trail of peaks and valleys. The effort to secure the necessary funds to pay eligible internees, many of whom were quite elderly, before they died was nearly as much of an ordeal as getting H.R. 442 passed in the first place. Another round of legislative battles and politicking was necessary to ensure that surviving internees or their heirs would actually receive their $20,000 checks. In 1989, over a year after the Civil Liberties Act was signed into law, an entitlement program that commenced distribution in fiscal year 1991 and aimed to complete payments by the end of fiscal year 1993 was established, appropriating $1.25 billion for redress. The number of former internees eligible for redress payments was considerably larger than had originally been estimated, however, and the funds set aside in the 1989 entitlement package were insufficient to cover all of the eligible recipients. As a result, Congress approved new legislation to increase the amount of money appropriated to the redress payments in September 1992, ensuring that all eligible recipients would receive their compensation. The long delay and political arm-twisting that were needed to set aside the funds raise a new set of questions about the significance of H.R. 442's passage. Does its passage lose significance because Congress took so long to appropriate the money necessary to compensate internees? If a significant percentage of eligible internees—i.e., all those living at the time H.R. 442 was signed—die before their redress checks arrive (and hence the checks go not to them but to their heirs), does the success of the redress movement lose some of its luster? What does the appropriations chapter tell us about the policy-making process?

The Second Round: The Appropriations Process

Once H.R. 442 had been signed into law, congressional supporters of redress faced the uphill task of securing the necessary funds just as the Gramm-Rudman-Hollings restrictions on the federal deficit were taking hold, which meant fierce competition with many other worthy causes for the same pool of federal monies. The battle to appropriate was almost as intense as the fight for H.R. 442. The main difference this time, however, was that the appropriations process is even more of an insiders' game. In general, lobbying by outside pressure groups plays at most a small role in persuading Congress to appropriate money for a particular program; behind-the-scenes political strong-arming and favor-trading among representatives and senators are much greater factors. Former Congressman Les AuCoin (D–Oreg.), who was a member of the House Appropriations Committee, has described the process of marking up appropriations legislation in subcommittee:

> To someone sitting on the sidelines, markup might look like a bunch of accountants flipping through pages and mumbling. That description disguises what is probably one of the fastest games in town. It's where the rubber meets the road, where the dollars are placed or taken away. If you go past a page and don't realize it, a whole agency can be passed over and millions of dollars lost because you're not on your toes and missed a chance to amend. It may be past history, because amending in full committee is so much more difficult.[1]

It is not so surprising, then, that the lobbying efforts that were a force in H.R. 442's success played a much more minor role in the appropriations process. What made the difference was politicking by the Japanese American members of Congress, particularly Senator Inouye.

Five months after he signed the redress bill into law, President Reagan dealt a blow to the redress movement when his proposed budget contained no redress funds for fiscal year 1989 and only $20 million for 1990. Although Reagan's last budget proposal was not taken seriously in Congress—Reagan was about to leave office—it was a forecast of the incoming Bush administration's attitude toward redress. Although he had supported redress during the 1988 presidential election campaign, in his first budget President George Bush followed Reagan's lead and proposed only $20 million for redress for 1990. As written into law, the Civil Liberties Act of 1988 authorized up to $500 million in each fiscal year until the total of $1.25 billion had been distributed. The legislation also imposed a ten-year time limit for the payments. Consequently, redress supporters were quite surprised and upset by President Reagan's proposal. Many expressed the opinion that Reagan's support of redress had been hypocritical, just lip service. It was good politics and good image-making for him to say that he supported redress, but when it came to backing up words with deeds, his support evaporated. As Congressman Mineta said:

> In 1988, the president said we made a mistake, that we admit a wrong and will provide a restitution payment. But today, in his fiscal year 1990 budget, the president asks for a $20 million appropriation to provide that payment for no more than 1,000 of the 60,000 individuals eligible.
>
> As president in 1988 and as a veteran of World War II in 1945, Ronald Reagan said that his idea of liberty and justice for all is "the American way." Why has the president's vision narrowed now? Why did he not fight for the full $500 million funding to honor his commitment and our nation's ideals?[2]

Others expressed regret that many eligible internees would not receive their payments before they died. The eligible recipients who had been interned as adults during the war were now in old age and about 200 of them were dying each month. Although the legislation allowed for immediate heirs to receive the payments of internees who were alive at the time of the bill's passage but died before payment arrived, the delay in appropriations seemed an insult to aging internees who had already waited 45 years for redress. According to Congressman Matsui, "The president's figure is far below what is needed to make payments on a timely basis. The law states that payments be made within a ten-year period. At the president's rate, they won't be completed for another 60 years. . . . There is no reason to delay the process now. We are talking about a majority of elderly citizens who may not be here in five or ten years, much less 60 years."[3] In an effort to increase the appropriation figure, redress supporters, specifically JACL-LEC and NCRR, embarked on a new letter-writing and phone-calling campaign targeting both the Oval Office and members of both the Senate and House Appropriations Committees. JACL-LEC staff asked civil-rights and religious groups that had supported redress throughout the authorization fight to activate their state telephone trees in districts of

Appropriations Committee members. Nonetheless, no provisions for redress were included in the supplemental budget for fiscal year 1989. Fiscal year 1990 was the first chance for redress funds to be appropriated.

When the matter came before the two Appropriations subcommittees, the outlook for payments in the near future seemed bleak. On July 25, 1989, the House approved $50 million for redress in fiscal year 1990, well above the Bush Administration's recommendation, but still well below the ceiling of $500 million. Fifty million dollars would be enough to pay only 2,500 of the oldest eligible internees. The Senate recommendation was even worse—zero dollars for fiscal year 1990.

Changes in the institutional setting for the issue had created a new situation for supporters of the redress movement. Although the new leadership was not hostile to redress, some of its strongest supporters in the House were no longer in power. Both Jim Wright and Tony Coelho, the Speaker and Majority Whip during the 100th Congress, had resigned during the summer of 1989 as a result of ethics scandals involving financial wheeling and dealing. In addition, Barney Frank, whose commitment to redress had ensured that the legislation would not die in committee, had also come under critical national scrutiny for his handling of personal matters and was reprimanded by the House. Although he still held his congressional seat, the scandal cast doubt on his judgment and undercut his effectiveness as a legislator. Thus, redress had lost some pivotal support. The new House leadership—Tom Foley (D–Wash.) as Speaker, Richard Gephardt (D–Mo.) as Majority Leader, and William Gray (D–Pa.) as Majority Whip—all supported H.R. 442 and were generally in favor of appropriating federal funds for it quickly. The change in leadership caused the redress movement to lose momentum and to alter its strategy, however, making it more difficult for the appropriations process to get under way.

The basic problem facing redress appropriations was competition from other federal programs for the same pool of funds, limited in size by Gramm-Rudman-Hollings. The relevant subcommittees of both chambers' Appropriations Committees were responsible for making recommendations about funding not only redress, but also the war on drugs and the 1990 census. Logistically, the census required a certain amount of money that the subcommittee had to set aside, and it was difficult for representatives and senators to take away any funds from such a "politically correct" cause as fighting illegal drug use. In the appropriations process, redress had a turbulent time competing with two highly visible and high-priority programs for a piece of the fiscal pie.

Despite these obstacles, redress had one last hope—Senator Daniel Inouye. As the second-ranking Democrat on the Appropriations Committee, he was in a prime position to execute the necessary maneuvers to increase and accelerate the appropriations for redress. The Japanese American community understood that its chances rested with Inouye, and that only if he pulled the necessary strings would redress have a chance of being paid out before most of the eligible internees had died or become too old for the payment to make a difference in their lives. Letters from people across the nation flooded Inouye's office.

Although he did not immediately agree to fight for redress appropriations, in the end the 442d Regimental Combat Team veteran responded to the lobbying campaign. At the suggestion of JACL-LEC strategist Grant Ujifusa, former members of Inouye's Company E, officers close to Inouye, and various other Nikkei veterans in Seattle, Denver, Los Angeles, and San Francisco contacted the senator and strongly urged him to lead the appropriations battle. In the end, it was Inouye's loyalty and dedication to his fellow veterans that persuaded him to propose to the Senate that redress should be made an entitlement program, so that its supporters would not have to battle through the appropriations process each year for another few million dollars. As an entitlement program, redress would be paid out over three years, starting in fiscal year 1991. For fiscal years 1991 and 1992, $500 million would be distributed in payments each year, with the remaining $250 million to be paid in fiscal year 1993. Inouye's proposal would take redress out of the discretionary funding pool and ensure that payments would be made each year through the Office of Redress Administration (ORA), which had been established with the passage of H.R. 442 to implement the legislation. Inouye sent out an impassioned "Dear Colleague" letter to Appropriations Committee members that explained why he felt so deeply about this issue. Describing his role in getting H.R. 442 passed as "minimal" and saying that his reluctance to speak out for the issue had been "a grave disservice to many Americans, especially those with whom I served in the Army during World War II,"[4] Inouye related his experiences as a member of the 442d, a unit composed of young Americans whose families were behind barbed wire. "I am certain you must have concluded that this letter has been most difficult to compose,"[5] wrote the normally reserved Inouye:

> It is with some measure of reluctance that I share it with you. I hope that when the time for decision is upon us, you will join me in remembering those men from the internment camps who proudly and courageously

demonstrated their "last full measure of devotion" in the defense of their country. Although these men will not receive benefits from the provisions of this bill, I am certain that they will gratefully rest in peace.[6]

Inouye kept his promise to the Japanese American community to do whatever it would take to get the funds appropriated as soon as possible.

Inouye's plea was successful. In a 74–22 vote on September 29, 1989, the Senate approved a $17.3 billion appropriations package for the Commerce, Justice, and State departments that included the redress entitlement program.[7] Only Senator Jesse Helms attempted to block the appropriation through a parliamentary motion, stating that "the committee's asking us to purge someone else's guilt—that's about the size of it."[8] The legislation then went to conference committee with the House, which had approved a $50 million down payment in the fiscal year that was to start the next day. At that time, one letter signed by eighteen of the member organizations of the Washington Interreligious Staff Council and another from members of the Leadership Conference on Civil Rights were sent to conference committee members, urging them to include both the 1990 funds in the House bill and the Senate entitlement program in the appropriations bill. On October 19, 1989, House and Senate negotiators settled on the entitlement plan, with the House representatives accepting the Senate's proposal intact.[9] A week later, on October 26, the House approved the appropriations bill that included the entitlement program by a vote of 249–166, sending the legislation to the Senate for final approval.[10] On November 1, the Senate passed the legislation, but because of three amendments that it made to the House bill (unrelated to redress), the legislation had to go back to the House for another vote.[11] After another go-round in the House, the Senate approved the bill for the last time on November 8, finally sending the legislation to President Bush's desk. On November 21, 1989, President Bush signed H.R. 2991, Appropriations for Commerce, State, and the Judiciary, thus establishing redress as an entitlement program.

A Promise Fulfilled

The response to President Bush's signature on the appropriations legislation was predictable: the Japanese American community erupted in celebration, marking the end to a long, difficult, and often frustrating trek through the legislative process. In a public statement, Congressman Matsui described the feelings of all involved, from his colleagues in support of the legislation to the grass-roots workers who kept their faith in the American system throughout the entire process: "President Bush's signature on the entitlement legislation marks the appropriate end to a regrettable chapter in American history. Happily, this chapter ends constructively with a reaffirmation of the values this country was built on. This is the end of a long ordeal—an arduous national march toward redemption."[12]

October 9, 1990, marked the distribution of the first nine redress payment checks. At a ceremony at the Department of Justice, U.S. Attorney General Richard Thornburgh handed $20,000 checks to a cross-section of the oldest living former internees, ranging in age from 73 to 107 and hailing from cities across the nation. Throughout October, Justice Department and ORA officials handed out checks at regional presentation ceremonies in Los Angeles, Fresno, San Francisco, San Jose, Sacramento, Seattle, and Honolulu. By the end of the first year, 25,000 Japanese Americans had received in person or in the mail their $20,000 checks accompanied by a letter of apology from President Bush. On White House letterhead, the letter said:

> A monetary sum and words alone cannot restore lost years or erase painful memories; neither can they fully convey our Nation's resolve to rectify injustice and to uphold the rights of individuals. We can never fully right the wrongs of the past. But we can take a clear stand for justice and recognize that serious injustices were done to Japanese Americans during World War II.
>
> In enacting a law calling for restitution and offering a sincere apology, your fellow Americans have, in a very real sense, renewed their traditional commitment to the ideals of freedom, equality, and justice. You and your family have our best wishes for the future.[13]

The Final Hurdle

At the time, former internees thought they were assured that they would receive their redress payments by the end of fiscal year 1993. The first two years of payment distribution went along smoothly, but by the end of 1991, the ORA realized that the number of eligible recipients was larger than originally anticipated and that the $1.25 billion appropriated to fund the program would not be enough for them all, nor would it cover the education fund. The ORA's original estimate of eligible recipients was 62,500. Once ORA staff members clarified classes of people eligible for payment and began identifying and locating individual recipients, they learned that the actual number was closer to 80,000. The main reason for the large discrepancy was the underestimation of (1) former internees as a result of the inaccuracy of the actuarial tables used to estimate longevity; (2) "voluntary evacuees," those Japanese Americans who left the exclusion areas on their own before the formal evacuation and internment program began; and (3) eligible former evacuees and internees in Hawaii whose rights were violated similarly to the way in which mainland Japanese Americans' were. In addition, a clarification in the eligibility of Japanese Americans who served in the armed forces during the war increased the number of eligible veterans, some of whom never stayed in the camps, but whose freedom was still curtailed because they were excluded from their home communities on the West Coast.

As a result, H.R. 4551 and S. 2553, companion bills that were both entitled the Civil Liberties Act Amendments of 1992, were introduced in March 1992 in order to extend redress benefits to the estimated 20,000 eligible recipients who would not receive payments under the entitlement program. In August, both the House Judiciary Committee and the Senate Governmental Affairs Committee held hearings on the legislation, reporting it out to their respective chambers for consideration. Although passage during an atypical election year was uncertain at first, the House and Senate both passed the legislation by voice vote in September, and H.R. 4551 became Public Law no. 102-371 when President Bush signed the bill on September 27, 1992. The Civil Liberties Act Amendments increased the amount of funds authorized by the 1988 act by an additional $400 million. By late March 1994, 79,342 former internees had received their compensation.

The 1992 amendments also created a new group of eligible redress recipients: non–Japanese American spouses and parents who were evacuated or interned during the war. This group primarily consisted of women who chose to be interned with their husbands and children to keep their families together. Because they represented a new recipient category, these non–Japanese Americans were not included in the 1989 entitlement program, and as a result, funds to cover their redress payments had to be secured separately. The conference report on the fiscal year 1993 appropriations bill for the Commerce, Justice, and State Departments allowed the Justice Department to reprogram $800,000 from other accounts within the agency to cover these redress payments. In late 1992, Attorney General William Barr transferred the necessary funds from the Bureau of Prisons, which had a surplus in its account, to the Civil Rights Division, in order to ensure that the 40 individuals in this group, many of whom were elderly, received their compensation.

In 1993, once the vast majority of the individual compensation payments had been distributed, attention shifted to the financing of the Public Education Fund. H.R. 442 authorized the creation of this fund and stated its purpose is to finance efforts to educate the American public about the internment. President Bill Clinton's budget for fiscal year 1994 included $5 million for the Education Fund, but, in a time of increasing concern about fiscal restraint and the ballooning federal deficit, Congress did not appropriate any money for the fund. President Clinton's budget for fiscal year 1995 again included $5 million for the fund, but legislation to appropriate the money faces an uphill battle, as it did for fiscal year 1994.

The Significance of the Entitlement Program

The question that arises out of the successful maneuver to make redress an entitlement program, immune from political bargaining, is what this chapter of the redress struggle reveals about the significance of the initial passage of the Civil Liberties Act in August 1988. When Congress seemed to be hedging on the appropriations issue, it appeared that its commitment to redress was only superficial. The president and Congress said they supported redress for Japanese Americans, but when it came to actually appropriating the necessary funds, their support waned. During the summer of 1989, when it appeared that the executive and legislative branches would balk at payments, their inaction came as a slap in the face to former internees, dying at the rate of 2,500 a year, who had already waited over 40 years to receive compensation. To pass H.R. 442 and then not appropriate the funds it called for demonstrated a "lack of moral integrity" on Congress's part, said Belle Cummins, counsel to the House Judiciary subcommittee that handled H.R. 442.[14]

Even members of Congress who had voted against H.R. 442 realized the hypocrisy of passing legislation and then not funding it. To the surprise of many, Congressman Jim Kolbe (R-Ariz.), a member of the relevant House Appropriations subcommittee who had voted against H.R. 442, was a strong proponent of funding the bill as quickly as possible. Acknowledging that the government's wartime treatment of Japanese Americans was a black mark on American history, Kolbe did not vote for redress because he believed that "it is not possible to make right the acts of discrimination through a cash payment."[15] As a member of the Appropriations Committee, however, he believed that since Congress had decided monetary compensation was the way that the nation was going to apologize to those Americans who suffered unjustly during the war, Congress now had an obligation to fund the legislation promptly.[16] Kolbe spoke out in subcommittee discussions of the matter and even wrote a letter to the chair urging Congress to fund the bill as fully as possible.

As we have seen, Congress did eventually vote for the entitlement program and an accelerated payment schedule. Had Congress not done so, the appropriations loophole might have explained why the redress law had passed despite the odds against it: representatives and senators who had no electoral reason to vote for redress did so, knowing that if their constituents' needs came into conflict with it, they could always refuse to fund the program. Thus, they could reap the benefits of appearing to be moral legislators committed to sound public policy, without suffering the potential political consequences of the substantial price tag. Since Congress did come up with the votes to guarantee funding, this hypothesis about the policy-making process fails to hold. The fact that Congress and the president agreed to the funding needed to complete the national apology to Japanese Americans supports the reasons set out earlier in this book that reelection-minded representatives and senators voted for a potentially politically disadvantageous piece of legislation: that the constitutional nature of the issue addressed led members to vote in accord with what they thought was constitutionally correct, rather than respond to constituent pressures; that the demographics of the Japanese American community and the lack of effective opposition allowed members to vote on the issue without worrying about electoral consequences; that a successful educational and lobbying campaign persuaded members of the merits of the bill; and that inside lobbying by key members of Congress played a critical part in gathering the necessary votes. The fact that many eligible internees died in the two years between passage of the bill and distribution of the first checks does lessen the symbolic significance of the legislation as restitution to those very victims of mass discrimination. But the passage of the entitlement program confirms that policy is not always driven by congressional desires for reelection.

Only when the last payment is made will the final chapter be written for individual Japanese Americans. As Congressman Mineta remarked:

> For 47 years, Americans of Japanese ancestry have sought to right the wrongs of the internment. We did so not out of any rancor or bitterness, but from our deep faith in the United States, in our Constitution, and in the American people. The 10-year legislative struggle which brought us the victory we celebrate today would not have been possible otherwise, nor would it hold the special meaning it does for all those who fought with us for justice. We now hope, and pray, that the tragedies of the internment never again occur.[17]

Conclusion

On February 19, 1942, President Franklin Delano Roosevelt issued Executive Order 9066, which led to the evacuation of West Coast Japanese Americans and their incarceration in inland concentration camps for the duration of World War II. Forty-six and a half years later, on August 10, 1988, President Ronald Reagan signed into law the Civil Liberties Act of 1988, awarding a national apology and monetary compensation to the surviving Japanese Americans affected by Roosevelt's wartime order. Never before had the government granted redress to an entire group of citizens for a deprivation of their constitutional rights. By October 1993, most of the eligible former internees (or their immediate heirs) should receive $20,000 checks from the federal government as restitution for that deprivation and for their suffering. At that time, one of the most shameful episodes in American history will formally come to a close. But it will not be forgotten or diminish in importance. On the contrary, the story of the internment and the subsequent redress campaign has already left an indelible mark on the conscience of the nation. The internment episode left the nation ashamed and disturbed. The victorious redress effort—remarkable for so many reasons—has begun to pull away the veil of shame, beginning a cleansing of the American conscience. Even more important, it has cleared the record on one of the most questionable actions ever taken by the federal government. It has restored the Japanese American community's faith in the American system and has made Japanese Americans feel whole for the first time in nearly half a century, symbolically granting them full rights to partake in all that American society has to offer. Finally, the redress victory promises all Americans that no other group will ever be incarcerated solely because of its race, religion, ethnicity, or any other unexceptional characteristic. As Senator Dan Inouye said after President Bush signed the legislation making redress an entitlement program:

> We are now at the end of a long and most painful process. It has been said that the wheels of justice grind slowly—it may seem intolerably slowly, to the victims of injustice. However, I hope that it restores a measure of faith in our nation's system of government to see it do its best to redress a wrong that has been committed. While we, individually and as a nation, must put the pain and bitter memories behind us, we must not forget them. Rather, this chapter must remain in our collective conscience as a grave reminder of what we are capable of in a time of crisis, and what we must not allow to happen again to any group, regardless of race, religion, or national origin.[1]

As this study has shown, the Japanese American redress movement is also significant for another reason: it provides a new vantage point on the legislative process. Its success qualifies the proposition that concern for re-election is the primary driving force behind congressional voting behavior; demonstrates how effective even a small and geographically concentrated interest group can be; and highlights the importance of individual legislative champions. In addition, it underscores the importance of institutional factors, which can make or break a piece of legislation, regardless of electoral interest and external pressures. Finally, it demonstrates how factors besides constituent pressures, especially political bargaining and ideology, can affect legislative outcomes.

The success of the redress campaign was the result of two forces: the nature of the legislation itself, and the convergence of a favorable institutional environment with strong community support. Because the legislation was constitutional in nature, redress supporters were able to frame the issue to appeal to members of Congress across the ideological spectrum as an all-American issue rather than a special interest. Many members agreed that redressing the loss of constitutional rights of Japanese Americans during World War II would secure the rights of all Americans, because if the government could take away the rights of one group with impunity, what was to stop it from taking away the rights of others in the future? Only by officially apologizing and paying compensation could the federal government restore the constitutional rights of all Americans. By framing the argument this way, the redress campaign built a winning coalition of diverse supporters in Congress—ideological liberals and conservatives, westerners and northerners, Democrats and Republicans.

Furthermore, the 100th Congress proved to be a nearly ideal forum for the redress law. The Senate had returned to Democratic control after six years of Republican rule. As a result, the median voter shifted leftward, to a position more favorable toward redress; more important, Democrats took over the leadership positions previously held by staunch Republican opponents of redress. Moreover, the inclusion of provisions for the Aleutian Islanders mistreated during the war gained the legislation the backing of Senator Ted Stevens, ranking member of the relevant subcommittee, and moved it to a more sympathetic committee. Together, these institutional factors all but determined the fate of the legislation. Meanwhile, in the House, an extremely advantageous leadership lineup emerged, with three strong redress supporters—Speaker Jim Wright, Majority Leader Tom Foley, and Majority Whip Tony Coelho—in the three top positions and Barney Frank, wholly committed to redress, chairing the relevant subcommittee. With institutional barriers removed by the support of leading members of both houses and of the key committee and subcommittee chairs, redress had the opportunity to come to the floor for a full vote. Finally, in both the House and the Senate, well-respected and well-liked Japanese American members made redress a personal issue, giving the redress campaign the inside connections without which few bills have a chance of passage.

At the same time, the Japanese American redress community had put the pieces in place for an effective lobbying campaign. After years of apathy, infighting, and political naïveté, the community had developed an organized and effective lobbying strategy. The Commission on Wartime Relocation and Internment of Civilians prompted Japanese Americans to come to terms with their wartime experience and enabled them to convert years of bottled-up anger and shame into the energy needed to fuel a successful campaign. Dedicated leaders emerged and developed a highly effective legislative strategy. Other civil-rights and lobbying organizations also provided support, creating a diverse coalition that mounted a strong campaign of letter-writing and personal lobbying.

Finally, the overall external environment created a relatively auspicious setting for the legislation. Related redress efforts in the courts increased congressional and public awareness and strengthened the case for redress. The sympathetic media also proved a great boon; throughout the prolonged legislative battle, articles and broadcasts on topics related to redress were common. It was the convergence of all these factors—the nature of the issue, the institutional structure of Congress, the emergence of the Japanese American community, and the prevailing attitude in American society—that made possible the passage of the Civil Liberties Act of 1988.

The success of the redress movement testifies to the limited ability of electoral interest theory to predict legislative outcomes. Had redress been a straight electoral interest story, it would have had an abrupt and dismal end. As an interest group, Japanese Americans hardly appeared to have the makings of a successful lobbying machine. Their population was too small, too geographically concentrated, too politically inactive, and too splintered to have much clout with Congress. Yet, as we have seen, this view of the legislative process is too narrow. A much more comprehensive conception of the policy-making process is needed to explain the bill's passage and the role of electoral politics in it. Reelection-minded members of the House and Senate from the majority of districts and states that had few Asian American voters faced one of two situations. If voters actively and vocally opposed redress, the lack of electoral benefit and the potential for political backlash made it difficult for a member to support H.R. 442. If there was little or no opposition to redress, however, H.R. 442 became a "free vote" with no electoral cost or benefit. This allowed members to vote their own preferences, follow their party leadership, or return favors done by other members. This was the situation in which most members found themselves. Accordingly, the support of both parties' leadership became even more important than usual; it was vital that Congressmen Mineta and Matsui and Senators Inouye and Matsunaga used their personal leverage and called in favors owed them; grass-roots lobbying in favor of redress became critical; and related judicial actions and media coverage had some influence. Thus, the success of redress can be attributed, on the one hand, to the failure of opposition groups to organize a strong attack, and, on the other, to the coordinated efforts of the Japanese American community, of the other groups that joined the campaign, and of Mineta, Matsui, Inouye, and Matsunaga. Finally, the simple merits of the redress cause should not be overlooked. Only when we take all these factors into account can we explain the passage of the Civil Liberties Act of 1988.

H.R. 442 was just one of hundreds of pieces of legislation that were passed by the 100th Congress and signed by President Reagan. Yet its passage was neither typical nor trivial. The success of the redress movement proved that the Japanese American community, despite its divisions and distaste for politics, could mount an effective lobbying campaign, and, more important, that Asian Americans could become an influential force in American politics. This is important not only to the Asian American community, but to the nation as a whole, particularly as the population of the United States moves toward a nonwhite majority by the mid–twenty-first century. The advent of a truly multiracial society will make it all the more difficult for the federal government to accommodate a citizenry of diverse races, religions, ethnicities, cultures, values, and beliefs. And in this changing political landscape, with no single effective majority, it will be crucial that all minority groups be able to articulate their needs and wants and that the government be able to respond. As the fastest-growing minority group, Asian Americans may be called on to take the lead in the next century and beyond. And if the success of the redress movement is any indication, the Asian American community should be in an adequate position to take on that responsibility and challenge.

Finally, the passage of the Civil Liberties Act breathed new life into the U.S. Constitution as it entered its third century. The Smithsonian chose the internment as the subject of its exhibit celebrating the bicentennial of the Constitution, in memory of what can happen when bigotry and war hysteria lead to a disregard for the basic principles of this country. Similarly, the story of the redress bill's success serves as a reminder of the need for the people of this nation to fight for adherence to constitutional principles in the coming decades of dramatic social change. As former Chief Justice Charles Evans Hughes once said:

> You may think that the Constitution is your security—it is nothing but a piece of paper. You may think that the statutes are your security—they are nothing but words in a book. You may think that elaborate mechanism of government is your security—it is nothing at all, unless you have sound and uncorrupted public opinion to give life to your Constitution, to give vitality to your statutes, to make efficient your government machinery.[2]

The truth of this statement is uncanny. Just ask Japanese Americans.

Appendixes

Organizational Endorsements of Redress

The following is a list of major endorsements for JACL-LEC's legislative campaign for redress. "Endorsement" often denotes organizational support for the recommendations made by the Commission on Wartime Relocation and Internment of Civilians, including individual monetary compensation for former internees. The term may also mean that an organization acknowledged the injustice of the internment, but had not addressed the question of monetary redress. As of March 17, 1987. Source: Office of Congressman Norman Y. Mineta (D-Calif.).

National Governmental Bodies and Political Organizations

Americans for Democratic Action, National Board
Congressional Black Caucus
Congressional Hispanic Caucus
Democratic Party (Platform)
National League of Cities
Republican Party (Platform)
U.S. Conference of Mayors

Statewide Governmental Bodies and Political Organizations

California State Assembly
California State Senate
California Association of Human Rights Organizations
Hawaii House of Representatives
State of Hawaii
Governor of Illinois
Illinois Committee on Intergovernmental Relations
Governor of Massachusetts
Minnesota State Legislature
State of Missouri
New Jersey General Assembly

New York State Legislature
Oregon State Legislature
Oregon State Rainbow Coalition
Washington State Democratic Central Committee
State of Washington
Governor of Washington
Western Governors' Conference
State of Wisconsin

Countywide Governmental Bodies and Political Organizations

California 2d District Board of Supervisors
Contra Costa County, California, Supervisors
King County, Washington, Democratic Central Committee
Marin County Human Rights Association
Marin County Human Rights Commission
Monterey, California, Board of Supervisors
Multnomah, Oregon, County Commissioners
Placer County, California, Supervisors
Sacramento County, California, Supervisors
San Francisco City and County, California, Supervisors
San Mateo County, California, Supervisors
Santa Clara County, California, Supervisors
Santa Cruz County, California, Board of Supervisors
Ventura County, California, Supervisors

Citywide Governmental Bodies and Political Organizations

City of Cambridge, Massachusetts
City of Chicago City Council
Cleveland, Ohio, City Council
El Cerrito, California, City Council
Marina, California, City Council
Orinda-Lafayette-Moraga, California, Council for Civic Unity
Orinda-Moraga Democratic Club
New York City Council
Mayor, City of New York
City of Philadelphia, Pennsylvania
Portland, Oregon, City Council
Richmond, California, City Council
Sacramento, California, City Council Members
Salinas, California, City Council
Salinas Valley Democratic Club
San Jose, California, City Council

Seaside, California, City Council
Seattle, Washington, City Council
Watsonville, California, City Council

Ethnic / Civil-Rights Organizations

ACLU of Monterey County
American Civil Liberties Union Foundation
Asian Pacific American Advocates of California
American Jewish Committee
American Jewish Congress
American Jewish Congress Executive Committee
American Jewish Congress, Northern California Division
Anti-Defamation League of B'nai B'rith
Anti-Defamation League, National Civil Rights Executive Committee
Chinese American Citizens Alliance
Chinese American Service League
Jewish Community Council of Greater Washington, D.C.
Jewish Community Relations Council of Greater Eastern Bay
Jewish Community Relations Council of South New Jersey
Jewish Community Relations Council of Greater Philadelphia
Jewish Community Relations Council of Seattle
Jewish Community Relations Council, National Advisory Board
National Council of La Raza
Office of Hawaiian Affairs
Pan American Nikkei Association
U.S. Commission on Civil Rights, State Advisory Chairs

Professional Organizations

American Bar Association
American Federation of Teachers
American Immigration Lawyers Association
American Orthopsychiatric Association
American Psychiatric Association
American Public Health Association
Association of Asian American Educators
California State Bar Association
California Flower Cooperative
California State Teachers' Association
Civil Rights in Education Committee, State Council, California Teachers'
    Association
National Association of Social Workers, Minority Issues Conference
National Education Association

Peralta Federation of Teachers
Philadelphia Federation of Teachers

Labor Organizations

AFL-CIO Executive Council
AFL-CIO of Florida
California Labor Federation, AFL-CIO
California Labor Federation, Executive Council, AFL-CIO
International Brotherhood of Teamsters; Chauffeurs, Warehousemen, and
    Helpers of America
International Brotherhood of Teamsters; American Communications
    Association
International Longshoremen's and Warehouse Union
Federated ILWU Auxiliaries (1985 Convention)
ILWU Auxiliaries (1986 Convention)
ILWU California Auxiliaries Nos. 16 and 17
ILWU Locals Nos. 6, 8, 10, 12, 28, 40, 50, 53, and 92
ILWU Columbia River and Northern California District Councils
Office and Professional Employees International Union (1986 Convention)
Office and Professional Employees, Local 29, AFL-CIO
Service Employees International Union, Local 87, AFL-CIO

Veterans' Groups

34th Infantry Division Association of Chicago
34th Infantry Division of Minneapolis
503 Parachute RCT Association
American Legion, Chicago Nisei Post 1183
American Legion, 6th District Council, Department of Illinois
American Legion (66th National Convention)
Jewish War Veterans of the USA
Veterans of Foreign Wars
Veterans of Foreign Wars, Americanism Committee, Department of
    California (64th Annual Convention)
Veterans of Foreign Wars, Department of California
Veterans of Foreign Wars, USA (85th National Convention)
Veterans of Foreign Wars, Department of North Dakota

Civic/Cultural Organizations

Committee on Police and Fire, Illinois
League of Women Voters, Salinas, California
Northshore Kiwanis
Salinas Bonsai Club

Satsuma Bonsai Club
Urban League of Portland

Religious Organizations

American Friends Service Committee
American Baptist Churches, USA
Asian American Baptists
Buddhist Churches of America
Buddhist Temple of Salinas
Christ Church, Diocese of California
Christian Church (Disciples of Christ), General Board
Church of Brethren, General Board
Congregation of Nevah Shalom
Disciples of Christ, General Board
Ecumenical Ministries of Oregon
Episcopal Church Center
Episcopal Church, Executive Council
Episcopal Church (Trinity) Rector, Warden and Vestry
Episcopal Asiamerica Strategies Task Force, Bay Area Convocation
Immanuel Lutheran Church Society
Japanese Presbyterian Conference
Lutheran Church in America, Committee of Reference and Counsel
Association of Evangelical Lutheran Churches
Lutheran Church, Red River Valley Synod
Presbyterian Churches: Lincoln Avenue and Parkview
Presbyterian Church of USA (1984 General Assembly)
Presbyterian Synod of Alaska
Presbytery of the Cascades
Presbytery of Riverside
Religious Society of Friends, San Francisco
Second United Unitarian Church
United Church of Christ, 14th General Synod
United Methodist Church (California-Nevada Annual Conference)
United Methodist Church (California-Pacific Annual Conference)
United Methodist Church (Pacific / Southwest Conference)
United Methodist Church, National Federation of Asian Americans
United Methodist 1987 Convocation
United Methodist Church, Board of Church and Society
United Methodist Church (1980 General Conference)
United Methodist Church, USA General Assembly
United Presbyterian Church

APPENDIX B

Executive Order 9066 Authorizing the
Secretary of War to Prescribe Military Areas

WHEREAS the successful prosecution of the war requires every possible protection against espionage and against sabotage to national-defense material, national-defense premises, and national-defense utilities as defined in Section 4, Act of April 20, 1918, 40 Stat. 533, as amended by the Act of November 30, 1940, 54 Stat. 1220, and the Act of August 21, 1941, 55 Stat. 655 (U.S.C., Title 50, Sec. 104):

Now, THEREFORE, by virtue of the authority vested in me as President of the United States, and Commander in Chief of the Army and Navy, I hereby authorize and direct the Secretary of War, and the Military Commanders whom he may from time to time designate, whenever he or any designated Commander deems such action necessary or desirable, to prescribe military areas in such places and of such extent as he or the appropriate Military Commander may determine, from which any or all persons may be excluded, and with respect to which, the right of any person to enter, remain in, or leave shall be subject to whatever restrictions the Secretary of War or the appropriate Military Commander may impose in his discretion. The Secretary of War is hereby authorized to provide for residents of any such area who are excluded therefrom, such transportation, food, shelter, and other accommodations as may be necessary, in the judgment of the Secretary of War or the said Military Commander, and until other arrangements are made, to accomplish the purpose of this order. The designation of military areas in any region or locality shall supersede designations of prohibited and restricted areas by the Attorney General under the Proclamations of December 7 and 8, 1941, and shall supersede the responsibility and authority of the Attorney General under the said Proclamations in respect of such prohibited and restricted areas.

I hereby further authorize and direct the Secretary of War and the said Military Commanders to take such other steps as he or the appropriate Military Commander may deem advisable to enforce compliance with the restrictions applicable to each Military area hereinabove authorized to be designated, including the use of Federal troops and other Federal Agencies, with authority to accept assistance of state and local agencies.

I hereby further authorize and direct all Executive Departments, independent establishments and other Federal Agencies, to assist the Secretary of War or the said Military Commanders in carrying out this Executive Order, including the furnishing of medical aid, hospitalization, food, clothing, transportation, use of land, shelter, and other supplies, equipment, utilities, facilities, and services.

This order shall not be construed as modifying or limiting in any way the authority heretofore granted under Executive Order No. 8972, dated December 12, 1941, nor shall it be construed as limiting or modifying the duty and responsibility of the Federal Bureau of Investigation, with respect to the investigation of alleged acts of sabotage or the duty and responsibility of the Attorney General and the Department of Justice under the Proclamations of December 7 and 8, 1941, prescribing regulations for the conduct and control of alien enemies, except as such duty and responsibility is superseded by the designation of military areas hereunder.

FRANKLIN D. ROOSEVELT

The White House, February 19, 1942.

Source: 3 C.F.R. (1938–43).

APPENDIX C

Public Law 100-383 [H.R. 442]
Aug. 10, 1988, 102 Stat. 903–16

An Act

To implement recommendations of the Commission on Wartime Relocation and Internment of Civilians.

Be it enacted by the Senate and House of Representatives of the United States of America in Congress assembled,

SECTION 1. PURPOSES.

The purposes of this Act are to—

(1) acknowledge the fundamental injustice of the evacuation, relocation, and internment of United States citizens and permanent resident aliens of Japanese ancestry during World War II;

(2) apologize on behalf of the people of the United States for the evacuation, relocation, and internment of such citizens and permanent resident aliens;

(3) provide for a public education fund to finance efforts to inform the public about the internment of such individuals so as to prevent the recurrence of any similar event;

(4) make restitution to those individuals of Japanese ancestry who were interned;

(5) make restitution to Aleut residents of the Pribilof Islands and the Aleutian Islands west of Unimak Island, in settlement of United States obligations in equity and at law, for—

(A) injustices suffered and unreasonable hardships endured while those Aleut residents were under United States control during World War II;

(B) personal property taken or destroyed by United States forces during World War II;

(C) community property, including community church property, taken or destroyed by United States forces during World War II; and

(D) traditional village lands on Attu Island not rehabilitated after World War II for Aleut occupation or other productive use;

(6) discourage the occurrence of similar injustices and violations of civil liberties in the future; and

(7) make more credible and sincere any declaration of concern by the United States over violations of human rights committed by other nations.

SEC. 2. STATEMENT OF THE CONGRESS.

(a) WITH REGARD TO INDIVIDUALS OF JAPANESE ANCESTRY.—The Congress recognizes that, as described by the Commission on Wartime Relocation and Internment of Civilians, a grave injustice was done to both citizens and permanent resident aliens of Japanese ancestry by the evacuation, relocation, and internment of civilians during World War II. As the Commission documents, these actions were carried out without adequate security reasons and without any acts of espionage or sabotage documented by the Commission, and were motivated largely by racial prejudice, wartime hysteria, and a failure of political leadership. The excluded individuals of Japanese ancestry suffered enormous damages, both material and intangible, and there were incalculable losses in education and job training, all of which resulted in significant human suffering for which appropriate compensation has not been made. For these fundamental violations of the basic civil liberties and constitutional rights of these individuals of Japanese ancestry, the Congress apologizes on behalf of the Nation.

(b) WITH RESPECT TO THE ALEUTS.—The Congress recognizes that, as described by the Commission on Wartime Relocation and Internment of Civilians, the Aleut civilian residents of the Pribilof Islands and the Aleutian Islands west of Unimak Island were relocated during World War II to temporary camps in isolated regions of southeast Alaska where they remained, under United States control and in the care of the United States, until long after any potential danger to their home villages had passed. The United States failed to provide reasonable care for the Aleuts, and this resulted in widespread illness, disease, and death among the residents of the camps; and the United States further failed to protect Aleut personal and community property while such property was in its possession or under its control. The United States has not compensated the Aleuts adequately for the conversion or destruction of personal property, and the conversion or destruction of community property caused by the United States military occupation of Aleut villages during World War II. There is no remedy for injustices suffered by the Aleuts during World War II except an Act of Congress providing appropriate compensation for those losses which are attributable to the conduct of United States forces and other officials and employees of the United States.

Title I—United States Citizens of Japanese Ancestry and Resident Japanese Aliens

SEC. 101. SHORT TITLE.

This title may be cited as the "Civil Liberties Act of 1988".

SEC. 102. REMEDIES WITH RESPECT TO CRIMINAL CONVICTIONS.

(a) REVIEW OF CONVICTIONS.—The Attorney General is requested to review any case in which an individual living on the date of the enactment of this Act was, while a United States citizen or permanent resident alien of Japanese ancestry, convicted of a violation of—

(1) Executive Order Numbered 9066, dated February 19, 1942;

(2) the Act entitled "An Act to provide a penalty for violation of restrictions or orders with respect to persons entering, remaining in, leaving, or committing any act in military areas or zones", approved March 21, 1942 (56 Stat. 173); or

(3) any other Executive order, Presidential proclamation, law of the United States, directive of the Armed Forces of the United States, or other action taken by or on behalf of the United States or its agents, representatives, officers, or employees, respecting the evacuation, relocation, or internment of individuals solely on the basis of Japanese ancestry; on account of the refusal by such individual, during the evacuation, relocation, and internment period, to accept treatment which discriminated against the individual on the basis of the individual's Japanese ancestry.

(b) RECOMMENDATIONS FOR PARDONS.—Based upon any review under subsection (a), the Attorney General is requested to recommend to the President for pardon consideration those convictions which the Attorney General considers appropriate.

(c) ACTION BY THE PRESIDENT.—In consideration of the statement of the Congress set forth in section 2(a), the President is requested to offer pardons to any individuals recommended by the Attorney General under subsection (b).

SEC. 103. CONSIDERATION OF COMMISSION FINDINGS BY DEPARTMENTS AND AGENCIES.

(a) REVIEW OF APPLICATIONS BY ELIGIBLE INDIVIDUALS.—Each department and agency of the United States Government shall review with liberality, giving full consideration to the findings of the Commission and the statement of the Congress set forth in section 2(a), any application by an eligible individual for the restitution of any position, status, or entitlement lost in whole or in part because of any discriminatory act of the United States Government against such individual which was based upon the individual's Japanese ancestry and which occurred during the evacuation, relocation, and internment period.

(b) NO NEW AUTHORITY CREATED.—Subsection (a) does not create any authority to grant restitution described in that subsection, or establish any eligibility to apply for such restitution.

SEC. 104. TRUST FUND.

(a) ESTABLISHMENT.—There is established in the Treasury of the United States the Civil Liberties Public Education Fund, which shall be administered by the Secretary of the Treasury.

(b) INVESTMENT OF AMOUNTS IN THE FUND.—Amounts in the Fund shall be invested in accordance with section 9702 of title 31, United States Code.

(c) USES OF THE FUND.—Amounts in the Fund shall be available only for disbursement by the Attorney General under section 105 and by the Board under section 106.

(d) TERMINATION.—The Fund shall terminate not later than the earlier of the date on which an amount has been expended from the Fund which is equal to the amount authorized to be appropriated to the Fund by subsection (e), and any income earned on such amount, or 10 years after the date of the enactment of this Act. If all of the amounts in the Fund have not been expended by the end of that 10-year period, investments of amounts in the Fund shall be liquidated and receipts thereof deposited in the Fund and all funds remaining in the Fund shall be deposited in the miscellaneous receipts account in the Treasury.

(e) AUTHORIZATION OF APPROPRIATIONS.—There are authorized to be appropriated to the Fund $1,250,000,000, of which not more than $500,000,000 may be appropriated for any fiscal year. Any amounts appropriated pursuant to this section are authorized to remain available until expended.

SEC. 105. RESTITUTION.

(a) LOCATION AND PAYMENT OF ELIGIBLE INDIVIDUALS.—

(1) IN GENERAL.—Subject to paragraph (6), the Attorney General shall, subject to the availability of funds appropriated to the Fund for such purpose, pay out of the Fund to each eligible individual the sum of $20,000, unless such individual refuses, in the manner described in paragraph (4), to accept the payment.

(2) LOCATION OF ELIGIBLE INDIVIDUALS.—The Attorney General shall identify and locate, without requiring any application for payment and using records already in the possession of the United States Government, each eligible individual. The Attorney General should use funds and resources available to the Attorney General, including those described in subsection (c), to attempt to complete such identification and location within 12 months after the date of the enactment of this Act. Any eligible individual may notify the Attorney General that such individual is an

eligible individual, and may provide documentation therefor. The Attorney General shall designate an officer or employee to whom such notification and documentation may be sent, shall maintain a list of all individuals who submit such notification and documentation, and shall, subject to the availability of funds appropriated for such purpose, encourage, through a public awareness campaign, each eligible individual to submit his or her current address to such officer or employee. To the extent that resources referred to in the second sentence of this paragraph are not sufficient to complete the identification and location of all eligible individuals, there are authorized to be appropriated such sums as may be necessary for such purpose. In any case, the identification and location of all eligible individuals shall be completed within 12 months after the appropriation of funds under the preceding sentence. Failure to be identified and located by the end of the 12-month period specified in the preceding sentence shall not preclude an eligible individual from receiving payment under this section.

(3) NOTICE FROM THE ATTORNEY GENERAL.—The Attorney General shall, when funds are appropriated to the Fund for payments to an eligible individual under this section, notify that eligible individual in writing of his or her eligibility for payment under this section. Such notice shall inform the eligible individual that—

(A) acceptance of payment under this section shall be in full satisfaction of all claims against the United States arising out of acts described in section 108(2)(B), and

(B) each eligible individual who does not refuse, in the manner described in paragraph (4), to accept payment under this section within 18 months after receiving such written notice shall be deemed to have accepted payment for purposes of paragraph (5).

(4) EFFECT OF REFUSAL TO ACCEPT PAYMENT.—If an eligible individual refuses, in a written document filed with the Attorney General, to accept any payment under this section, the amount of such payment shall remain in the Fund and no payment may be made under this section to such individual at any time after such refusal.

(5) PAYMENT IN FULL SETTLEMENT OF CLAIMS AGAINST THE UNITED STATES.—The acceptance of payment by an eligible individual under this section shall be in full satisfaction of all claims against the United States arising out of acts described in section 108(2)(B). This paragraph shall apply to any eligible individual who does not refuse, in the manner described in paragraph (4), to accept payment under this section within 18 months after receiving the notification from the Attorney General referred to in paragraph (3).

(6) EXCLUSION OF CERTAIN INDIVIDUALS.—No payment may be made under this section to any individual who, after September 1, 1987, accepts

payment pursuant to an award of a final judgment or a settlement on a claim against the United States for acts described in section 108(2)(B), or to any surviving spouse, child, or parent of such individual to whom paragraph (6) applies.

(7) PAYMENTS IN THE CASE OF DECEASED PERSONS.—(A) In the case of an eligible individual who is deceased at the time of payment under this section, such payment shall be made only as follows:

(i) If the eligible individual is survived by a spouse who is living at the time of payment, such payment shall be made to such surviving spouse.

(ii) If there is no surviving spouse described in clause (i), such payment shall be made in equal shares to all children of the eligible individual who are living at the time of payment.

(iii) If there is no surviving spouse described in clause (i) and if there are no children described in clause (ii), such payment shall be made in equal shares to the parents of the eligible individual who are living at the time of payment.

If there is no surviving spouse, children, or parents described in clauses (i), (ii), and (iii), the amount of such payment shall remain in the Fund, and may be used only for the purposes set forth in section 106(b).

(B) After the death of an eligible individual, this subsection and subsections (c) and (f) shall apply to the individual or individuals specified in subparagraph (A) to whom payment under this section will be made, to the same extent as such subsections apply to the eligible individual.

(C) For purposes of this paragraph—

(i) the "spouse" of an eligible individual means a wife or husband of an eligible individual who was married to that eligible individual for at least 1 year immediately before the death of the eligible individual;

(ii) a "child" of an eligible individual includes a recognized natural child, a stepchild who lived with the eligible individual in a regular parent-child relationship, and an adopted child; and

(iii) a "parent" of an eligible individual includes fathers and mothers through adoption.

(b) ORDER OF PAYMENTS.—The Attorney General shall endeavor to make payments under this section to eligible individuals in the order of date of birth (with the oldest individual on the date of the enactment of this Act (or, if applicable, that individual's survivors under paragraph (6)) receiving full payment first), until all eligible individuals have received payment in full.

(c) RESOURCES FOR LOCATING ELIGIBLE INDIVIDUALS.—In attempting to locate any eligible individual, the Attorney General may use any facility or resource of any public or nonprofit organization or any other record, document, or information that may be made available to the Attorney General.

(d) ADMINISTRATIVE COSTS NOT PAID FROM THE FUND.—No costs incurred by the Attorney General in carrying out this section shall be paid from the Fund or set off against, or otherwise deducted from, any payment under this section to any eligible individual.

(e) TERMINATION OF DUTIES OF ATTORNEY GENERAL.—The duties of the Attorney General under this section shall cease when the Fund terminates.

(f) CLARIFICATION OF TREATMENT OF PAYMENTS UNDER OTHER LAWS.— Amounts paid to an eligible individual under this section—

(1) shall be treated for purposes of the internal revenue laws of the United States as damages for human suffering; and

(2) shall not be included as income or resources for purposes of determining eligibility to receive benefits described in section 3803(c)(2)(C) of title 31, United States Code, or the amount of such benefits.

SEC. 106. BOARD OF DIRECTORS OF THE FUND.

(a) ESTABLISHMENT.—There is established the Civil Liberties Public Education Fund Board of Directors, which shall be responsible for making disbursements from the Fund in the manner provided in this section.

(b) USES OF FUND.—The Board may make disbursements from the Fund only—

(1) to sponsor research and public educational activities, and to publish and distribute the hearings, findings, and recommendations of the Commission, so that the events surrounding the evacuation, relocation, and internment of United States citizens and permanent resident aliens of Japanese ancestry will be remembered, and so that the causes and circumstances of this and similar events may be illuminated and understood; and

(2) for reasonable administrative expenses of the Board, including expenses incurred under subsections (c)(3), (d), and (e).

(c) MEMBERSHIP.—

(1) APPOINTMENT.—The Board shall be composed of 9 members appointed by the President, by and with the advice and consent of the Senate, from individuals who are not officers or employees of the United States Government.

(2) TERMS.—(A) Except as provided in subparagraphs (B) and (C), members shall be appointed for terms of 3 years.

(B) Of the members first appointed—

(i) 5 shall be appointed for terms of 3 years, and

(ii) 4 shall be appointed for terms of 2 years,

as designated by the President at the time of appointment.

(C) Any member appointed to fill a vacancy occurring before the expiration of the term for which such member's predecessor was appointed shall be appointed only for the remainder of such term. A member may serve after the expiration of such member's term until such member's successor has taken office. No individual may be appointed as a member for more than 2 consecutive terms.

(3) COMPENSATION.—Members of the Board shall serve without pay, except that members of the Board shall be entitled to reimbursement for travel, subsistence, and other necessary expenses incurred by them in carrying out the functions of the Board, in the same manner as persons employed intermittently in the United States Government are allowed expenses under section 5703 of title 5, United States Code.

(4) QUORUM.—5 members of the Board shall constitute a quorum but a lesser number may hold hearings.

(5) CHAIR.—The Chair of the Board shall be elected by the members of the Board.

(d) DIRECTOR AND STAFF.—

(1) DIRECTOR.—The Board shall have a Director who shall be appointed by the Board.

(2) ADDITIONAL STAFF.—The Board may appoint and fix the pay of such additional staff as it may require.

(3) APPLICABILITY OF CIVIL SERVICE LAWS.—The Director and the additional staff of the Board may be appointed without regard to section 5311(b) of title 5, United States Code, and without regard to the provisions of such title governing appointments in the competitive service, and may be paid without regard to the provisions of chapter 51 and subchapter III of chapter 53 of such title relating to classification and General Schedule pay rates, except that the compensation of any employee of the Board may not exceed a rate equivalent to the minimum rate of basic pay payable for GS-18 of the General Schedule under section 5332(a) of such title.

(e) ADMINISTRATIVE SUPPORT SERVICES.—The Administrator of General Services shall provide to the Board on a reimbursable basis such administrative support services as the Board may request.

(f) GIFTS AND DONATIONS.—The Board may accept, use, and dispose of gifts or donations of services or property for purposes authorized under subsection (b).

(g) ANNUAL REPORTS.—Not later than 12 months after the first meeting of the Board and every 12 months thereafter, the Board shall transmit to the President and to each House of the Congress a report describing the activities of the Board.

(h) TERMINATION.—90 days after the termination of the Fund, the Board shall terminate and all obligations of the Board under this section shall cease.

SEC. 107. DOCUMENTS RELATING TO THE INTERNMENT.

(a) PRESERVATION OF DOCUMENTS IN NATIONAL ARCHIVES.—All documents, personal testimony, and other records created or received by the Commission during its inquiry shall be kept and maintained by the Archivist of the United

States who shall preserve such documents, testimony, and records in the National Archives of the United States. The Archivist shall make such documents, testimony, and records available to the public for research purposes.

(b) PUBLIC AVAILABILITY OF CERTAIN RECORDS OF THE HOUSE OF REPRE-SENTATIVES.—(1) The Clerk of the House of Representatives is authorized to permit the Archivist of the United States to make available for use records of the House not classified for national security purposes, which have been in existence for not less than thirty years, relating to the evacuation, relocation, and internment of individuals during the evacuation, relocation, and internment period.

(2) This subsection is enacted as an exercise of the rulemaking power of the House of Representatives, but is applicable only with respect to the availability of records to which it applies, and supersedes other rules only to the extent that the time limitation established by this section with respect to such records is specifically inconsistent with such rules, and is enacted with full recognition of the constitutional right of the House to change its rules at any time, in the same manner and to the same extent as in the case of any other rule of the House.

SEC. 108. DEFINITIONS.

For the purposes of this title—

(1) the term "evacuation, relocation, and internment period" means that period beginning on December 7, 1941, and ending on June 30, 1946;

(2) the term "eligible individual" means any individual of Japanese ancestry who is living on the date of the enactment of this Act and who, during the evacuation, relocation, and internment period—

(A) was a United States citizen or a permanent resident alien; and

(B)(i) was confined, held in custody, relocated, or otherwise deprived of liberty or property as a result of—

(I) Executive Order Numbered 9066, dated February 19, 1942;

(II) the Act entitled "An Act to provide a penalty for violation of restrictions or orders with respect to persons entering, remaining in, leaving, or committing any act in military areas or zones", approved March 21, 1942 (56 Stat. 173); or

(III) any other Executive order, Presidential proclamation, law of the United States, directive of the Armed Forces of the United States, or other action taken by or on behalf of the United States or its agents, representatives, officers, or employees, respecting the evacuation, relocation, or internment of individuals solely on the basis of Japanese ancestry; or

(ii) was enrolled on the records of the United States Government during the period beginning on December 7, 1941, and ending on June 30, 1946, as being in a prohibited military zone;

except that the term "eligible individual" does not include any individual who, during the period beginning on December 7, 1941, and ending on September 2, 1945, relocated to a country while the United States was at war with that country;

(3) the term "permanent resident alien" means an alien lawfully admitted into the United States for permanent residence;

(4) the term "Fund" means the Civil Liberties Public Education Fund established in section 104;

(5) the term "Board" means the Civil Liberties Public Education Fund Board of Directors established in section 106; and

(6) the term "Commission" means the Commission on Wartime Relocation and Internment of Civilians, established by the Commission on Wartime Relocation and Internment of Civilians Act (Public Law 96-317; 50 U.S.C. App. 1981 note).

SEC. 109. COMPLIANCE WITH BUDGET ACT.

No authority under this title to enter into contracts or to make payments shall be effective in any fiscal year except to such extent and in such amounts as are provided in advance in appropriations Acts. In any fiscal year, total benefits conferred by this title shall be limited to an amount not in excess of the appropriations for such fiscal year. Any provision of this title which, directly or indirectly, authorizes the enactment of new budget authority shall be effective only for fiscal year 1989 and thereafter.

Title II—Aleutian and Pribilof Islands Restitution

SEC. 201. SHORT TITLE.

This title may be cited as the "Aleutian and Pribilof Islands Restitution Act".

SEC. 202. DEFINITIONS.

As used in this title—

(1) the term "Administrator" means the person appointed by the Secretary under section 204;

(2) the term "affected Aleut villages" means the surviving Aleut villages of Akutan, Atka, Nikolski, Saint George, Saint Paul, and Unalaska, and the Aleut village of Attu, Alaska;

(3) the term "Association" means the Aleutian/Pribilof Islands Association, Inc., a nonprofit regional corporation established for the benefit of the Aleut people and organized under the laws of the State of Alaska;

(4) the term "Corporation" means the Aleut Corporation, a for-profit regional corporation for the Aleut region organized under the laws of the

State of Alaska and established under section 7 of the Alaska Native Claims Settlement Act (Public Law 92-203; 43 U.S.C. 1606);

(5) the term "eligible Aleut" means any Aleut living on the date of the enactment of this Act—

(A) who, as a civilian, was relocated by authority of the United States from his or her home village on the Pribilof Islands or the Aleutian Islands west of Unimak Island to an internment camp, or other temporary facility or location, during World War II; or

(B) who was born while his or her natural mother was subject to such relocation;

(6) the term "Secretary" means the Secretary of the Interior;

(7) the term "Fund" means the Aleutian and Pribilof Islands Restitution Fund established in section 203; and

(8) the term "World War II" means the period beginning on December 7, 1941, and ending on September 2, 1945.

SEC. 203. ALEUTIAN AND PRIBILOF ISLANDS RESTITUTION FUND.

(a) ESTABLISHMENT.—There is established in the Treasury of the United States the Aleutian and Pribilof Islands Restitution Fund, which shall be administered by the Secretary. The Fund shall consist of amounts appropriated to it pursuant to this title.

(b) REPORT.—The Secretary shall report to the Congress, not later than 60 days after the end of each fiscal year, on the financial condition of the Fund, and the results of operations of the Fund, during the preceding fiscal year and on the expected financial condition and operations of the Fund during the current fiscal year.

(c) INVESTMENT.—Amounts in the Fund shall be invested in accordance with section 9702 of title 31, United States Code.

(d) TERMINATION.—The Secretary shall terminate the Fund 3 years after the date of the enactment of this Act, or 1 year following disbursement of all payments from the Fund, as authorized by this title, whichever occurs later. On the date the Fund is terminated, all investments of amounts in the Fund shall be liquidated by the Secretary and receipts thereof deposited in the Fund and all funds remaining in the Fund shall be deposited in the miscellaneous receipts account in the Treasury.

SEC. 204. APPOINTMENT OF ADMINISTRATOR.

As soon as practicable after the date of the enactment of this Act, the Secretary shall offer to undertake negotiations with the Association, leading to the execution of an agreement with the Association to serve as Administrator under this title. The Secretary may appoint the Association as Administrator if such agreement is reached within 90 days after the date of the enactment of this title. If no such agreement is reached within such period, the Secretary shall appoint another person as Administrator under this title, after consultation with leaders of affected Aleut villages and the Corporation.

SEC. 205. COMPENSATION FOR COMMUNITY LOSSES.

(a) IN GENERAL.—Subject to the availability of funds appropriated to the Fund, the Secretary shall make payments from the Fund, in accordance with this section, as restitution for certain Aleut losses sustained in World War II.

(b) TRUST.—

(1) ESTABLISHMENT.—The Secretary shall, subject to the availability of funds appropriated for this purpose, establish a trust for the purposes set forth in this section. Such trust shall be established pursuant to the laws of the State of Alaska, and shall be maintained and operated by not more than seven trustees, as designated by the Secretary. Each affected Aleut village may submit to the Administrator a list of three prospective trustees. The Secretary, after consultation with the Administrator, affected Aleut villages, and the Corporation, shall designate not more than seven trustees from such lists as submitted.

(2) ADMINISTRATION OF TRUST.—The trust established under this subsection shall be administered in a manner that is consistent with the laws of the State of Alaska, and as prescribed by the Secretary, after consultation with representatives of eligible Aleuts, the residents of affected Aleut villages, and the Administrator.

(c) ACCOUNTS FOR THE BENEFIT OF ALEUTS.—

(1) IN GENERAL.—The Secretary shall deposit in the trust such sums as may be appropriated for the purposes set forth in this subsection. The trustees shall maintain and operate 8 independent and separate accounts in the trust for purposes of this subsection, as follows:

(A) One account for the independent benefit of the wartime Aleut residents of Attu and their descendants.

(B) Six accounts for the benefit of the 6 surviving affected Aleut villages, one each for the independent benefit of Akutan, Atka, Nikolski, Saint George, Saint Paul, and Unalaska, respectively.

(C) One account for the independent benefit of those Aleuts who, as determined by the Secretary, upon the advice of the trustees, are deserving but will not benefit directly from the accounts established under subparagraphs (A) and (B).

The trustees shall credit to the account described in subparagraph (C) an amount equal to 5 percent of the principal amount deposited by the Secretary in the trust under this subsection. Of the remaining principal amount, an amount shall be credited to each account described in subparagraphs (A) and (B) which bears the same proportion to such remaining principal amount as the Aleut civilian population, as of June 1, 1942, of the village with respect to which such account is established bears to the total civilian Aleut population on such date of all affected Aleut villages.

(2) USES OF ACCOUNTS.—The trustees may use the principal, accrued interest, and other earnings of the accounts maintained under paragraph (1) for—

(A) the benefit of elderly, disabled, or seriously ill persons on the basis of special need;

(B) the benefit of students in need of scholarship assistance;

(C) the preservation of Aleut cultural heritage and historical records;

(D) the improvement of community centers in affected Aleut villages; and

(E) other purposes to improve the condition of Aleut life, as determined by the trustees.

(3) AUTHORIZATION OF APPROPRIATIONS.—There are authorized to be appropriated $5,000,000 to the Fund to carry out this subsection.

(d) COMPENSATION FOR DAMAGED OR DESTROYED CHURCH PROPERTY.—

(1) INVENTORY AND ASSESSMENT OF PROPERTY.—The Administrator shall make an inventory and assessment of real and personal church property of affected Aleut villages which was damaged or destroyed during World War II. In making such inventory and assessment, the Administrator shall consult with the trustees of the trust established under subsection (b), residents of affected Aleut villages, affected church members and leaders, and the clergy of the churches involved. Within 1 year after the date of the enactment of this Act, the Administrator shall submit such inventory and assessment, together with an estimate of the present replacement value of lost or destroyed furnishings and artifacts, to the Secretary.

(2) REVIEW BY THE SECRETARY; DEPOSIT IN THE TRUST.—The Secretary shall review the inventory and assessment provided under paragraph (1), and shall deposit in the trust established under subsection (b) an amount reasonably calculated by the Secretary to compensate affected Aleut villages for church property lost, damaged, or destroyed during World War II.

(3) DISTRIBUTION OF COMPENSATION.—The trustees shall distribute the amount deposited in the trust under paragraph (2) for the benefit of the churches referred to in this subsection.

(4) AUTHORIZATION OF APPROPRIATIONS.—There are authorized to be appropriated to the Fund $1,400,000 to carry out this subsection.

(c) ADMINISTRATIVE AND LEGAL EXPENSES.—

(1) REIMBURSEMENT FOR EXPENSES.—The Secretary shall reimburse the Administrator, not less often than annually, for reasonable and necessary administrative and legal expenses in carrying out the Administrator's responsibilities under this title.

(2) AUTHORIZATION OF APPROPRIATIONS.—There are authorized to be appropriated to the Fund such sums as are necessary to carry out this subsection.

SEC. 206. INDIVIDUAL COMPENSATION OF ELIGIBLE ALEUTS.

(a) PAYMENTS TO ELIGIBLE ALEUTS.—In addition to payments made under section 205, the Secretary shall, in accordance with this section, make per capita payments out of the Fund to eligible Aleuts. The Secretary shall pay, subject to the availability of funds appropriated to the Fund for such payments, to each eligible Aleut the sum of $12,000.

(b) ASSISTANCE OF ATTORNEY GENERAL.—The Secretary may request the Attorney General to provide reasonable assistance in locating eligible Aleuts residing outside the affected Aleut villages, and upon such request, the Attorney General shall provide such assistance. In so doing, the Attorney General may use available facilities and resources of the International Committee of the Red Cross and other organizations.

(c) ASSISTANCE OF ADMINISTRATOR.—The Secretary may request the assistance of the Administrator in identifying and locating eligible Aleuts for purposes of this section.

(d) CLARIFICATION OF TREATMENT OF PAYMENTS UNDER OTHER LAWS.—Amounts paid to an eligible Aleut under this section—

(1) shall be treated for purposes of the internal revenue laws of the United States as damages for human suffering, and

(2) shall not be included as income or resources for purposes of determining eligibility to receive benefits described in section 3803(c)(2)(C) of title 31, United States Code, or the amount of such benefits.

(e) PAYMENT IN FULL SETTLEMENT OF CLAIMS AGAINST THE UNITED STATES.—The payment to an eligible Aleut under this section shall be in full satisfaction of all claims against the United States arising out of the relocation described in section 202(5).

(f) AUTHORIZATION OF APPROPRIATIONS.—There are authorized to be appropriated to the Fund such sums as are necessary to carry out this section.

SEC. 207. ATTU ISLAND RESTITUTION PROGRAM.

(a) PURPOSE OF SECTION.—In accordance with section (3)(c) of the Wilderness Act (78 Stat. 892; 16 U.S.C. 1132(c)), the public lands on Attu Island, Alaska, within the National Wildlife Refuge System have been designated as wilderness by section 702(1) of the Alaska National Interest Lands Conservation Act (94 Stat. 2417; 16 U.S.C. 1132 note). In order to make restitution for the loss of traditional Aleut lands and village properties on Attu Island, while preserving the present designation of Attu Island lands as part of the National Wilderness Preservation System, compensation to the Aleut people, in lieu of the conveyance of Attu Island, shall be provided in accordance with this section.

(b) ACREAGE DETERMINATION.—Not later than 90 days after the date of the enactment of this Act, the Secretary shall, in accordance with this subsection, determine the total acreage of land on Attu Island, Alaska, that, at the beginning of World War II, was subject to traditional use by the Aleut villagers of that island for subsistence and other purposes. In making such acreage determination, the Secretary shall establish a base acreage of not less than 35,000 acres within that part of eastern Attu Island traditionally used by the Aleut people, and shall, from the best available information, including information that may be submitted by representatives of the Aleut people, identify any such additional acreage on Attu Island that was subject to such use. The combination of such base acreage and such additional acreage shall constitute the acreage determination upon which payment to the Corporation under this section is-based. The Secretary shall promptly notify the Corporation of the results of the acreage determination made under this subsection.

(c) VALUATION.—

(1) DETERMINATION OF VALUE.—Not later than 120 days after the date of the enactment of this Act, the Secretary shall determine the value of the Attu Island acreage determined under subsection (b), except that—

(A) such acreage may not be valued at less than $350 per acre nor more than $500 per acre; and

(B) the total valuation of all such acreage may not exceed $15,000,000.

(2) FACTORS IN MAKING DETERMINATION.—In determining the value of the acreage under paragraph (1), the Secretary shall take into consideration such factors as the Secretary considers appropriate, including—

(A) fair market value;

(B) environmental and public interest value; and

(C) established precedents for valuation of comparable wilderness lands in the State of Alaska.

(3) NOTIFICATION OF DETERMINATION; APPEAL.—The Secretary shall promptly notify the Corporation of the determination of value made under this subsection, and such determination shall constitute the final determination of value unless the Corporation, within 30 days after the determination is made, appeals the determination to the Secretary. If such appeal is made, the Secretary shall, within 30 days after the appeal is made, review the determination in light of the appeal, and issue a final determination of the value of that acreage determined to be subject to traditional use under subsection (b).

(d) IN LIEU COMPENSATION PAYMENT.—

(1) PAYMENT.—The Secretary shall pay, subject to the availability of funds appropriated for such purpose, to the Corporation, as compensation for the Aleuts' loss of lands on Attu Island, the full amount of the value of the acreage determined under subsection (c), less the value (as determined under subsection (c)) of any land conveyed under subsection (e).

(2) PAYMENT IN FULL SETTLEMENT OF CLAIMS AGAINST THE UNITED STATES.—The payment made under paragraph (1) shall be in full satisfaction of any claim against the United States for the loss of traditional Aleut lands and village properties on Attu Island.

(e) VILLAGE SITE CONVEYANCE.—The Secretary may convey to the Corporation all right, title, and interest of the United States to the surface estate of the traditional Aleut village site on Attu Island, Alaska (consisting of approximately 10 acres) and to the surface estate of a parcel of land consisting of all land outside such village that is within 660 feet of any point on the boundary of such village. The conveyance may be made under the authority contained in section 14(h)(1) of the Alaska Native Claims Settlement Act (Public Law 92-203; 43 U.S.C. 1613(h)(1)), except that after the enactment of this Act, no site on Attu Island, Alaska, other than such traditional Aleut village site and such parcel of land, may be conveyed to the Corporation under such section 14(h)(1).

(f) AUTHORIZATION OF APPROPRIATIONS.—There are authorized to be appropriated $15,000,000 to the Secretary to carry out this section.

SEC. 208. COMPLIANCE WITH BUDGET ACT.

No authority under this title to enter into contracts or to make payments shall be effective in any fiscal year except to such extent and in such amounts as are provided in advance in appropriations Acts. In any fiscal year, the Secretary, with respect to—

(1) the Fund established under section 203,

(2) the trust established under section 205(b), and

(3) the provisions of sections 206 and 207,

shall limit the total benefits conferred to an amount not in excess of the appropriations for such fiscal year. Any provision of this title which, directly or indirectly, authorizes the enactment of new budget authority shall be effective only for fiscal year 1989 and thereafter.

SEC. 209. SEVERABILITY.

If any provision of this title, or the application of such provision to any person or circumstance, is held invalid, the remainder of this title and the application of such provision to other persons not similarly situated or to other circumstances shall not be affected by such invalidation.

Title III—Territory or Property Claims against United States

SEC. 301. EXCLUSION OF CLAIMS.

Notwithstanding any other provision of law or of this Act, nothing in this Act shall be construed as recognition of any claim of Mexico or any other country or any Indian tribe (except as expressly provided in this Act with respect to the Aleut tribe of Alaska) to any territory or other property of the United States, nor shall this Act be construed as providing any basis for compensation in connection with any such claim.

Approved August 10, 1988.

Reference Matter

Notes

Complete references for the works and interviews cited in short form are given in the References, pp. 241–46.

Introduction

1. Original estimates of surviving internees ranged from 60,000 to 65,000. The estimate of the Commission on Wartime Relocation and Internment of Civilians was 62,500. As I will explain further in Chapter Twelve, the process of identifying and locating eligible recipients of the redress money revealed the actual number to be approximately 80,000.

Chapter One

1. Chan, *Asian Americans*, p. 11.
2. Daniels, *Asian America*, p. 100.
3. Kitano, *Japanese Americans*, p. 15.
4. Chan, *Asian Americans*, pp. 27–28.
5. Nee and Nee, *Longtime Californ'*, p. 33.
6. Chan, *Asian Americans*, p. 46.
7. Ibid., pp. 30–32.
8. Chen, *The Chinese of America*, pp. 147–48.
9. Daniels, *Concentration Camps*, p. 7.
10. Daniels, "Japanese Immigrants," p. 86.
11. Takaki, *Strangers from a Different Shore*, p. 203.
12. Kitano, *Japanese Americans*, p. 28.
13. Daniels, *Concentration Camps*, p. 21.

14. Ibid., p. 24.
15. Masaoka, with Hosokawa, *Moses Masaoka*, p. 44.
16. Daniels, *Asian America*, pp. 179–82.
17. Tateishi, *And Justice for All*, p. xiii.
18. TenBroek, Barnhart, and Matson, *Prejudice*, p. 29.
19. Weglyn, *Years of Infamy*, p. 34.
20. Ibid.
21. Ibid.
22. Commission on Wartime Relocation and Internment of Civilians (CWRIC), *Personal Justice Denied*, p. 55.
23. Ibid., pp. 54–55.
24. Japanese American Citizens League (JACL), National Committee for Redress, *Japanese American Incarceration*, p. 10.
25. Lieutenant General John L. DeWitt, quoted in Takahata, "Case," p. 118.
26. Daniels, Taylor, and Kitano, eds., *Japanese Americans*, p. xvi.
27. Ibid.
28. Henry L. McLemore, quoted in Kitano, *Japanese Americans*, p. 32.
29. Daniels, *Concentration Camps*, p. 33.
30. Bosworth, *America's Concentration Camps*, pp. 46–47.
31. Kitano, *Japanese Americans*, p. 28. Kitano also mentions the American Civil Liberties Union, while Daniels, in *Asian America*, p. 218, contends that the ACLU later reluctantly urged Japanese Americans to comply with the government's evacuation orders.
32. DeWitt, quoted in Tateishi, *And Justice for All*, p. xv.
33. JACL, National Committee for Redress, *Japanese American Incarceration*, p. 11.
34. Tateishi, *And Justice for All*, pp. xv–xvi.
35. Masaoka, with Hosokawa, *Moses Masaoka*, p. 85.
36. Ibid., p. 86.
37. Executive Order 9066, 7 Fed. Reg. 1407 (1942).
38. Ibid.
39. JACL, National Committee for Redress, *Japanese American Incarceration*, pp. 12–13.
40. CWRIC, *Personal Justice Denied*, p. 289.
41. Tateishi, *And Justice for All*, p. xviii.
42. Chuman, *Bamboo People*, p. 152.
43. Myer, *Uprooted Americans*, p. 23.
44. Public Proclamation no. 1, 7 Fed. Reg. 2320 (1942).
45. Executive Order 9102, 7 Fed. Reg. 2165 (1942).
46. Myer, *Uprooted Americans*, p. 12.
47. Restrictions in Military Areas and Zones Act, Pub. L. no. 503, ch. 191, 56 Stat. 173 (1942).

48. Masaoka, with Hosokawa, *Moses Masaoka*, p. 93.

49. Ibid., p. 92.

50. Daniels, *Asian Americans*, pp. 221–22.

51. Chuman, *Bamboo People*, p. 161.

52. Tateishi, *And Justice for All*, p. xvii.

53. Takahata, "Case," p. 161. DeWitt reasoned as follows: The Japanese in the United States maintained close ties with Japan and failed to assimilate to American culture because of nonacceptance by other Americans and because of strong bonds of tradition and culture. As a result, Japanese born in America identified with their alien parents and their traditions. The Japanese also situated themselves at strategic military points on the West Coast. There had to be some disloyal Japanese who posed a security threat to the nation, and because of their strong cultural identification, it was impossible to distinguish the loyal Japanese from the disloyal.

54. JACL, National Committee for Redress, *Japanese American Incarceration*, p. 14.

55. CWRIC, *Personal Justice Denied*, pp. 284–86.

56. Ibid., p. 264.

57. Okihiro, *Cane Fires*, p. 209.

58. CWRIC, *Personal Justice Denied*, pp. 266–73.

59. Ibid., p. 277, and Okihiro, *Cane Fires*, p. 267. Some of the internees at Hawaii's army-administered camps later were sent to the WRA or Justice Department camps on the mainland.

60. Rostow, "The Japanese American Cases," p. 508.

61. Ibid., p. 494.

62. Tateishi, *And Justice for All*, p. xx.

63. Wilson and Hosokawa, *East to America*, p. 212.

64. CWRIC, *Personal Justice Denied*, pp. 2–3.

65. Japanese American Curriculum Project, *Japanese Americans*, p. 17.

66. JACL, National Committee for Redress, *Japanese American Incarceration*, p. 16.

67. CWRIC, *Personal Justice Denied*, p. 192.

68. Tateishi, *And Justice for All*, pp. xxii–xxiii.

69. CWRIC, *Personal Justice Denied*, pp. 247–51; Chan, *Asian Americans*, pp. 138–39.

70. CWRIC, *Personal Justice Denied*, pp. 251–52.

71. Masaoka, with Hosokawa, *Moses Masaoka*, p. 119.

72. CWRIC, *Personal Justice Denied*, p. 251.

73. As later chapters will show, this belief in the importance of a Japanese American military record proved correct, as pressure from Japanese American veterans precluded official and active opposition to the redress legislation by the national organizations of the Veterans of Foreign Wars and the American

Legion. Also, during the redress fight, the contributions of the Japanese American World War II units proved to be effective arguments in persuading members of Congress to support the legislation.

74. President Franklin D. Roosevelt, quoted in Masaoka, with Hosokawa, *Moses Masaoka*, p. 127.

75. O'Brien and Fugita, *Japanese American Experience*, pp. 66–68.

76. CWRIC, *Personal Justice Denied*, p. 257; Tanaka, *Go for Broke*, pp. 17, 146.

77. CWRIC, *Personal Justice Denied*, pp. 253–59.

78. Ibid., p. 254.

79. JACL, National Committee for Redress, *Japanese American Incarceration*, pp. 18-19.

80. Wilson and Hosokawa, *East to America*, p. 253.

81. 320 U.S. 81 (1943).

82. 320 U.S. 115 (1943).

83. 323 U.S. 215 (1944).

84. Tateishi, *And Justice for All*, p. xxi.

85. 323 U.S. 283 (1944).

86. Ibid.

87. Chuman, *Bamboo People*, p. 235.

88. Daniels, Taylor, and Kitano, *Japanese Americans*, p. xxi.

89. Chuman, *Bamboo People*, p. 237. The $400 million figure was in 1942 dollars.

Chapter Two

1. The general phrase "contemporary political theory of how Congress operates" refers to an amalgam of related writings and lectures of currently active political scientists that presents a widely accepted view of how Congress deals with legislation. This chapter draws on the works of Nelson Polsby, David Mayhew, Gary Jacobson, David Brady, David Baron, Kenneth Shepsle, David Rohde, and Richard Fenno, which together form a cohesive description and explanation of how institutions and other forces in the policy-making process affect the final legislative outcomes.

2. Fiorina, "Case of the Vanishing Marginals," pp. 30–38.

3. From 1932 to 1946, the outcome of the race for the presidency was predicted by which party won a majority of seats in the previous off-year congressional election. For example, in the 1930 elections, Democrats held control of the House; in 1932, Franklin D. Roosevelt, a Democrat, was elected president.

4. Mayhew, *Congress*, p. 16.

5. Jacobson, "Running Scared," pp. 39–90. The thesis of Jacobson's article is that the same conditions that made it possible for members of Congress to develop a personal vote, through casework and new campaign technologies, have made their own electoral fates more uncertain. Because challengers now

have greater access to PAC money and other campaign funds, as well as advanced polling techniques, incumbents try to raise as much money as possible either to prevent threatening challengers from entering the race or to mount expensive public-relations campaigns if they do. Members of Congress may have greater control over their own electoral fates, but at the price of continuously living on the campaign trail, even in off-election years.

6. Polsby, *Congress and the Presidency*, pp. 141–46.

7. Ibid., pp. 155–56.

8. Rohde and Shepsle, "Democratic Committee Assignments," pp. 179–201.

9. Fenno, *Congressmen*, pp. xiii–xv.

10. Ibid., pp. 1, 5–13.

11. Ibid., pp. 15, 26–30.

12. Smith and Deering, *Committees*, p. 178.

13. Ibid., p. 182.

14. Polsby, *Congress and the Presidency*, p. 154.

15. Ibid.

Chapter Three

1. For the purposes of this study, H.R. 4110, introduced by Congressman Jim Wright (D–Tex.) in October 1983, and S. 2116, introduced by Senator Spark Matsunaga (D–Hawaii) in November 1983, are considered the direct precursors to the Civil Liberties Act of 1988. As we shall see in Chapter Five, in November 1979 Congressman Mike Lowry (D–Wash.) introduced H.R. 5977 as the first bill to deal with redress. Introduced around the same time as the bill creating the Commission on Wartime Relocation and Internment of Civilians, the Lowry bill lacked support within Congress and the Japanese American community. H.R. 4110 and S. 2116 were the first bills introduced after the release of the findings and recommendations of the CWRIC. These two bills explicitly called for acceptance and implementation of the commission's findings and recommendations. Although the two bills that were finally passed in 1988 to become the Civil Liberties Act of 1988 were numbered H.R. 442 and S. 1009, they were essentially identical to the original Wright and Matsunaga bills of 1983.

2. Barone and Ujifusa, *Almanac 1984*, p. 1125. ADA ratings for a given year are based on the percentage of time each member of Congress voted in accordance with the ADA position on selected votes in that year. A high ADA rating typically suggests that the member has a relatively liberal voting record; conversely, a low ADA rating suggests a nonliberal voting record.

3. Ibid. ACLU ratings for a given year are based on the percentage of time each member of Congress voted in accordance with the ACLU position on selected votes in that Congress; a rating for 1982 is the rating for the entire 97th Congress (1981–82). A high ACLU rating typically indicates that the

member has a relatively strong voting record in defense of civil liberties during that Congress. In contrast, a low ACLU rating indicates a weak voting record in defense of civil liberties.

4. Barone and Ujifusa, *Almanac 1982*, p. 1056, and idem, *Almanac 1986*, p. 1286. From 1979 to 1984, Hall's ACU rating averaged in the 80s, peaking at 100 percent in 1984. ACU ratings for a given year are based on the percentage of time a member voted with the ACU position on selected votes for that year. A high ACU rating tends to indicate a conservative voting record for that year.

5. Barone and Ujifusa, *Almanac 1982*, p. 200.

6. Ibid. According to the 1980 census, only about 1 percent of Delaware's population was Asian American.

7. U.S. Bureau of the Census, *U.S. Census of Population: 1980*. There were 716,331 Japanese Americans in the total U.S. population of 226,545,805.

8. U.S. Bureau of the Census, *U.S. Census of Population: 1990*. The total U.S. population in 1990 was 248,709,873, of which there were 791,275 Japanese Americans.

9. U.S. Bureau of the Census, *U.S. Census of Population: 1980*.

10. U.S. Bureau of the Census, *U.S. Census of Population: 1990*.

11. Ibid.

12. Carole Uhlaner, professor at the University of California, Irvine, who conducted an Asian voter survey, quoted in Stokes, "Learning the Game," p. 2653.

13. Stokes, "Learning the Game," p. 2651.

14. Ibid., p. 2652.

15. According to the 1980 census, Asian Americans only made up 1 percent of California's Third Congressional District, which Matsui represents, and 6 percent of Mineta's Thirteenth District. In 1990, Matsui's district was 5.6 percent Asian American, while Mineta's had decreased to 5.2 percent.

16. Judy Chu, quoted in Chua-Eoan, "Strangers in Paradise," p. 35.

17. Tateishi, telephone conversation with author, Nov. 1, 1989.

18. Hohri, telephone conversation with author.

19. Ibid.

20. Hohri, *Repairing America*, p. 191.

21. Nakano, telephone conversation with author.

22. Kitashima, interview with author.

23. CWRIC, *Personal Justice Denied*, p. 18.

24. Correspondence and press releases by the American Ex-Prisoners of War and American Defenders of Bataan and Corregidor, Inc., in the files of JACL's Washington, D.C., office.

25. Baker, *Concentration Camp Conspiracy*.

26. Uyehara, interview with author.

27. *Congressional Quarterly Weekly Report* 46, no. 8 (Feb. 20, 1988): 338. The

deficit rose to $220.7 billion in 1986, decreasing to $155.1 billion in 1988, the year the Civil Liberties Act was enacted into law.

28. Willard, interview with author.

29. Japanese American Evacuation Claims Act of 1948, 50 U.S.C. App., sec. 1981.

30. CWRIC, *Personal Justice Denied*, pp. 118–21.

31. CWRIC, *Recommendations*, p. 7.   32. Ibid.

33. Ibid.   34. Willard, interview with author.

35. Congressman Dan Lungren (R–Calif.), quoted in *Congressional Record*, 100th Congress, 1st sess., 1987, vol. 133, no. 141, p. H7575.

36. Congressman Norm Shumway (R–Calif.), quoted ibid., p. H7564.

37. *Congressional Quarterly Weekly Report* 46, no. 1 (Jan. 2, 1988): 31.

38. *Fortune*, quoted in Burress, "Dark Heart," p. 7.

39. Lieutenant General John L. DeWitt, quoted in Johnson, *Japanese Through American Eyes*, p. 145.

40. O'Hare and Felt, *Asian Americans*, p. 7.

41. Givens, "Drive to Excel," p. 4.

42. O'Hare and Felt, *Asian Americans*, p. 7.

43. Ibid., p. 12.

44. Shumway, quoted in *Congressional Record*, 100th Cong., 1st sess., 1987, vol. 133, no. 141, p. H7564.

45. Lungren, quoted ibid., p. H7575.

Chapter Four

1. The content of these bills was basically the recommendations of the CWRIC, which were issued in a report in 1983. The commission, its findings and recommendations, and its impact on subsequent redress legislation will be further discussed in Chapter Five.

2. All House ADA ratings are for 1987, the year in which H.R. 442 was first passed; all Senate ratings are for 1988.

3. All House ACU ratings are for 1987; all Senate ratings are for 1988.

4. All House and Senate ACLU ratings are for the 100th Congress (1987–88).

5. The U.S. Bureau of the Census uses a category consisting of persons of Asian or Pacific Islander ancestry. The Asian subgroups include Chinese, Japanese, Filipino, Asian Indian, Korean, Vietnamese, Cambodian, Hmong, Laotian, and Thai. The Pacific Islander designation includes Hawaiians, Samoans, and Guamanians.

6. Percentages come from the 1980 census, as reported in Barone and Ujifusa, *Almanac 1986*.

7. All percentages, except those explicitly referring only to those representatives or senators physically present at the time of the vote, include the preferences of those members whose votes were paired or announced. The number of members not present who did not previously make their stances known is also

taken into account; 435 in the House and 100 in the Senate are the base numbers used for all percentages, unless otherwise noted. Thus, the percentages reflect not just the votes as recorded in the *Congressional Record*, but also the opinions of all representatives and senators, whether present or not.

8. The other three senators to vote with Helms and oppose the motion to table the amendment were Republicans: Steven Symms and James McClure of Idaho, and Hecht of Nevada.

9. Senator Jesse Helms (R–N.C.), quoted in *Congressional Record*, 100th Cong., 2d sess., 1988, vol. 134, no. 51, p. 41.

10. Senator Spark Matsunaga (D–Hawaii), quoted ibid., p. 42.

11. A study by researchers of the University of California, Irvine, and the California Institute of Technology found that in 1984, only 77 percent of Asian Americans in California were registered to vote, whereas 87 percent of whites and 88 percent of blacks were registered. A 1990 study by the Field Institute of San Francisco concluded that only 39 percent of California's Asian Americans were registered to vote, compared to 65 percent of whites, 58 percent of blacks, and 42 percent of Hispanics.

12. Stokes, "Learning the Game," p. 2652.

13. Kelly, interview with author. Kolbe eventually voted for the Lundgren Amendment to strike the monetary provisions from the legislation and against H.R. 442 in the final vote. According to Kolbe, while the internment was "indeed a sorry chapter in American history . . . it is not possible to make right the acts of discrimination through a cash payment."

Chapter Five

1. Nakano, telephone conversation with author; Mineta, interview with author.

2. Matsui, interview with author.

3. Tateishi, telephone conversation with author, Nov. 1, 1989. S. I. Hayakawa, a Republican, was the junior senator from California for one term from 1977 to 1982; thus, he was in office when redress first came to Congress's attention with the commission bill in 1979. A native of Canada, neither he nor any member of his family had experienced wartime relocation or internment. Senator Hayakawa had already publicly announced his opposition to redress, and as a result, he was not included in this meeting.

Although Hayakawa cosponsored the commission legislation because he supported the idea of a study commission to set straight the facts of the wartime episode, he never supported the concept of redress in the form of monetary compensation; in fact, he was staunchly against the idea. Because he left office before the 100th Congress, he was not a factor for or against H.R. 442, although some of his statements were later used as support for the opposition.

4. Ibid.

5. Ibid.

6. The other original cosponsors were Democrats Alan Cranston of California and Frank Church of Idaho, and Republicans S. I. Hayakawa of California and James A. McClure of Idaho. Other senators who later signed on as cosponsors included Democrats Bill Bradley of New Jersey, Mike Gravel of Alaska, Henry M. Jackson and Warren G. Magnuson of Washington, Patrick Leahy of Vermont, and John Melcher of Montana, and Republicans Barry Goldwater of Arizona and David Durenberger of Minnesota.

7. Mineta, interview with author.

8. The nine Democrats included Majority Leader Jim Wright of Texas, Majority Whip John Brademas of Indiana, Norman Mineta, Bob Matsui, Phil Burton, and Glenn Anderson of California, Peter Rodino of New Jersey, and Sidney Yates and Paul Simon of Illinois.

9. Hohri, *Repairing America*, pp. 39, 52–53.

10. Even though NCJAR opposed the commission idea, once the commission was created NCJAR supporters reluctantly gave it whatever help they could. They testified at the CWRIC hearings and offered to provide research assistance.

11. President Jimmy Carter, quoted in Hosokawa, *JACL*, p. 352.

12. Public Law no. 96-317, 94 Stat. 964 (1980).

13. Joan Bernstein, quoted in Hosokawa, *JACL*, p. 353.

14. CWRIC, *Personal Justice Denied*, p. 1. Aiko Herzig-Yoshinaga, a research associate for the CWRIC, produced much of the commission's archival research. Herzig-Yoshinaga was also active with the NCJAR and its battle for redress through the court system, as outlined in Chapter Eleven.

15. Ibid., p. 18.   16. Ibid., p. 23.

17. CWRIC, *Recommendations*, p. 6.   18. Ibid., pp. 8–10.

19. Ibid., pp. 11–12.

20. Tateishi, telephone conversation with author, Nov. 3, 1989.

21. U.S. Bureau of the Census, *Statistical Abstract*, p. 39.

22. Ibid.

23. From the testimony of Akiyo Deloyd during the Los Angeles hearings, Aug. 4, 1981. The testimony of individuals before the CWRIC are from the unpublished transcripts of the hearings.

24. From the testimony of Albert Kurihara during the Los Angeles hearings, Aug. 4, 1981.

25. From the testimony of Mary Sakaguchi Oda during the Los Angeles hearings, Aug. 4, 1981.

26. From the testimony of Amy Iwasaki Mass during the Los Angeles hearings, Aug. 4, 1981.

27. From the testimony of William Hohri during the first Washington, D.C., hearings, July 16, 1981.

28. From the testimony of Bert Nakano during the first Washington, D.C., hearings, July 16, 1981.

29. From the testimony of Min Yasui during the first Washington, D.C., hearings, July 16, 1981.

30. Hiroshi Kasigawa, quoted on KCRA-TV (Sacramento) television show, "Finnerty and Company," 1983.

31. Minami, interview with author.

Chapter Six

1. From the testimony of Senator Daniel Inouye (D–Hawaii) during the first Washington, D.C., hearings, July 14, 1981.

2. In the 97th (1981–82) and 99th (1985–86) Congresses, the Republicans' edge was 53–47. In the 98th Congress (1983–84), that margin increased to 55–45.

3. Cranston, interview with author.

4. The significance of the inclusion of the Aleutian Islander redress provisions and of the presence of Senator Ted Stevens (R–Alaska) on the Governmental Affairs Committee will be discussed in more detail in Chapter Eight.

5. Mineta, interview with author.

6. Polsby, *Congress and the Presidency*, p. 117.

7. Ibid., p. 119.

8. Ibid., p. 130.

9. Newhouse, "Profiles," p. 48.

10. Congressman Dick Cheney (R–Wyo.), quoted ibid., p. 54.

11. Carlson, "Fallen Angel," p. 18.   12. Ibid., p. 20.

13. Newhouse, "Profiles," pp. 48–49.   14. Mineta, interview with author.

15. Morganthau, with Fineman, Clift, Starr, and Turque, "Barney Frank's Story," p. 16.

16. Cummins, interview with author.

17. Fleming, interview with author.

18. Patricia Saiki, a Japanese American, represented the First District of Hawaii from 1987 to 1990. As the only Republican ever elected to the House from Hawaii, she first took office in 1987 at the beginning of the 100th Congress. Thus, she entered the redress fight late in the game, and even though she supported the redress legislation, as a freshman representative with few connections who was just trying to find her own way around the Hill, she did not play a pivotal role in getting redress passed. Also, as a native Hawaiian, she was not interned during the war and therefore had no direct personal stake in the legislation.

Although not a Japanese American, as the congressman representing the Second District of Hawaii and a friend of Senators Inouye and Matsunaga, Daniel Akaka played a small role in the redress fight. As a member of the Appropriations Committee, he was especially helpful during the funding battle.

He served in the House from 1977 to 1990 and was appointed to the Senate to fill the seat vacated by Senator Matsunaga's death in 1990.

19. Mineta, interview with author.

20. Uyehara, interview with author.

21. Other members of the conference committee included Congressmen Peter Rodino, Howard Berman, and Pat Swindall, managers on behalf of the House, and Senators John Glenn, David Pryor, Spark Matsunaga, Ted Stevens, and Warren Rudman, managers for the Senate.

22. Joint Explanatory Statement of the Committee of Conference, 1988.

Chapter Seven

1. Fleming, interview with author.

2. Henderson, interview with author.

3. A recent example of such one-on-one lobbying was Senator John Danforth's (R–Mo.) effort in the bruising confirmation battle over Clarence Thomas's nomination to the U.S. Supreme Court in 1991. Danforth put his reputation on the line for Thomas, a former aide of his, by lobbying his colleagues on Thomas's behalf and preparing the nominee for the Judiciary Committee's confirmation hearings. In a controversial vote, the Senate confirmed Thomas, 52–48. Just like Matsunaga's efforts on redress, Danforth's commitment in this case was rare and nearly unparalleled.

4. Maxa, "Front Page People," p. 4.

5. A typical example of Matsunaga's legislative accomplishments and his ability to see a vision through to the end was his commitment to peace. In his first year as a congressman from Hawaii in 1963, he introduced a bill to create a United States Peace Academy; although it seemed like an idea to which few could object, at that time Matsunaga was able to persuade only five representatives to cosponsor the legislation. Yet the idea, which appeared to be little more than a dream, became a reality 22 years later, when Congress created the U.S. Institute of Peace, despite Reagan Administration opposition. Vickie Ong, "Peace Academy, 700 Celebrate Matsunaga's Dream Come True," *Honolulu Advertiser*, Nov. 10, 1984, p. A5.

6. News Release by "The Lawmakers," June 17, 1982. Public television's "The Lawmakers," a regularly scheduled television series devoted to covering the activities of the U.S. Congress, is a production of WETA/26, Washington, D.C. At the end of 1981, "The Lawmakers" sent two surveys to all members of Congress, asking them to rate each other in a wide variety of categories; about 20 percent of each body responded, and responses were well balanced according to region, seniority, and party.

7. Masaoka, "In Tribute to Sen. Spark Matsunaga: 'Initiated Probably More Statutes of Benefit to Those of Japanese Ancestry,'" in *Pacific Citizen*, 110, no. 17, May 4, 1990, p. 6.

8. From the written testimony of Congressmen Mineta (D–Calif.) and Matsui (D–Calif.) during the first Washington, D.C., hearings, July 14, 1981.

9. Mineta, quoted in *Congressional Record*, 100th Cong., 1st sess., vol. 133, no. 141, p. H7585.

10. Matsui, quoted ibid., p. H7584.

11. Ibid.

12. Fleming, interview with author.

Chapter Eight

1. Jones, *Century of Servitude*, p. 107.

2. CWRIC, *Personal Justice Denied*, pp. 19–20.

3. Jones, *Century of Servitude*, pp. 107–9.

4. CWRIC, *Personal Justice Denied*, pp. 337–41.

5. Ibid., p. 318.

6. Cherry Kinoshita, board member, JACL–Legislative Education Committee, personal correspondence to David Eun, September 1989.

7. CWRIC, *Personal Justice Denied*, p. 1.

Chapter Nine

1. In this chapter and the next, I focus almost exclusively on the Japanese American community because the provisions for Japanese American redress made up the largest and most substantial part of H.R. 442. The Aleut community played a very small role in getting the legislation passed and essentially rode on the coattails of the Japanese American movement. The larger and more costly issue of Japanese American redress was the primary topic of the discussions surrounding the legislative battle over H.R. 442, and the success of the Japanese American community in mobilizing an effective lobbying campaign was critical to the passage of the legislation. The emphasis on the Japanese American community and the minimal attention given the Aleut community are in no way meant to denigrate the latter.

2. CWRIC, *Personal Justice Denied*, p. 117.

3. U.S. Bureau of the Census, *Statistical Abstract*, p. 39.

4. From the testimony of Harry Kawahara during the Los Angeles CWRIC hearings, Aug. 4, 1981.

5. Kinoshita, telephone conversation with author.

6. Some may question my assertion that children interned suffered less emotionally because children are the most impressionable of all age groups. Since many interned children do not have vivid memories of the experience and at the time did not really understand what was happening or feel shamed by it, however, I believe that their emotional scars are not as deep as those of the Issei and older Nisei.

7. Presidential Proclamation no. 4417, 41 Fed. Reg. 7741 (Feb. 20, 1976).

8. Ibid.

9. Hohri, *Repairing America*, pp. 29–35.

10. Hosokawa, *JACL*, p. 343.

11. Thomas, *Democracy*, p. 36.

12. Hosokawa, *JACL*, p. 344.

13. Tateishi, telephone conversation with author, Nov. 1, 1989.

14. Masaoka, with Hosokawa, *Moses Masaoka*, p. 321.

15. Tateishi, telephone conversation with author, Nov. 1, 1989; Hosokawa, *JACL*, p. 345.

16. Tateishi, telephone conversation with author, Nov. 1, 1989. William Marutani was later added to the committee.

17. *Salt Lake City Tribune* article, quoted in Hosokawa, *JACL*, p. 347.

18. Tateishi, telephone conversation with author, Nov. 1, 1989.

19. Ibid.

20. Nakano, telephone conversation with author; Kitashima, interview with author.

21. Ujifusa, interview with author.

22. Tateishi, telephone conversation with author, Nov. 3, 1989.

23. Ibid.

Chapter Ten

1. Bauer, interview with author.

2. Andrew Young, quoted in Stokes, "Learning the Game," p. 2651.

3. Stokes, "Learning the Game," p. 2651.

4. Lillian Baker, statement in opposition to S. 1009, for inclusion as testimony, Hearing on S. 1009 before the Subcommittee on Federal Services, Post Office, and Civil Service of the Committee on Governmental Affairs, United States Senate, 100th Cong., 1st sess., 1987, p. 336.

5. Mineta, interview with author.

6. Grant Ujifusa, strategy chair, JACL–LEC, speech to Spokane JACL, Feb. 1990.

7. Ujifusa, interview with author.   8. Ibid.

9. Uyehara, interview with author.   10. Roberts, interview with author.

11. Laurie Goodman, interview with author; Ujifusa, telephone conversation with author.

12. Laurie Goodman, interview with author; Ujifusa, telephone conversation with author.

13. Laurie Goodman, interview with author.

14. Uyehara, interview with author.

15. Ibid.

16. From the testimony of William L. Robinson, ABA, in Hearing on S. 1009 before the Subcommittee on Federal Services, Post Office, and Civil Service of the Committee on Governmental Affairs, p. 313.

17. Uyehara, interview with author.

18. Ibid., and Mineta, interview with author.

19. Congressmen Jack Kemp, Pat Swindall, Newt Gingrich, and Henry Hyde, "Dear Colleague" letter, June 14, 1988.

20. Kinoshita, telephone conversation with author.

21. Ibid.

22. Uyehara, interview with author.

23. Ujifusa, quoted in Naito and Scott, "Against All Odds," p. C-13.

24. Willard, interview with author.

25. Sato, interview with author; Hayashino, interview with author.

26. Ibid.

27. Stokes, "Learning the Game," p. 2652.

28. Ibid., pp. 2650, 2652.

29. Stroebel, interview with author.

30. Ujifusa, interview with author.

31. Nakano, telephone conversation with author.

Chapter Eleven

1. It should be noted that JACL leaders during the war opposed Yasui's, Hirabayashi's, and Korematsu's challenges. Although it was not reopened with the three *coram nobis* cases, a fourth case, *Ex Parte Endo*, 323 U.S. 283 (1944), also challenged the constitutionality of the evacuation and internment orders, as we saw in Chapter One. JACL supported Endo, contending that the proper way to challenge the government's orders was to comply with them first and willingly enter the camps in order to prove one's loyalty, and then to test their constitutionality in the courts.

2. Irons, *Justice at War*, pp. 81–87.

3. Minoru Yasui, quoted ibid., p. 84.

4. Irons, *Justice at War*, pp. 87–93.

5. Gordon Hirabayashi, quoted ibid., p. 88.

6. Ibid.   7. Irons, *Justice at War*, pp. 93–99.

8. 320 U.S. 81 (1943).   9. 320 U.S. 115 (1943).

10. *Hirabayashi v. United States*, 320 U.S. 81 (1943).

11. Ibid.   12. 323 U.S. 214 (1944).

13. Ibid. at 217–18.   14. Ibid. at 218–19.

15. Ibid. at 231 (Roberts, J., dissenting).

16. Ibid. at 226.

17. Ibid. at 243 (Jackson, J., dissenting).

18. Ibid. at 242 (Murphy, J., dissenting).

19. Ibid. at 238.

20. Ibid. at 240.

21. Although Judge Patel announced her opinion at the Korematsu hearing on November 10, 1983, her formal written opinion was not issued until April 19, 1984.

22. *Korematsu v. United States*, 584 F. Supp. 1406 (N.D. Cal. 1984).

23. Ibid.

24. Irons, ed., *Justice Delayed*, pp. 28–30.

25. *Hirabayashi v. United States*, 627 F. Supp. 1445 (W.D. Wash. 1986).

26. Irons, ed., *Justice Delayed*, pp. 30–46.

27. To be sure, the vacated convictions did not overturn the 1943–44 Supreme Court rulings, which still stand on the books. Rather, they only vacated the convictions and declared that evidence showed that the three men had suffered fundamental injustices in their original trials. Only the Supreme Court can overturn one of its own opinions.

28. 586 F. Supp. 769 (D.D.C. 1984), *rev'd in part*, 782 F.2d 227 (D.C. Cir. 1986), *vacated and remanded*, 482 U.S. 64 (1987), *district court ruling aff'd*, 847 F.2d 779 (Fed. Cir. 1988), *cert. denied*, 488 U.S. 925 (1988).

29. NCJAR Complaint, quoted in Hohri, *Repairing America*, p. 200.

30. Ibid.   31. Ibid.

32. Ibid., p. 201.   33. Ibid., pp. 201–2.

34. 463 U.S. 206 (1983). In *Mitchell*, the Court found that the federal government's mismanagement of timberlands on an Indian reservation breached the fiduciary duty that the United States owed to the Indians as a trustee under various statutes. NCJAR argued that the United States had assumed fiduciary duties to the internees by exercising comprehensive control over their lives, and that it had breached those duties.

35. 586 F. Supp. 769, 785 (D.D.C. 1984).

36. Hohri, *Repairing America*, p. 224.

37. Hohri, telephone conversation with author.

38. Herzig-Yoshinaga, interview with author.

39. Ibid.

Chapter Twelve

1. Congressman Les AuCoin, quoted in Dan Morgan, "Collegiality Closes Deals in '13 Sovereign States': Hill Panels Work Mostly Behind Closed Doors," *Washington Post*, July 17, 1989, p. A1.

2. Congressman Norman Mineta (D–Calif.), quoted in "Redress Activists Angry over Reagan Budget," *Hokubei Mainichi*, Jan. 11, 1989.

3. Congressman Robert Matsui (D–Calif.), quoted ibid.

4. Senator Daniel Inouye (D–Hawaii), "Dear Colleague" letter, reprinted in *Pacific Citizen* 109, no. 4, Aug. 18–25, 1989, p. 5.

5. Ibid.

6. Ibid.

7. It is ironic that redress ultimately became an entitlement program, since one of the arguments originally used by those urging passage of H.R. 442 was that redressing the wartime loss of constitutional rights was not an "entitlement" like welfare payments or affirmative-action programs. In order to ensure its full funding, however, Inouye and other redress strategists decided that creating a time-limited entitlement program—that is, setting aside federal money for redress each year for three years—was the most promising stratagem.

8. Senator Jesse Helms (R–N.C.), quoted in "Senate Votes to Pay World War II Internees," *San Francisco Chronicle*, Sept. 30, 1989, p. A20.

9. "Panel OKs Guaranteed Payments to Internees," in *Sacramento Bee*, Oct. 20, 1989, p. A4.

10. "Japanese Internees Would Get Money Under a House Bill," *New York Times*, National Edition, Oct. 27, 1989, p. A11.

11. "Senate Sends Reparations Bill to the House," *San Francisco Chronicle*, Nov. 2, 1989, p. A24.

12. Matsui, quoted in "Congressional Response to President's Signature," *Nichi Bei Times*, no. 12,285, Nov. 23, 1989, p. 1.

13. Letter of official national apology to redress recipients from President George Bush, 1990.

14. Cummins, interview with author.

15. Congressman Jim Kolbe (R–Ariz.), statement of position in defense of roll-call vote on H.R. 442, released from Kolbe's office, Sept. 18, 1988.

16. Kelly, interview with author.

17. Mineta, quoted in "Congressional Response to President's Signature," p. 1.

Conclusion

1. Senator Daniel Inouye (D–Hawaii), quoted in JACL-LEC news release, Nov. 22, 1989.

2. Chief Justice Charles Evans Hughes, quoted in Weglyn, *Years of Infamy*, p. 282.

References

Baker, Lillian. *The Concentration Camp Conspiracy: A Second Pearl Harbor.* Lawndale, Calif.: AFHA Publications, 1981.

————. *Dishonoring America: The Collective Guilt of American Japanese.* Medford, Oreg.: Webb Research Group, 1988.

Barone, Michael, and Grant Ujifusa. *Almanac of American Politics 1982.* Washington, D.C.: National Journal, 1981.

————. *Almanac of American Politics 1984.* Washington, D.C.: National Journal, 1983.

————. *Almanac of American Politics 1986.* Washington, D.C.: National Journal, 1985.

————. *Almanac of American Politics 1988.* Washington, D.C.: National Journal, 1987.

————. *Almanac of American Politics 1990.* Washington, D.C.: National Journal, 1989.

Bauer, Gary. Former assistant to President Reagan for domestic policy development. Interview with author. Washington, D.C., July 20, 1989.

Blanco, Marie. Legislative assistant to Senator Daniel K. Inouye (D–Hawaii). Interview with author. Washington, D.C., July 24, 1989.

Bosworth, Allan R. *America's Concentration Camps.* New York: W. W. Norton, 1967.

Brody, David. Special counsel and former director of the Washington, D.C., office of the Anti-Defamation League of B'nai B'rith. Interview with author. Washington, D.C., July 27, 1989.

Burress, Charles. "The Dark Heart of Japan-Bashing." *This World, San Francisco Chronicle* (Mar. 18, 1990): 7–8, 13–14.

Carlson, Margaret. "Fallen Angel." *New Republic* 200, no. 24 (June 12, 1989): 18–21.

Chan, Sucheng. *Asian Americans: An Interpretive History.* Boston: Twayne, 1991.

Chen, Jack. *The Chinese of America.* San Francisco: Harper and Row, 1980.

Chua-Eoan, Howard G. "Strangers in Paradise." *Time* 135, no. 15 (Apr. 9, 1990): 32–35.

Chuman, Frank F. *The Bamboo People: The Law and Japanese Americans.* Del Mar, Calif.: Publisher's, 1976.

Commission on Wartime Relocation and Internment of Civilians. *Personal Justice Denied.* Washington, D.C.: G.P.O., 1982.

———. *Personal Justice Denied.* Part II, *Recommendations.* Washington, D.C.: G.P.O., 1983.

———. Unpublished hearings transcripts, July–Dec. 1981. Record Group 220. National Archives.

Congressional Quarterly Weekly Report 46, no. 1 (Jan. 2, 1988): 31.

——— 46, no. 8 (Feb. 20, 1988): 388.

Congressional Record. 100th Cong., 1st sess., 1987. Vol. 133, no. 141.

———. 100th Cong., 2d sess., 1988. Vol. 134, no. 50.

———. 100th Cong., 2d sess., 1988. Vol. 134, no. 51.

Cranston, Alan. Then Democratic Senator from California. Interview with author. Washington, D.C., July 25, 1989.

Cummins, Belle. Then majority assistant counsel to House Judiciary Committee, Subcommittee on Administrative Law and Governmental Relations. Interview with author. Washington, D.C., July 25, 1989.

Daniels, Roger. *Asian America: Chinese and Japanese in the United States Since 1850.* Seattle: University of Washington Press, 1988.

———. *Concentration Camps: North America, Japanese in the United States and Canada During World War II.* Rev. ed. Malabar, Fla.: Robert E. Kriegler, 1981.

———. "Japanese Immigrants on a Western Frontier: The Issei in California, 1890–1940." In Hilary Conroy and T. Scott Miyakawa, eds., *East Across the Pacific,* 76–91. Santa Barbara, Calif.: American Bibliographical Center, Clio Press, 1972.

Daniels, Roger, Sandra C. Taylor, and Harry H. L. Kitano, eds. *Japanese Americans: From Relocation to Redress.* Salt Lake City: University of Utah Press, 1986.

Ekstrom, Ingrid. Then legislative assistant to Senator Alan Cranston (D–Calif.). Interview with author. Washington, D.C., July 25, 1989.

Fenno, Richard F., Jr. *Congressmen in Committees.* Boston: Little, Brown, 1973.

Fiorina, Morris. "The Case of the Vanishing Marginals: The Bureaucracy Did It." In Mathew D. McCubbins and Terry Sullivan, eds., *Congress: Structure and Policy,* 30–38. New York: Cambridge University Press, 1987.

Fleming, Roger. Then minority counsel to House Judiciary Committee, Subcommittee on Administrative Law and Governmental Relations. Interview with author. Washington, D.C., July 26, 1989.

Givens, Ron. "The Drive to Excel." *Newsweek on Campus* (Apr. 1984): 4–13.

Goodman, Laurie. Then legislative assistant to Senator Alan K. Simpson (R–Wyo.). Interview with author. Washington, D.C., July 20, 1989.

Goodman, Rick. Majority staff aide to Senate Governmental Affairs Committee, Subcommittee on Federal Services, Post Office, and Civil Service. Interview with author. Washington, D.C., July 26, 1989.

Hayashino, Carole. Associate director, Japanese American Citizens League, national headquarters. Interview with author. San Francisco, July 22, 1991.

Henderson, Elma. Then legislative assistant to Senator Spark M. Matsunaga (D–Hawaii). Interview with author. Washington, D.C., July 21, 1989.

Henry, William A., III. "Beyond the Melting Pot." *Time* 135, no. 15 (Apr. 9, 1990): 28–31.

Herger, Wally. Republican Congressman from the Second District of California. Interview with author. Washington, D.C., July 26, 1989.

Herzig-Yoshinaga, Aiko. Former research associate for the Commission on Wartime Relocation and Internment of Civilians and member of the National Council for Japanese American Redress. Interview with author. Falls Church, Va., Jan. 11, 1992.

Hohri, William. Chair of National Council for Japanese American Redress. Telephone conversation with author. Aug. 25, 1989.

———. *Repairing America: An Account of the Movement for Japanese-American Redress.* Pullman: Washington State University Press, 1988.

Hordes, Jess N. Director of the Washington, D.C., office of the Anti-Defamation League of B'nai B'rith. Interview with author. Washington, D.C., July 27, 1989.

Hosokawa, Bill. *JACL: In Quest of Justice.* New York: William Morrow, 1982.

———. *Nisei: The Quiet Americans.* New York: William Morrow, 1969.

Irons, Peter. *Justice at War.* New York: Oxford University Press, 1983.

———, ed. *Justice Delayed: The Record of the Japanese American Internment Cases.* Middletown, Conn.: Wesleyan University Press, 1989.

Jacobson, Gary C. "Running Scared: Elections and Congressional Politics in the 1980s." In Mathew D. McCubbins and Terry Sullivan, eds., *Congress: Structure and Policy,* 39–90. New York: Cambridge University Press, 1987.

Japanese American Citizens League, National Committee for Redress. *The Japanese American Incarceration: A Case for Redress.* 4th ed. San Francisco, 1981.

Japanese American Curriculum Project. *Japanese Americans: The Untold Story.* New York: Holt, Rinehart and Winston, 1971.

Johnson, Sheila K. *The Japanese Through American Eyes.* Stanford, Calif.: Stanford University Press, 1988.

Jones, Dorothy Knee. *A Century of Servitude: Pribilof Aleuts Under U.S. Rule.* Lanham, Md.: University Press of America, 1980.

Kagiwada, JoAnne H. Then executive director, Japanese American Citizens League–Legislative Education Committee. Interview with author. Washington, D.C., July 19, 1989.

Kelly, John B. Then legislative director to Congressman Jim Kolbe (R–Ariz.). Interview with author. Washington, D.C., July 27, 1989.

Kinoshita, Cherry. Board member, Japanese American Citizens League–Legislative Education Committee. Telephone conversation with author. Aug. 22, 1989.

Kitano, Harry H. L. *Japanese Americans: The Evolution of a Subculture.* Englewood Cliffs, N.J.: Prentice-Hall, 1969.

Kitashima, Sox. Member, National Coalition for Redress / Reparations. Interview with author. San Francisco, Aug. 21, 1989.

Mahan, Roger. Legislative director and press secretary to Congressman Wally Herger (R–Calif.). Interview with author. Washington, D.C., July 26, 1989.

Masaoka, Mike. Former Washington representative of the Japanese American Citizens League; president, Go for Broke National Nisei Veterans Organization. Interviews with author. San Francisco, June 9, 1989; Chevy Chase, Md., July 23, 1989.

Masaoka, Mike, with Bill Hosokawa. *They Call Me Moses Masaoka: An American Saga.* New York: William Morrow, 1987.

Matovcik, Ed. Then press secretary to Congressman Robert T. Matsui (D–Calif.). Interview with author. Washington, D.C., July 19, 1989.

Matsui, Robert T. Democratic Congressman from the Third District of California. Interview with author. Sacramento, Calif., Aug. 7, 1989.

Maxa, Rudy. "Front Page People." *The Washington Post Magazine* (Mar. 16, 1980): 4.

Mayhew, David R. *Congress: The Electoral Connection.* New Haven, Conn.: Yale University Press, 1974.

Minami, Dale. Lead counsel for Fred Korematsu *coram nobis* case. Interview with author. San Francisco, Aug. 25, 1989.

Mineta, Norman Y. Democratic Congressman from the Thirteenth District of California. Interview with author. Washington, D.C., July 19, 1989.

Morganthau, Tom, with Howard Fineman, Eleanor Clift, Mark Starr, and Bill Turque. "Barney Frank's Story." *Newsweek* 114, no. 13 (Sept. 25, 1989): 14–16.

Myer, Dillon S. *Uprooted Americans: The Japanese Americans and the War Relocation Authority During World War II.* Tucson: University of Arizona Press, 1971.

Naito, Calvin, and Esther Scott. "Against All Odds: The Japanese Americans' Campaign for Redress." Cambridge, Mass.: Harvard University, John F. Kennedy School of Government Case Program, 1990.

Nakano, Bert. National spokesperson, National Coalition for Redress / Reparations. Telephone conversation with author. Aug. 29, 1989.

Nee, Victor G., and Brett de Bary Nee. *Longtime Californ': A Documentary Study of an American Chinatown.* New York: Pantheon, 1972. Reissue: Stanford, Calif.: Stanford University Press, 1986.

Newhouse, John. "Profiles: The Navigator." *The New Yorker* (Apr. 10, 1989): 48–84.

O'Brien, David J., and Stephen S. Fujita. *The Japanese American Experience.* Bloomington: Indiana University Press, 1991.

O'Hare, William P., and Judy C. Felt. *Asian Americans: America's Fastest Growing Minority Group.* Washington, D.C.: Population Reference Bureau, 1991.

Okihiro, Gary Y. *Cane Fires: The Anti-Japanese Movement in Hawaii, 1865–1945.* Philadelphia: Temple University Press, 1991.

Polsby, Nelson W. *Congress and the Presidency.* 4th ed. Englewood Cliffs, N.J.: Prentice-Hall, 1986.

Reece, Michael, with Mary Lord and Richard Sandza. "America's Day of Infamy." *Newsweek* 98 (July 27, 1981): 28.

Roberts, Glenn. Former legislative director to Congressman Norman Y. Mineta (D–Calif.). Interview with author. Washington, D.C., July 24, 1989.

Rohde, David W., and Kenneth A. Shepsle. "Democratic Committee Assignments in the House of Representatives: Strategic Aspects of a Social Choice Process." In Mathew D. McCubbins and Terry Sullivan, eds., *Congress: Structure and Policy,* 179–206. New York: Cambridge University Press, 1987.

Rostow, Eugene V. "The Japanese American Cases—A Disaster." *Yale Law Journal* 54, no. 3 (June 1945): 489–533.

Sato, Frank. Former national president of the Japanese American Citizens League. Interview with author. Washington, D.C., Jan. 7, 1992.

Smith, Steven S., and Christopher J. Deering. *Committees in Congress.* Washington, D.C.: Congressional Quarterly Press, 1984.

Stokes, Bruce. "Learning the Game." *National Journal* 43 (Oct. 22, 1988): 2649–54.

Stroebel, Carol. Then legislative director to Congressman Norman Y. Mineta (D–Calif.). Interview with author. Washington, D.C., July 19, 1989.

Takahata, Sandra. "The Case of *Korematsu v. United States*: Could It Be Justified Today?" *University of Hawaii Law Review* 6 (1984): 109–75.

Takaki, Ronald. *Strangers from a Different Shore: A History of Asian Americans.* Boston: Little, Brown, 1989.

Tanaka, Chester. *Go for Broke: A Pictorial History of the Japanese American 100th Infantry Battalion and the 442nd Regimental Combat Team.* Richmond, Calif.: Go For Broke, Inc., 1982.

Tateishi, John. Former chair of the Japanese American Citizens League, National Redress Committee. Telephone conversations with author. Nov. 1, 1989; Nov. 3, 1989.

———. *And Justice for All: An Oral History of the Japanese American Detention Camps.* New York: Random House, 1984.

TenBroek, Jacobus, Edward Norton Barnhart, and Floyd W. Matson. *Prejudice, War, and the Constitution.* Berkeley: University of California Press, 1970.

Thomas, Norman. *Democracy and Japanese Americans.* New York: Post War World Council, 1942.

Ujifusa, Grant. Strategy chair, Japanese American Citizens League–Legislative Education Committee; coauthor of *Almanac of American Politics.* Telephone conversation with author. June 5, 1989. Interview with author. Chappaqua, N.Y., July 15, 1989.

U.S. Bureau of the Census. *Statistical Abstract of the United States.* Washington, D.C.: G.P.O., 1980.

———. *U.S. Census of Population: 1980.* Washington, D.C.: G.P.O.

———. *U.S. Census of Population: 1990.* Washington, D.C.: G.P.O.

U.S. Congress. House. Subcommittee on Administrative Law and Governmental Relations of the Committee on the Judiciary. *Hearings on Legislation to Implement the Recommendations of the Commission on Wartime Relocation and Internment of Civilians, H.R. 442, the Civil Liberties Act of 1987, H.R. 1631, the Aleutian and Pribilof Island Restitution Act.* 100th Cong., 1st sess., 1987.

———. Senate. Subcommittee on Federal Services, Post Office, and Civil Service of the Committee on Governmental Affairs. *Hearings on S. 1009, to Accept the Findings and to Implement the Recommendations of the Commission on Wartime Relocation and Internment of Civilians.* 100th Cong., 1st sess., 1987.

Uyehara, Grayce. Former executive director, Japanese American Citizens League–Legislative Education Committee. Interview with author. Medford, N.J., July 14, 1989.

Weglyn, Michi. *Years of Infamy: The Untold Story of America's Concentration Camps.* New York: William Morrow, 1976.

Willard, Richard. Former assistant attorney general, Civil Division. Interview with author. Washington, D.C., July 21, 1989.

Wilson, Robert A., and Bill Hosokawa. *East to America: A History of the Japanese in the United States.* New York: William Morrow, 1980.

Index

In this index "f" after a number indicates a separate reference on the next page, and "ff" indicates separate references on the next two pages. A continuous discussion over two or more pages is indicated by a span of numbers. *Passim* is used for a cluster of references in close but not consecutive sequence.

Adams, Ansel, 179

AFHA, 48f, 149

Akaka, Daniel, 108, 234n

Aleutian Islanders: H.R. 442 and redress of, 58, 108, 120–28 *passim*, 215–22 *passim*; S. 1647, 87; NCJAR report and recommendations for, 89f; internment of, 121ff

Alien Land Law (1913), 8

Almanac of American Politics (Ujifusa and Barone), 144

American Bar Association (ABA), 156f

American Civil Liberties Union (ACLU): importance of ratings, 39f, 59, 78; support of, 156f; Hirabayashi and Korematsu defense by, 167f; determining ratings of, 229–30n; ratings of 100th Congress, 231n

American Conservative Union (ACU) rating, 39f, 59, 78, 230n

American Defenders of Bataan and Corregidor, Inc., 49

American Ex–Prisoners of War, 49

American Legion, 12, 48f, 149

Americans for Democratic Action (ADA) rating, 39f, 58, 78, 229n

Americans for Historical Accuracy (AFHA), 48f, 149

Anderson, Glenn, 233n

Anti–Defamation League of B'nai B'rith (ADL), 156

Appropriations process, 182–90 *passim*, 240n

Article XIX, 7

Asian Americans: discrimination against Chinese, 7f; cultural values of, 43; diversity of, 43–47 *passim*; lack of political clout, 50; hostility toward, 52; census classification of, 74, 231n; developing political clout,

147f. *See also* Constituent district percentage; Japanese Americans

Asian Exclusion Act of 1924, 9

AuCoin, Les, 182

Australian ballot, 28

Backlash fears, 54f

Baker, Howard, 163

Baker, Lillian, 49, 149f

Balanced Budget and Emergency Control Act of 1985, 2, 50

Bannai, Paul, 42, 88f

Barnett, Arthur, 167

Barone, Michael, 144

Bauer, Gary L., 163

Belloni, Robert C., 171

Bendetsen, Karl, 171

Bennett, Charles, 82f

Bennett, William J., 163

Bentsen, Lloyd, 73

Berman, Howard, 235n

Bernstein, Joan Z., 88f

Besig, Ernest, 168

Biddle, Francis, 14, 102

Black, Hugo, 168

Boitano, Ida, 168

Brademas, John, 233n

Bradley, Bill, 233n

Brody, David, 156

Brooke, Edward W., 88

Brown v. Topeka Board of Education, 131

Burton, Phil, 233n

Bush, George, 148, 162, 183, 186f

Bushido, 136

Butler, Patrick, 163

Byrd, Robert, 102

California, 7–14 *passim*

California Gold Rush, 7

California State Grange, 12

Camp Harmony, 134

Carson, Ellen Godbey, 173

Carter, Jimmy, 87f, 100

Chafee, John, 101

Cheney, Dick, 105

Chicago Nisei Post 1183, 150

Chin, Frank, 141

Chin, Vincent, 52

Chinese American Citizens Alliance, 59

Chinese Exclusion Act of 1882, 8

Chu, Judy, 43

Church, Frank, 233n

Civilian Exclusion Order no. 57, 167

Civil Liberties Act Amendments of 1992, 188

Civil Liberties Act of 1988: signed by Reagan, 1, 177, 191; significance of, 1f, 6, 115, 118, 151–59 *passim*, 191–95 *passim*; economy as external factor, 37; barriers to passage of, 38–56 *passim*; electoral interest analysis of, 57–80 *passim*; Aleutian Islanders/Japanese Americans redress combination, 120–28 *passim*; battle for appropriations, 181–90 *passim*, 240n. *See also* Redress bill (Japanese Americans)

Civil rights, 131, 173–78 *passim*, 201. *See also* Civil Liberties Act of 1988; Discrimination

Civil Rights Act of 1964, 131

Cloture, 113

"Coalition Against the Falsification of U.S.A. History," 49. *See also* AFHA

Coble, Howard, 156

Coelho, Tony, 103ff, 184, 193

Collins, Wayne, 21

Commission on Wartime Relocation and Internment of Civilians (CWRIC), *see* CWRIC

Committee system, 32–36 *passim*. See also Congress

The Concentration Camp Conspiracy: A Second Pearl Harbor (Baker), 49

Concentration camps, 19ff, 24. *See also* Internment

Conference committee, 33

Conference report (1988), 58, 65ff

Congress: racist legislation considered by, 20; operations described, 27; rise of the personal vote in, 27–30 *passim*; power of interest groups on, 30ff; institutional features of policy–making process, 32–36 *passim*; three basic goals of membership, 34; emergence of redress camps in, 51f; redress bills introduced in 1985, 57; 100th Congress, 83f, 193, 231n; NCJAR report impact on, 90ff; lobbying by Nikkei members of, 110–19 *passim*; JACL strategy for lobbying, 154ff; hypocrisy of H.R. 442 in, 189. *See also* Electoral interest analysis; House; 100th Congress; Senate

Congressmen in Committees (Fenno), 34

Constituent district percentage: described, 58f, 73–80 *passim*; Lundgren Amendment vote and, 60f; House H.R. 442 vote and, 63f; Conference report (1988), 65ff; Hecht Amendment and, 67f; Redress bill Senate vote and, 71ff; of Mineta's district, 115. *See also* Asian Americans

Coram nobis cases, 165–73 *passim*

Cranston, Alan, 101ff, 233n

Cultural values, 43, 136, 227n

Cummins, Belle, 107, 189

Curfew: in Hawaii, 18; *Yasui v. United States*, 166f

CWRIC: redress recommendations of, 1, 44f, 57, 114f, 125; redress campaign and, 84–90 *passim*, 134; conclusions regarding Aleutian Islanders, 124; evacuation findings of, 132; significance of, 193; organizational support for recommendations listed, 199–203 *passim*; internee estimates by, 225n

Danforth, John, 235n

"Day of Remembrance" programs, 133f, 178

Deloyd, Akiyo, 95f

Democratic Congressional Campaign Committee (DCCC), 103

Democratic party: Lundgren Amendment vote and, 62f; Conference report (1988) vote, 63ff; House H.R. 442 vote, 63ff; Hecht Amendment and, 68f; First Helms Amendment vote, 69ff; Redress bill Senate vote, 71ff; control of 100th Congress Senate, 100–103 *passim*. *See also* Party affiliation

Detention centers, 16f

DeWitt, John L.: proposals regarding Japanese Americans, 11ff; issues Public Proclamation no. 1, 14; issues civilian exclusion orders, 16–19 *passim*, 48, 53, 166; 1943 justification report, 91; Supreme Court upholds, 168, 170; reasoning of Japanese cultural values by, 227n

Discrimination: against Chinese immigrant workers, 7f; against Issei and Nisei, 8ff, 93, 130f; following release of Japanese Americans, 24f. *See also* Civil rights; Prejudice

Dishonoring America: The Collective Guilt of American Japanese (Baker), 49

Doi, Gene, 159

Dole, Robert, 102
Douglas, William O., 168
Drinan, Robert F., 88
Duberstein, Kenneth, 163
Durenberger, David, 233n

1832–1946 rule, 29
Eighth Amendment, 174
Eisenhower, Dwight D., 29
Eisenhower, Milton S., 15
Election of 1956, 29
"Electoral connection" model, 30, 82
Electoral interest analysis: relevant factors listed, 58ff; Lundgren Amendment roll–call vote, 60–63 passim; House H.R. 442 vote, 63ff; House Conference report (1988) vote, 65ff; Civil Liberties Act of 1988 vote, 73–80 passim; of 100th Congress, 193f. See also Congress
Endo, Mitsuye, 23f
Ennis, Edward, 171
Eu, March Fong, 42
Evacuation: of Japanese Americans, 6, 13–19 passim, 225n; upheld by Supreme Court, 23f; of Aleutian Islanders, 121f. See also Internment
Ex ante power, 32f
Executive Order 9066: Roosevelt signs, 6, 13ff, 44, 191; German and Italian resident aliens and, 17f; upheld by Supreme Court, 23f; Ford formally rescinds, 135f; copy of, 204f
Ex Parte Endo (1944), 24, 238n
Ex post power, 33

Fair Play Committee, 22
Farewell to Manzanar (Houston), 179
Federal budget deficit, 2f, 50ff, 162
Federal Bureau of Investigation (FBI), 2f, 50ff, 162
Fenno, Richard, 34

Fifteenth Amendment, 174
Fifth Amendment, 81, 173–78 passim. See also Civil rights
Filibusters, 36, 113
Fiorina, Morris, 28
First Amendment, 174
First Helms Amendment, 69–71 passim
Fleming, Roger, 118
Flemming, Arthur S., 88
Foley, Thomas, 57, 103ff, 184, 193
Ford, Gerald, 135f
Formal rules (Congress), 36
442d Regimental Combat Team: achievements of, 22f; impact on veterans' groups, 49, 150; redress appeal of, 82f; Inouye and Matsunaga part of, 110, 112
Fourteenth Amendment, 174
Frank, Barney, 106–10 passim, 151, 184, 193
Funter Bay Cannery, 122f
Funter Bay Mine, 123

"Gains in trade" power, 33
Garza, E. (Kika) de la, 158f
Gatekeeping power, 33
"Gentleman's Agreement" of 1908, 9
Gephardt, Richard, 184
German Americans, 12, 17ff
Germany, 10
Gingrich, Newt, 147, 153, 159
Glenn, John, 101ff, 235n
Glickman, Dan, 106f
"Go for Broke" exhibit, 178
Go for Broke Nisei Veterans Association, 108
Goldberg, Arthur J., 88
Goldberg, Bernard, 141
Goldwater, Barry, 233n
Gramm–Rudman–Hollings, spending restrictions of, 2, 50, 182, 184
Grassley, Charles, 127

Gravel, Mike, 233n
Gray, William, 184
Gromoff, Father Ishmael Vincent, 88

Hall, Sam, 39, 106
Hatch, Orrin, 127
Hawaii, 18–22 *passim*, 47
Hawaii National Guard (1942), *see* 100th Infantry Battalion
Hayakawa, S. I., 42, 92, 140f, 232n
Hayes, Rutherford B., 28
Hearst newspapers, 12
Heart Mountain internment camp, 154
Hecht, Chic, 67–71 *passim*
Hecht Amendment, 67ff
Helms, Jesse, 69–71 *passim*, 186
Helms Amendment, 69–73 *passim*
Herzig, Jack, 173
Herzig–Yoshinaga, Aiko, 170, 173
Hirabayashi, Gordon, 23f, 157, 167, 179
Hirabayashi v. United States,' 23f, 103, 149, 167–73 *passim*
Hohri, William, 45, 97, 137
Hohri et al. v. United States, 173, 176ff
Hoover, J. Edgar, 14
Hosokawa, Bill, 137
House: institutional features of, 35f; S. 2116 opposition in, 39f; Lundgren Amendment roll–call vote, 60–63 *passim*; H.R. 442 vote, 63ff; Conference report (1988) vote, 65ff; Asian American constituencies of, 74f; 100th Congress changes in, 103–9 *passim*; influence of Mineta and Matsui on, 113–19 *passim*; redress funds allocations by, 184, 186. *See also* Congress; Senate
Houston, Jeanne Wakatsuki, 179
H.R. 442: community groups and passage of, 2; obstacles to, 39; introduced to 99th Congress, 57; House vote on, 58, 63ff; Lundgren Amendment roll–call vote on, 60–63 *passim*; Senate floor vote on, 71ff; significance of, 81ff; House vs. Senate versions of, 108f; Aleutian Islanders redress part of, 124–28 *passim*; support coalition for, 153–58 *passim*; Justice Department's opposing opinion, 161f; media coverage of, 165f, 178ff; NCJAR's class–action suit vs., 177f; copy of, 206–22 *passim*
H.R. 1631, 125
H.R. 2991, 186
H.R. 4110, *see* H.R. 442
H.R. 4551, 188
H.R. 5499, 86ff
Hughes, Charles Evans, 195
Humphrey, Gordon, 127
Hyde, Henry, 159

Ikejiri, Ron, 85, 141
Inouye, Daniel K.: combat record of, 23; meets with JACL leaders, 85f; success doubts expressed by, 99; as Secretary of the Majority, 101ff; lobbying influence of, 110ff, 154; proposes blue–ribbon study commission, 141f; fights for redress appropriations, 185f
Interest groups, 30ff
Internment: of Japanese American, 6, 13–19 *passim*; temporary detention centers, 16f; Baker's justification of, 49; historical ignorance regarding, 53, 133ff; unique circumstances of, 55f; testimony regarding, 95ff; of Aleutian Islanders, 121ff. *See also* Concentration camps; Evacuation
Irons, Peter, 169f
Issei: as agricultural labor, 8f; leave clearance form dilemma, 20f; impact

of internment on, 25, 132f. *See also* Japanese Americans

Italian Americans, 17f

Jackson, Henry M., 233n
Jackson, Robert H., 169
JACL: formation of, 9; cooperation with WRA, 15f; protests Class 4-C classification, 21; pushes for Nisei combat service, 22; redress strategy of, 45ff, 85f, 90f, 154ff; Seattle Plan, 87, 124f; early redress strategy of, 137-40 *passim*; supports NCJAR's suit, 177; support of *Ex Parte Endo* case, 238n. *See also* NCJAR
JACL–LEC: successful lobbying by, 4, 159ff; creation and growth of, 142–45 *passim*; redress funds allocation lobbying, 183; organizational endorsements listed, 199–203 *passim*
Japan, 10f, 52f, 121
Japan–bashing phenomenon, 52f
Japanese American Citizens League (JACL), *see* JACL
Japanese American Citizens League's Legislative Education Committee (JACL–LEC), *see* JACL–LEC
Japanese American Evacuation Claims Act (1948), 51, 175
Japanese Americans: evacuation and internment of, 6, 13–19 *passim*, 24ff, 225n; immigration history of, 7ff; Issei, 8f, 20f, 25, 132f; Kibei, 9; impact of Pearl Harbor on, 11f; in Hawaii, 18f, 47, 62; in the military, 21ff, 82f, 228n; renunciation by, 21; released from concentration camps, 24; obstacles to redress lobbying by, 40–48 *passim*; Japanese American Evacuation Claims Act (1948), 50f;

model minority myth of, 53ff; from Aleutian Islands, 62; impact of NCJAR report on, 92–98 *passim*; Sansei, 94, 133ff; Yonsei, 133; eligible redress recipients, 187f; DeWitt's view of cultural values, 227n. *See also* Asian Americans; Nisei; Redress movement
Japanese American Young Democrats, 9
Japanese American Young Republicans, 9
Japanese Association, 9
Johnson, Lyndon, 105
Justice Department, 161f

Kajihara, Harry, 108, 143
Kassebaum, Nancy, 113
Kawanami, Carol, 42
Kean, Thomas, 163
Kemp, Jack, 147, 159
Kennedy, Ted, 73, 127
Kibei, 9. *See also* Japanese Americans
Kido, Saburo, 15
Kinoshita, Cherry, 134, 159f
Kirtland, John C., 108
Kolbe, Jim, 75, 189
Korean Americans, 44
Korematsu, Fred, 23f, 157, 164–68 *passim*, 179
Korematsu v. United States, 23f, 103, 149, 167–73 *passim*
Kurihara, Albert, 96

"The Lawmakers" (Public television), 235n
Leadership Conference on Civil Rights, 46, 156, 186
Leahy, Patrick, 233n
Leave clearance form (WRA), 20f
Legislation process, 30–38 *passim*, 79f. *See also* Congress

Lobbying: by interest groups, 30ff; obstacles to Japanese American, 40–48 *passim*; against redress by veterans' groups, 48f; throwaway votes and inside, 75f; by 442d veterans, 82f; by four Nikkei Congress members, 110–19 *passim*, 194; evolution of redress, 136–40 *passim*, 153–58 *passim*, 193; impact of personal, 158–63 *passim*; to the executive branch, 161ff; NCRR approach to, 163f; for redress allocation funds, 183–86 *passim*; Inouye's redress appropriations, 185f; example of John Danforth's, 235n

"Lost Battalion," 22

Lowman, David, 106

Lowry, Mike, 86

Lungren, Daniel, 51, 55, 88, 90, 148

Lungren Amendment, 60–63 *passim*

Macbeth, Angus, 89, 108

McCloy, John J., 22, 171

McClure, James A., 233n

MacLeish, Archibald, 102

McLemore, Henry, 12

MAGIC cables, 106

Magnuson, Warren G., 233n

Mail censorship, 18

Majority Leader, 104

Mamiya, Ron, 140

Manzanar relocation camp, 179

Martial law, 18

Marutani, William, 88

Masaoka, Mike, 15f, 108, 113

Mass, Amy Iwasaki, 96f

Masuda, Kazuo, 162f

Matsui, Robert: Sacramento city councilman, 42; redress supporter, 84f, 92, 104; testifies at subcommittee hearing, 108; lobbying influence of, 110–19 *passim*, 163; on redress funds allocation, 183; public statement by, 186f

Matsunaga, Spark: combat record of, 23; introduces S. 1009 to 100th Congress, 57; introduces S. 1053 to 99th Congress, 57; motion to table First Helms Amendment, 69; redress supporter, 85f, 92, 102; lobbying influence of, 110–13 *passim*, 154; personal lobbying by, 158–61 *passim*

Mayhew, David, 29f, 82

Media: "yellow peril" hysteria of, 9f; impact on Congress visibility, 29; "Day of Remembrance" programs, 133f, 178; sympathetic coverage of H.R. 442, 165f, 178ff, 193f; focus on *coram nobis* cases, 171f

Melcher, John, 233n

Military, 21, 48f, 168f, 227n. *See also* 442d Regimental Combat Team; 100th Infantry Battalion

Military Intelligence Service Language School (MISLS), 22, 49, 150, 178f

Minami, Dale, 170

Mineta, Norman: political background of, 42; becomes redress supporter, 85f, 92; on Wright's redress support, 103f; testifies at subcommittee hearing, 108; lobbying influence of, 110–19 *passim*, 154, 158–61 *passim*; urges "A More Perfect Union" exhibit, 179f; on lack of redress funds, 183; final statement by, 190

Mitchell, Hugh B., 88

Mitchell v. United States, 175

Miyatake, Henry, 87, 124, 140

Model minority myth, 53ff

Monopoly, 33

"A More Perfect Union" exhibit, 179f, 195

Moss, John, 117
Multiple regression analysis, 76ff
Munson, Curtis B., 10
Murkowski, Frank, 126
Murphy, Frank, 169

Nakano, Bert, 97
Nakata, Mike, 87
National American Legion, 150
National Association for the Advance-
    ment of Colored People (NAACP),
    156
National Coalition for Redress/Repara-
    tions (NCRR), see NCRR
National Council for Japanese Ameri-
    can Redress (NCJAR), see NCJAR
National Education Association (NEA),
    156f
National Redress Committee (JACL's),
    45
Native Hawaiian Claims Commission
    Act, 86
Native Sons of the Golden West, 12
Naval Intelligence, 10
NCJAR: redress strategy of, 45ff; cre-
    ation of, 85–88 passim, 142; Personal
    Justice Denied report, 89f, 125, 149;
    recommendations of, 90ff; report
    impact on Japanese Americans,
    92–98 passim; class–action suit filed
    by, 165, 173–78 passim. See also
    JACL
NCRR: redress activities of, 46f, 97;
    creation and growth of, 138, 142–45
    passim; lobbying by, 163f; fails to
    support NCJAR's suit, 177; redress
    funds lobbying by, 183
Neas, Ralph, 156
Newhouse, John, 104f
Nisei: America–oriented, 9; leave clear-
    ance form dilemma, 20f; impact of

internment on, 25, 132f; relating
    internment experience, 94; redress
    movement support, 134f. See also
    Japanese Americans
"No–no boys," 21

Oberdorfer, Louis F., 175f
Oda, Mary Sakaguchi, 96
Office of Management and Budget
    (OMB), 162
Office of Redress Administration
    (ORA), 185, 187
Okamura, Ray, 138, 140
Okazaki, Steven, 172, 179
100th Congress, 83f, 193, 231n. See also
    Congress
100th Infantry Battalion, 22, 49, 112,
    150, 178
O'Neill, Tip, 103
Oyakodo, 136

Party affiliation, votes by, 61–78 passim.
    See also Democratic party; Republi-
    can party
Patel, Marilyn, 170ff
Pearl Harbor, 11
Personal Justice Denied (NCJAR re-
    port), 89f, 125, 149
Personal vote, 27–30 passim, 194. See
    also Congress
Policy–making process, 32–36 passim.
    See also Congress
The Politics of Inclusion (Kean), 163
Polsby, Nelson, 104
Post War World Council pamphlet, 138
Powell, Lewis, 176
Preference outlier theory, 33f
Prejudice, 10, 12f, 52f. See also Discrimi-
    nation
Pribilof Islands, 122ff
Pryor, David, 102f, 127, 235n

Public Law 77–503, 15, 44
Public Law 100–383, *see* H.R. 442
Public Law no. 503, 167
Public Proclamation no. 1, 14
Public Proclamation no. 3 (curfew), 167

Rayburn, Sam, 105
Reagan, Ronald: signs Civil Liberties Act, 1, 177, 191; conference report sent to, 58; conservatism of, 99f, 153; motivation of, 151; redress lobbying of, 161ff; 1989/1990 redress funds allocation, 182f
Redress bill (Aleutian Islanders), 124f. *See also* Civil Liberties Act of 1988
Redress bill (Japanese Americans): impact of W.W. II combat records on, 23; House and Senate barriers to, 39f; Japanese American obstacles to, 40–48 *passim*; opposition to, 48ff; external factors affecting, 50–56 *passim*; regarding Aleutian Islanders, 58; relevant factors influencing votes on, 58ff; Lundgren Amendment vote, 60–63 *passim*; Helms Amendments, 69ff; Senate floor vote on, 71ff; fortunate timing of, 83f; Nikkei Congress members lobby for, 110–19 *passim*; made into an American issue, 115–18 *passim*, 151–59 *passim*; support coalition for, 151–58 *passim*; maneuvered into entitlement program, 186–90 *passim*. *See also* Civil Liberties Act of 1988
Redress movement: Japanese American attitudes toward, 2, 45ff, 97f, 130–36 *passim*; range of activities of, 2; opposition to, 48f, 149f; *coram nobis* cases, 165f, 170–73 *passim*; NCJAR class–action suit, 165, 173–78

passim; significance of, 191–95 *passim*. *See also* JACL; NCJAR
Reed, Stanley F., 168
"Reelection mentality," 29f
Region affiliation, votes by, 61–73
Renunciants, 21
Republican party: Lundgren Amendment vote and, 62f; House H.R. 442 vote, 63ff; Conference report (1988) vote, 65ff; Hecht Amendment vote and, 68f; First Helms Amendment vote, 69ff; Redress bill Senate vote, 71ff; redress bill lobbying to, 154f. *See also* Party affiliation
Resolution 318 (National American Legion), 150
Reynolds, William Bradford, 153
Riders (legislation), 36
Roberts, Glenn, 115
Roberts, Owen J., 169
Robinson, William L., 108, 157
Rodino, Peter, 39, 106f, 233n
Roosevelt, Eleanor, 102
Roosevelt, Franklin D., 6, 13ff, 18, 22, 191
Roth, William V., 40, 42, 101f, 147
Rudman, Warren, 235n
Rutledge, Wiley B., 168

S. 1006, 39
S. 1009, 57f, 67–71, 113, 125ff
S. 1053, 57
S. 1647, 86f. *See also* CWRIC
S. 2116, *see* S. 1006
S. 2553, 188
Saiki, Pat, 108, 234n
Sansei, 94, 133ff, 142. *See also* Japanese Americans
Sasaki, Shosuke, 87, 124
Sato, Frank, 143, 162
Scobey, William, 22

Seattle Evacuation Redress Committee (JACL Seattle chapter), 87
Seattle Plan (JACL), 87, 124f
Second Helms Amendment, 71
Select Committee Investigating National Defense Migration of the House of Representatives, 77th Congress, Second Session, *see* Tolan Committee
Senate: institutional features of, 35f; opposition to S. 2116 in, 39f; S. 1009 roll–call vote, 67–73 *passim*; first Helms Amendment vote in, 69ff; 100th Congress changes in, 100–103 *passim*; Inouye's and Matsunaga's influence in, 111ff; redress funds allocations by, 184, 186. *See also* Congress; House
Shaw, E. Clay, 118
Shigekuni, Phil, 140
Shumway, Norm, 52, 55
Simon, Paul, 233n
Simpson, Alan, 101, 154f
Sixth Amendment, 174
Social Security Act, 51
Social Security Notch Adjustment Act, 79f
Speaker of the House, 104
Staggers, Harley, 160f
Stevens, Ted: redress bill supporter, 40; motion to table Hecht Amendment, 67; motion to table second Helms Amendment, 71; Aleutian Islanders' redress supported by, 87, 120, 124–27 *passim*; replaced by Pryor as subcommittee chair, 101
Stevenson, Adlai, 29
Stilwell, "Vinegar Joe," 162
Stimson, Henry L., 12ff, 18
Stone, Harlan F., 168
Stone, Victor, 171

Stroebel, Carol, 115, 163
Subcommittees, 33, 57. *See also* Committee system
Supreme Court: upholds Executive Order 9066, 23f, 103, 149, 168; petition for writ of error *coram nobis*, 165; *United States v. Mitchell* ruling, 175. *See also* United States
Svahn, John A. "Jack," 162
Swift, Al, 160
Swindall, Pat, 159, 235n

Tateishi, John, 45, 55f, 85, 139ff, 142f
Thirteenth Amendment, 174
Thomas, Norman, 138
Thornburgh, Richard, 187
Throwaway votes, 75f
Thurmond, Strom, 127
Ticket–splitting, 28
Tilden, Samuel J., 28
Tokiwa, Rudy, 82f
Tolan, John H., 13
Tolan Committee, 13
Topeka Board of Education v. Brown, 131
Truman, Harry S, 135
Tule Lake internment camp, 21, 24, 141

Ujifusa, Grant, 143f, 151, 154, 158–63 *passim*, 185
"Unfinished Business" (film), 172, 179
United States: federal budget deficit, 2f, 50ff, 162; declares war on Japan, 11; issues Executive Order 9066, 13ff; Japanese American political activism, 40–44 *passim*; Japanese trade relations with, 52f; H.R. 442 significance to, 81ff; rescinds Executive Order 9066, 135f; U.S. Constitution, 195. *See also* Civil Liberties Act of 1988; Supreme Court

United States v. Hirabayashi, 23f, 103, 149, 167

United States v. Hohri et al., 173–78 *passim*

United States v. Korematsu, 24, 103, 149, 167f

United States v. Mitchell, 175

United States v. Yasui, 24, 103, 149, 166f

Uno, Edison, 138f

Unruh, Jesse, 148

Uyeda, Clifford, 141

Uyehara, Grayce, 108, 143f, 152f, 158–61 *passim*

Veterans' groups, 202

Veterans of Foreign Wars (VFW), 48f, 149

"Visible Target" (PBS documentary), 179

Voorhees, Donald, 171

Votes: rise of the personal, 27–30 *passim*, 194; electoral interest analysis of, 73–80 *passim*, 193f; throwaway, 75f; multiple regression analysis of, 76ff; ideological variables and, 78f. *See also* Electoral interest analysis

Voting Rights Act of 1965, 131

Wakabayashi, Ron, 143

War Relocation Authority (WRA), *see* WRA

Warren, Earl, 12f

Washington Interreligious Staff Council, 186

Western Defense Command, 14

Willard, Richard K., 108 161, 163

Wilson, Pete, 148

Woo, Michael, 42

Woo, S. B., 42, 147

World War II, 10, 106, 121–26 *passim*. *See also* Internment

World War II Japanese American Human Rights Violation Redress Act, *see* H.R. 5977

WRA, 14ff, 20f, 24

Wright, Jim, 57, 103f, 115, 184, 193

Wright, Skelly, 176

"Yankee Samurai" exhibit, 179f

Yasui, Minoru: challenges curfew, 23f, 157, 166f, 179; on redress for Japanese Americans, 97; member of National Redress Committee, 140–43 *passim*

Yasui v. United States, 24, 103, 149, 166–73 *passim*

Yates, Sidney, 233n

"Yellow peril" hysteria, 9f

Yonsei, 133. *See also* Japanese Americans

Young, Don, 108, 126

Zelenko, Benjamin, 173

Library of Congress Cataloging-in-Publication Data

Hatamiya, Leslie T., 1969—
    Righting a wrong: Japanese Americans and the passage of the
    Civil Liberties Act of 1988/Leslie T. Hatamiya.
        p.   cm.—(Asian America)
    Includes bibliographical references.
    ISBN 0-8047-2144-0 (cl.) : ISBN 0-8047-2366-4 (pb.)
    1. Japanese Americans—Evacuation and relocation, 1942-1945.
2. Japanese Americans—Civil rights.   I. Title.   II. Series.
D769.8.A6H38   1993
940.53´1503956073—dc20

92-40402 CIP

∞This book is printed on acid-free paper.